HARD WON WISDOM FROM . . .

Judith Albino • Lenora Cole Alexander • Aida Alvarez •
Margaret Beckett • Mary-Ellis Bunim • Susan Butcher •
Linda Chavez-Thompson • Margaret Cho • Sheila Coates •
Frances Conley • Rev. Suzan Johnson Cook • Paula Coughlin •
Nancy Dickey • Ruth Dreifuss • Brooke Medicine Eagle •
Sylvia Earle • Teresa Edwards • Jocelyn Elders •
Shannon Faulkner • Carly Fiorina • Jane Goodall •
Ellen Goodman • Cammi Granato • Jill Gould • Gayle Greer •
Penny Harrington • Dr. Bernadine Healy • Judith Heumann •
Kristine Fugal Hughes • Gen. Claudia Kennedy • Claudia Laird •
Wilma Mankiller • Frances McDormand • Rita Moreno • Lisa Olson •
Cokie Roberts • Genevieve Sangudi • Phyllis Schlafly • Pat Schroeder •
Araceli Segarra • Jenny Shipley •Connie Stevens • Kathryn Sullivan •
Kathrine Switzer • Helen Thomas • Marilyn Van Derbur Atler •
Faye Wattleton • Sarah Weddington • Betty Williams • Jody Williams

HARD WON WISDOM

More Than 50 Extraordinary
Women Mentor You to Find
Self-Awareness, Perspective,
and Balance

Fawn Germer

Newhouse Books

To Jennifer
Keep Kickingass!
I'm Proud you are
making a real
life after newspapers
love,
Fawn

Published by Newhouse Books

This book was initially published by The Berkley Publishing Group
A division of Penguin Putnam Inc.

First Perigee hardcover edition: October 2001
First Perigee trade paperback edition: February 2003
First Newhouse edition: January 2008

ISBN Newhouse hardcover: 978-0-9795466-3-1
ISBN Newhouse trade paperback: 978-0-9795466-4-8

The Library of Congress has catalogued the Perigee hardcover edition as follows:

Germer, Fawn.
Hard won wisdom : today's extraordinary women mentor you to find self-awareness,
balance and perspective / by Fawn Germer
      p.   cm.
Includes index.
ISBN 0-399-52711-7
1. Women—United States—Psychology.   2. Women—United States—Life skills
guides.   3. Women—United States—Conduct of life.   4. Self-esteem in women—
United States.   I. Title.

Hq1221.G43 2001
305.4—dc21

                                                                    2001021091

Printed in the United States of America

This book is dedicated to my mother,
the strongest woman I know, who fought back after a massive stroke
and taught me how to live.

CONTENTS

ACKNOWLEDGMENTS

I T NEVER OCCURRED TO ME how important the author's acknowledgements are until the time came to write my own. The people mentioned here aren't just names listed on a page. They fill my world with life.

Imagine spending three years chasing your life's dream of publishing a book, then having it released days after the horrors of September 11. My friends kept me going, buying copies for every person on their Christmas list, sending e-mails to everyone they ever met in their lives and cheering me until I found success despite the obstacles.

To my beautiful mother, Betty Germer, who believes in me unconditionally and always knows how to make me feel good. To my incredible father, Fred Germer, the most loving, generous man on this earth who has made me feel so honored and thankful that I am his daughter. And, to my brother, Jim, who would not lift my bags in college because he wanted to teach me about "equal rights."

To Connie Bouchard, Joyce Duarte and Tina Proctor—the three life sisters who have shared the best moments of my life with me. To Rebecca Whitley, who has brought so much laughter, warmth and wild revelry to my world. To Linda Ambraz, Betsy Pinkerton and Pam Sarich—the "girls in the hood" who keep me sane with sage advice and trips to Super Wal-Mart. To Keri Douglas, a best friend and touchstone who has been there for me—no questions asked. To Hollie Ainbinder, who helped me cook up this idea and Christine Bichovsky, one of the truest believers. And to my new sisters, Liz Roberts, Heidi Shattuck, Carole L. "The Professor" Cole, Susan Edwards, Marty Rosen and Dianne Williams.

To Caroline Carney, my agent and compass in this journey. She is the wise woman who has made me think, stretch, laugh and love this moment. She is a mentor, a friend, a true sister in life.

To my extraordinary editor, Jennifer Repo, a bold women who immediately "got" my vision and embraced this book, challenging me both as a writer and a person. You made this book everything I dreamed it could be.

To those who just read what I said about Jennifer Repo and Caroline Carney, my partners in this experience: Look at what happens when determined women work *together*. We have so much power as women—we just have to take it and use it.

To Michelle Howry, the wonder woman who stepped in after Jen left to chase her own dream. And Christel Winkler, the one who did the legwork that kept us all from going out of our minds.

To Liz Perl, who came up with such a great title, and to the rest of the marketing and sales team at Perigee: Thanks for making my dream come alive. To Gina Anderson, my protector.

Thanks to Pat Schroeder, Gen. Claudia Kennedy, Helen Thomas and Betty Williams for saying yes at the very beginning, giving me the ability to shamelessly name-drop so others would join in. And, to everyone who *did* join in. You all did this for the right reason, and I hope others will be as touched by your wise words as I have been.

To Sheila Coates, Aida Alvarez and Liz Perl, thanks for playing hardball so I got my fair shake on television.

To Teresa Searcy, Jody Williams, Betty Williams, Ellen Goodman, Jennifer Repo, Caroline Carney, Rebecca Whitley, Pam Iorio, Mary Figg, Penny Styponias, Jeff Himelhoch, Steffie Allen, Keri Douglas and the others who gave me encouragement and strategic advice to help deal with a book release so soon after September 11.

To the memory of Evelyn Hirsch, so much more than an aunt, who showed such true valor in her fight against leukemia.

To my beautiful friend Bette Hasse, who died this year of ovarian cancer but showed me that our ultimate purpose in life is to *live* our lives.

To Sisses #1, 2 and 3: Jayne Bray, Betsy Buffo and Lisa Pritchard. To the Preds: Brian Campbell, Jeanne Elliot, Jackie St. Joan and Kathleen Bowers.

To Capt. Miriam Reed, my heroic friend who has set an example for every one of us.

To my other cheering section: Merrilee Stanley, Ed Primeau, Clark Taylor, Lisa Rary, Carolyn DiPaolo, Geoff Roth and Evelyn Tovar.

To the Himelhoch, Hirsch, and Rubinstein clans. Thanks to Keri Smith, for an injection of much-needed encouragement. To Meredith Tupper, the Internet wiz who electrified my vision.

My wonderful friends, too many to name, but some so giving during this project they must be noted, in alphabetical and geographic order, so no one gets offended: The Florida Crew: Marilyn Allen, Jonathan Alpert, Pete

Ambraz, Jim Baldridge, Huguette Baldridge, Rebecca Blanco, Jane Boles, Leah Cash, Vickie Chachere, Gary Duarte, Chris Elzner, Carol Folsom, Malea Guiriba, Chante Ishta, Barb Jiannetti, Victoria Jorgensen, Dana Kuehn, Harold Linde, Marty Matthews, Erika Morton, Candace Mundy, Lindsay Peterson, Larry Pinkerton, Lou Price, Pat Price, Hope Pulido, Lynn Cotner Rau, Linda Robertson, Alex Sarich, Dave Sarich, Nicholas Sarich, Judie Taggart, Patricia Tucker, Jackie Walker, Pamela Woods. To WomanQuest: Kathy Donohue, Victoria Duran, Teresa Hoover, Barb Zingg, Jean Rockwell, Tami Wingard.

The Old Colorado Crew: Martha Bailey, Betsy Cannon, Laurie Cannon, Katherine Jens, Erin Johansen, Janet Kacskos, Diane King, Carolyn Little, Rachel Moore, Joe Moran, Geri Reinardy, Dorothy Rupert, Kay Sheehan, George Thomas. To other new friends who stepped in to help along the way: Julie Fiore, Joyce Meskis, Anton Mueller, Nancy Rawlinson, Mary Ward.

And my gratitude to my many mentors in life who helped me to be who I am: Grace Allen, Stephanie Allen, Pat Andrews, Rabbi Andrew Bossov, Nick Bournias, Chris Broderick, Marie Diebler, Beth Dutkowski, George Edmonson, Mickie Edwardson, Mike Finney, Susan Gembrowski, Mary Louise Gerard, Bobbie Campbell Gonzales, Gayle Greer, Fred Hartmann, Susan Kirk, Mark Leib, Rob Lorei, David Nelson, Chris Niederpruem, Robert Nierescher, Laurie Prochazka, Rubin Rabinovitz, Jackie St. Joan, John Sanko, Sonia Schork, the late Rabbi Gerald Schuster, Billie Stanton, Mary Winter.

I am so blessed.

INTRODUCTION:
OUR MOMENT

B Y NOW, I'VE LOST COUNT of the number of times I have left work wondering if it was me who was crazy—or everybody else. Believe me, I have had enough of those days, weeks, months, and even years when I've felt worn out and wondered how I'd survive emotionally, much less professionally.

We all have. What's the deal? I read the same newspapers you do. Every day there is another headline telling us how far we've come. Why, here's a story about a woman, a CEO in a Fortune 500 company! And look at that one: *She* plays soccer. There's one running for president. That one's directing films, publishing books, commanding the space shuttle—not to mention the one who was in charge of foreign affairs . . .

Before I started connecting with this kind of woman in search of the hard-won wisdom from which the rest of us could benefit, I wondered whether we were even working on the same planet. They were leaping tall buildings in a single bound, and I was running head-on into the wall of office politics as a newspaper editor. I wondered why there were so many books telling us how to dress, how to talk, how to act and how to break through the glass ceiling—but *none* telling us how to survive it all emotionally.

Hopefully, with some of our generation's boldest women as our mentors, *Hard Won Wisdom* will fill that void. The idea for this book was to get the women who paved the road to show us how they did it, and let them mentor us from afar. They are joined by some of the nation's foremost experts in women's psychology, business and sociology who help synthesize the advice, inspiration and insight into a prescription for success. This book is the result of hundreds of interviews—done in person or by phone—with women leaders who have experienced the same obstacles and challenges that we encounter as we try to balance our professional and personal lives.

What surprised me most when I talked to these women was their willingness to speak so openly, sharing their own pain and triumph while relating what they have learned to our struggle today. What emerged was a concept of boldness that, once embraced, gives us permission to succeed, to fail, to try, to live. Their collective wisdom, which was certainly hard-won, is now a permanent resource that you and I can consult every time we need a little coaching or emotional boost.

These women give us validation, hope, and a game plan that will guide us through the minefield of competitive work environments that aren't always nice, fair or nurturing. They urge us to embrace chance, opportunity and the spirit by finding the right balance to support every personal challenge. And, they show us how to live a more fulfilling life.

What shocked me was how much I learned from women whose experiences are so removed from my own. I *never* imagined that a hockey player, dogsled racer, oceanographer or an anthropologist who focuses on primates would have advice that would apply to my world. But, they did. These women cut their paths in male-dominated fields, fighting the very same battles that many of us face. They have experienced as many tough days as the rest of us, and they've kept pushing.

These women didn't just "happen" upon greatness. They focused on it. They achieved what once seemed so impossible, not because they sought glory, but because they didn't have a choice. It burned inside of them. They latched on to what meant most to them and chased their passions. Their reward was the same sense of purpose that we all can experience by finding our own calling and doing what matters most to us.

So, we aren't the crazy ones. We are women who want to read and learn from others who have something to share. The women who share their wisdom here don't pretend to have every answer or to be any more worldly than the rest of us. They've had their share of battles, too, and hate that any of us still have to struggle. That's why they're talking now.

Imagine what we can do next, if only we listen.

SELF-AWARENESS

ONE

HAVING VISION

"What separates an ordinary woman from
an extraordinary woman?
The belief that she is ordinary."

—Jody Williams, 1997 winner of the
Nobel Peace Prize for the crusade against land mines

S HEILA COATES WAS NO ORDINARY woman, although she thought she was. One evening, she prepared dinner like she had done every other day in the twenty-five years since she'd married. Her sister dropped by and watched as the forty-two-year-old homemaker and teacher's aide cooked, pulled down the dishes, cut the food into portions, put the food on the plates, buttered the bread, and even salt and peppered the corn for her husband and three sons.

"Are you going to eat it for them too?" her sister asked.

Coates looked at her, dumbfounded.

"How old is Leo?" her sister inquired.

"Sixteen," Coates answered.

"He's not a baby," her sister said. "Why are you doing this for your sons?"

That was the moment when Sheila Coates woke up. She'd found her moment, and maybe, when you see what she and the other women mentors in this book did with their moments, you'll find yours. Fifteen years after her sister challenged her in her kitchen, Coates stands as one of America's most revered advocates for African-American families—a woman whose influence has stretched from the home to Congress to the White House. "It was the catalyst for the change," Coates remembers. "I reevaluated my life. I never realized how frustrated and unhappy I was. Not only was I concerned about my own frustration, but I was teaching my three sons to be dependent on women. I couldn't live like that anymore."

After that discussion with her sister, she became serious about changing her life, quit her job and went back to school full time to study public administration and pre-law. She took a required course in organizational theory, which taught her how to turn issues into action. Coates emerged at the forefront of a powerful group of activists for African-American families, founding Black Women United for Action, an Arlington, Virginia–based community service organization with ties throughout the United States, in Africa and in Canada. The organization focuses on improving the lives of vulnerable families, and as its leader, Coates has testified before national committees, spoken at the White House and consulted on public policy with White House staffers, cabinet members—even the vice president. In addition, she has served in a succession of gubernatorial appointments and fought relentlessly to make a difference for others.

She accomplished all of that in just fifteen years. She says that it took knowing what she wanted. Her mother had long taught her that the sky was the limit and Coates saw education as her vehicle to free flight. In her studies, she learned that 80 percent of the people in the world want to be led. Twenty percent will help out in the core action group, but only 10 percent will be actual leaders. Coates wanted to lead. "It would have been easier to walk out the door and say, 'Hell, I'll go get a real job.' But there was this nagging piece, the 'what if' piece. What if I do that? Once I made up my mind, that was it. A lady once told my mother I'd go bear hunting with a switch. I was that fearless."

She remembers coaxing a caterer into helping her put together a fund-raiser with just $8.22 in her organizational treasury. She was asked what the group had to spend. "I said, '$8.22, so you can't spend over $6,000 for catering.'" One man who watched her finesse the arrangements said, "Don't even try to figure it out. It'll be done." Her colleague said, "This doesn't even make sense, but I'm going to stay with the group just to see. There's no way she can do it." The event took in $32,000, with $16,000 in profit. All out of $8.22. "You can do some crazy things when you believe," Coates says. "Every human being on this earth has a purpose. Everyone has something they can give. The need is there and you rise to the need."

Whoa. Who has time to rise to the need? We're pretty busy here, just "livin' the dream." "Sure, Boss, I can do that before I leave . . . No problem, I'll pick up the kids . . . Yes, of course I can do that. I'll fit it in . . . Have you finished your homework?" Good grief! Sometimes we get so caught up in the demands of daily living that we forget to take time to make sure that the dream we are living is *our* dream. We're so busy pleasing other people and meeting *their* expectations of *us* that we neglect to satisfy our own needs.

Most of us limit ourselves, deciding that we will only focus on our jobs and/or our families, rather than carving out the time and space we need to satisfy what really matters to us, deep down. We think that what we've got is all we're going to get. But, some dare to go beyond those limits, testing themselves and the rest of the world to see how much possibility really exists. They have vision, and you do too—if you just open up your eyes. You don't have to go out and win a Nobel Prize or an Academy Award, you don't have to fight your way to the top of the corporate hierarchy, and you don't have to get yourself elected to public office in order to fulfill yourself. What you have to do is explore what *you* want out of life and move forward with your own plan so you don't let other people and external influences control how you live your life.

Living in Florida, I see so many retirees struggling with their identities because their kids are grown and they no longer have job titles by which they can quickly distinguish themselves. It doesn't matter what their job used to be, whether they were brain surgeons or janitors. What matters now is who they *are*. But, lacking work to give them identity and generate respect from others, many are lost. Why not find out who you are *now*, so you can spend the rest of your life enjoying the reward of such awareness?

If you want to do something outrageous, spectacular or different with your life, *do it*! Seize your moment. Just focus on what you want, figure out how to make it happen, then make that the dream you live. *Your* dream. Fill it with passion and energy, and decide whether it will be the new direction where you will lead your family or career. Your reward becomes something much larger and more personal than a paycheck. It's fulfillment.

Betty Williams found fulfillment through her passion, and her accomplishments show what every one of us can do if we have vision. Back when she found her moment, the press was still referring to her as "an ordinary housewife." Hardly. Williams turned her outrage over the violence in Northern Ireland into the beginnings of the peace movement there and won the Nobel Peace Prize in 1976. "Quite honestly," she said, "I've never met an ordinary housewife."

Williams grew up Catholic and raised her family in a neighborhood mixed with Catholics and Protestants because she did not want her children isolated among one group. The tension in the mixed area was ever present, as was the violence. In 1973, the fury took the life of a British soldier, who fell near Williams's feet after he was shot. She knelt beside him and prayed—an act that brought her scorn from neighbors who said he was the enemy.

Three years later, as Anne Maguire and her three children walked home from her daughter's school in Belfast, an IRA guerrilla lost control of his car after being shot by British soldiers. The car careened into Maguire and her children, Andrew, 6 weeks, John, 2, and Joanna, 8. The children were killed, and Maguire was seriously injured. Three years later, she would commit suicide. Williams was there when the children were killed, and what she witnessed changed her forever. "I still don't know what happened inside of me that day. There was an explosion within. I just knew I couldn't continue to live like that."

After the deaths, Williams quickly collected 6,000 signatures from Catholics and Protestants all demanding that the violence end. She called the newspaper to ask for help building this movement by publicizing her telephone number—a brazen act in Northern Ireland. She united with Maguire's sister, Mairead Corrigan, and together they called for a show of solidarity from the women of Northern Ireland. Williams knocked on doors and awakened the mothers of Northern Ireland, calling on them to band together for peace. Just four days after the children were killed, 10,000 Catholic and Protestant women marched through the streets of Belfast. The Community of the Peace People was born. Weeks later, 250,000 people crowded into Trafalgar Square to join her in protest. When Williams was awarded the Peace Prize, Egil, Aarvik, vice-chairman of the Nobel committee, praised Williams and Corrigan for having the courage to take the first step. "Someone had to start forgiving," he said.

That was Williams's destiny. She now lives in Florida, where she works as a university professor and coordinates a global initiative for the protection of children. Williams believes that every one of us changes this world in some way and it is up to us to decide how. Whether we give or take. Whether we solve problems or manufacture them.

Her path was her own, a journey that others couldn't have dreamed up or designed for her, and one that she could not have achieved if she had hinged every turn on needing the approval of others. It serves as a lesson to all of us that we have to stretch and live our own vision, despite what we think we are supposed to be doing to impress or please others. It is time to live for ourselves, to stop waiting to get permission and to start defining who we are as individuals.

It all begins with vision, and with vision comes self-awareness. Even though you can't always control what happens to you, you *can* control who you are. And as you become more aware of this true center in your self, you will have a greater command over what occurs around you, defining your dreams and goals, and owning the responsibility for growing into them. Listen to that voice inside of you that tells you when something isn't working for you, when you're wearing down, or when you are feeling held back. Whenever you catch yourself thinking "If only this would happen, then I could . . ." write down the idea. If you ignore your dreams and turn off your imagination, you let go of what you really want in life. So, instead of saying, "If only I could . . ." or, "I could never . . ." ask yourself, "Why not?" You are allowed to dream! This doesn't mean you should abandon your job or family or your current life. It means you should focus on yourself, listening to that inner voice, because it will tell you what matters most.

Listen to Cammi Granato, captain of the 1998 women's U.S. Olympic hockey team. "I don't think you should limit yourself—ever," she says. "I definitely don't think you should let others limit you. If you have a passion, you have to go for it. You have to live that passion. That's what life is about. It's also about challenging yourself. You have to go for it. If you fall short, you get up and either try it again or figure out another way."

The game is mental, whether it is in an ice rink or in your office. It always comes down to endurance, and when you feel exhausted or like giving up, calm down, reassess and tap back into the energy that put you on your path. Even when it's tough, you are still living your dream. Keep that dream—your vision—right in front of you so you find the inspiration to persevere and make it come to life. "Your body can probably go ten times more than you think it can go, or fifty more times," Granato said. "Your mind has to take over and say, 'I can do it. I can do this.' You have to have a mental picture to come through it. I use the Olympic rings as a visual in my head. I picture them. How bad do I want it? I'm not quitting. Or, I picture the gold medal. Or, I say the word *gold*. I can overcome what I'm going through, whether it's sports or anything else."

She realizes the lessons learned in sports translate into the rest of her life. "I am a driven person. I've learned that when you want something, you've got to be the one to go after it. If you want to be happy, you have to be the one who makes the decision to be happy. I truly believe if you work hard and you are determined, you are going to be successful. Your work ethic, your sacrifice and determination will get you somewhere. That works off the ice, whether in relationships or in work."

So, even though we are all sick of books that promise us our dreams will come true if we only believe in ourselves and visualize, visualize, visualize, we need to buy into the concept: Vision is all powerful, especially when it is bolstered by our *passion*. It doesn't matter who you are, where you were born, what your economic circumstances are or your age. We all have the same power to create and re-create ourselves into extraordinary women by focusing on those callings we hear inside.

Focus Your Vision

Everybody has days when they don't feel like diving into their routine. Every work environment has its share of office jerks, crummy assignments and injustice. So, even when you have found your true center and are doing the work that is most important to you, you're going to have days when you aren't having a good time. Still, the bad days don't feel so bad when you are tending to your passions.

Look at where you are right now and ask yourself: Are you doing what you really want to be doing? Is it important to you? Challenging? Does it make you feel good? Is it worth the routine aggravation that comes with it? Do you have more good days than bad? If not, stop trying to force it. Make your current situation as tolerable as possible while you look inside and figure out what it is that will change your outlook and excite you. Do what you want. You don't have to change your entire world and you don't even have to walk away from your job—unless that's what you want. There are many other ways to grow by volunteering, taking classes, devoting spare time to sports, writing, music or artwork, focusing greater attention on family, friends and spirituality.

I went through a spell when I got bored being a reporter. I'd done it since I was fifteen years old, and after a while, the stories started to repeat themselves. I took a course in screenwriting—something completely out of my realm—and suddenly, I welled with creative energy that spilled over into my newspaper work and made me appreciate reporting again. I had a blast writing fiction and that made me much happier on my day job.

Ask yourself: What is your vision, and how are you going to live it? "The first step, for me, is always this flash of imagination," says Kathryn Sullivan, the first American woman to walk in space. "It's a soft watercolor image of how neat it will be, and then I follow along with it. That's an easy style for me to work with. Get a glimmer in the eye and see what it's about. It's the same flash of imagination that makes an individual decide to be a professional athlete, a naval officer, a mother, a painter or even an actress. When the details are messy, nasty, ugly and frustrating, you see this little beacon."

Sullivan hadn't planned on being an astronaut, but rather, a marine geophysicist. "This astronaut stuff was very, very, very late-breaking news for me. NASA started advertising for shuttle astronauts. It meant exploring a new domain, my capabilities, and how my abilities would serve me in a new domain. I was a committed earth scientist at that point, but then somebody offered the chance to see that sight out the window instead of looking at somebody's pictures of it. Well, it didn't strike me as a total fantasy to go do that."

> "It's like a ladder—when you put your hand on one rung and your foot on another, you ought to be eyeballing something two rungs up. There is always something else."
>
> —Dr. Nancy Dickey, first woman president of the American Medical Association

So, she did.

"I absolutely never put it in the context that it was cool just because other people would like it. Never. It wouldn't have mattered to me if 743 million people had done this before or zero had done it before," said Sullivan, now president and CEO of the Center of Science and Industry, located in Columbus and Toledo, Ohio. "All the big deal about being the first American woman to walk in space was nice, but my first space walk would have been my first space walk, regardless of how many women had done it before me. That's how I look at it. Do what feels right and look for the flash."

Permission to Succeed

Give yourself permission to succeed, to fail, to try, to live. But, do it *your way*, so you define your own dreams and expectations. What is real success? Is it a corner office and a big, fat paycheck? Or is it the certainty that you are doing what you love, and giving it everything you have to give?

If you care about what you are doing, if you love what you are doing, you will succeed. Don't measure your success by what anyone else does or what other people might expect of you. And, take a good, long look at what you really care about. That's where the magic is, and it is where you will find your power.

"Passion for what you do is an important ingredient for success, and if you don't love what you do, it's not worth the time or the energy. I really need to love it. That keeps me motivated and interested. It keeps me sharp."

—*Carly Fiorina, CEO, Hewlett-Packard*

The problem is that life isn't always easy and we often find ourselves stuck in environments that aren't fair or nurturing. Not that we expect them to be all the time, but it's easy to get worn down by the emotional challenge. The most powerful antidote for rough times is purpose. Knowing that you are doing what you were meant to do, even though it is difficult, will help you get up and try again on those days when things get heavy.

Don't wait for someone else to come along and validate your dreams before you dare to pursue them. What are you waiting for? Isn't it enough to know inside that you are daring to chase a vision that has meaning for you? Sometimes, you have to define yourself without the accolades or support you might want to have. If you are waiting for others to approve of your vision, it isn't *your* vision. It's everyone else's.

"As a kid, I was told to prepare for the worst as well as the best. I was prepared for what the world wouldn't give me. I knew I had to go out and make it happen. I accept my gift for what it is, my strengths for what they are. I'm not going to be Michael Jordan, because that's not me. This is who I am. I think women are better at accepting our strengths and making the most of them. Men get in mind what they want to be and what they want to happen, and when it doesn't happen, they are devastated."

—*Teresa Edwards, Olympic champion, pioneer of women's basketball*

Consultant Jean Isberg Stafford has helped thousands of women focus their vision through her consulting firm, Executive Coaching for Women Inc. "Look at the number of businesses women are starting—at a rate of two to one compared to men." The latest U.S. Census numbers, from 1997, show women now own 5.4 million businesses in this country, with $819 billion in receipts.

Stafford said the traditional path to success doesn't work for women—or men anymore, but women feel freer to do something about it. That may mean starting a business, it may mean pursuing a muse—whatever. "First, we live our lives the way other people think we should," she says. "We do what we are told. Then, we get to the point where we have to reorder our priorities if we are going to live the lives we have to live. We have to shed our skin, so to speak. Things that were important to us when we first graduated college may not matter anymore. New things do." She tells us to evaluate what we care about, make new priorities, then use them as the foundation for the rest of our lives. "It's very liberating, very freeing to be able to do what you want to do for yourself," she says.

"The most important challenge is self-awareness," she says. "Know what you want. We have a terrible time articulating what we want because it requires that we get past a lifetime of trying to find out what everybody else wants. We need to commit to a vision, to say 'I'm going to do this,' rather than waiting for someone else to come along and say that. That involves a lot of internal work. We abdicate our power when we don't take the time to figure out what we want. Write it down. The gains will come from inside us, not from breaking down external barriers. Those still exist, but, right now, we are the biggest obstacle to ourselves," Stafford says.

Figuring it out

So, you need to figure out what you're going to do when you grow up. Again. Sometimes, the hardest part is figuring out exactly what it is that you want to do. When I was working in the field as a newspaper reporter, people were always telling me, "You know, I always wanted to be a reporter . . ." or, "I majored in journalism and never did anything with it. I've always regretted that." Well, if there is something you meant to do but haven't done, consider that path. Is that what you want to do with your life now?

If not, start thinking about what you are doing when time gets away from you and you are completely enjoying yourself. What skills are you using? Go over your personal priorities. What matters most? Often, it's not the list of accomplishments on your resume, but the personal connections you have built. Is there a way to tap into those outlets? Would you rather pursue something that touches on your political or social values? Start talking to people who know you best and ask them what kind of career they can see you chasing. Don't ask one or two people—ask a dozen. Are any ideas coming up again and again? Which ones?

It's not enough to know what you want, but also, *why* you want it. The stronger your reasons, the easier it will be for you to commit to making changes.

Next comes the planning phase, which is vital. Let's say you decide you want to leave corporate America to teach high school. Do your research and find out what it will take to get certified and into the classroom, then figure out the steps you'll need to take in order to make it happen. Write it all down.

Figure out what kind of time commitment the change will entail, and how you can make it work with your schedule. Start taking the required courses and filling out applications. Think about the financial implications making this move will have on your life. Talk to your significant other.

A dreamer without a plan is just a dreamer. Come up with a plan of action and become its project-manager. Write down every step that stands between you and your goals, and start checking them off as you achieve them. Create a reasonable timetable that will keep you on track without killing you. Enlist those people who are closest to you for support, so you have help juggling your schedule and other obligations. They will help you out.

Then, GET BUSY. There is always, always, ALWAYS an excuse to put a major change off for six months, a year, a decade, a lifetime. But, if you break your plan down into small enough pieces and start working on them one or two at a time, you will be on your way to new success. If you see it as one big obstacle, it's never going to happen. I remember doing a story on a woman who had been taking classes for more than a decade to get her bachelor's degree. One class at a time, she inched toward her goal until she had it licked.

Enjoy the process. Every day, remind yourself of what you have done to move toward your own goal. Visualize. Trite as it may sound, this action step is critical. It's a daily commitment—and recommitment—to your future. You don't have to give up your current life on the way to your new destination, but you must see to it that you stay focused and keep moving forward. It is up to you to make it happen. You can count on family and friends to support you through the transition, but the success of your mission must be born within you.

Celebrate every time you achieve a personal milestone on this path. Get a massage or go out for a special dinner. Get a baby-sitter so you have time to enjoy the outdoors on your own. Constantly remind yourself of how much you are accomplishing and be your own cheerleader. Try to give yourself a few minutes of quiet time each day so you can look at what you are doing and feel good about it, and use that time to unwind and connect with what it was that started you on your path in the first place. When you begin to lose momentum or feel discouraged, think positive! Look

> "I had peers who went to the officers' club—who *still* go to the officers' club—in hopes of marrying an officer. I used to think, 'Good God. Why marry one when you can be one and fly a plane?'"
>
> —*Paula Coughlin, the ex–U.S. Navy pilot who forever changed the armed forces after she fought back in Tailhook*

ahead to how much better off you will be once you have bitten the bullet and met the challenge. Think of how you are growing and taking care of yourself.

Give yourself permission to make it happen.

Making it Happen

1. Figure out what you want to do. Think of what has always intrigued, challenged and excited you.
2. Come up with a set of personal priorities. What matters most to you, and why?
3. Talk to people. Ask friends in your support group what kind of future they see you pursuing.
4. Make your plan. Figure out exactly what steps you must go through in order to make your dream a reality. Set a reasonable timetable to keep you on track.
5. Do it. Don't make excuses and don't procrastinate. You deserve to do what is most important to you. Break your plan into small, achievable steps and click them off one at a time.
6. Stay on track. Every day, ask what you have done to push yourself closer to your goal.
7. Count on yourself. Nobody else can make it happen.
8. Celebrate your successes along the way.
9. Visualize. If you catch yourself losing momentum, imagine what your life will be like once you finish the hard work and live your dream.
10. Give yourself permission to succeed.

One-Track Helen

You've seen Helen Thomas, the journalism legend who was the longstanding dean of the White House press corps. She is a perfect example of a woman doing what she wanted to do in spite of societal pressures that could have held her back. "Thank you, Mr. President," she has always said, closing press conferences. She fell in love with journalism when she received her first by-line in a school paper and, tradition be damned, pushed her way into the media, which was a hard-charging, practically all-male boys' club. "I had a one-track mind and never changed my mind about what I wanted to do. I focused on that, and remained determined. I certainly never expected to be at the White House. I just wanted to be a reporter . . . I didn't know women weren't supposed to be hired as journalists." And it wouldn't have mattered. She had her vision, and lived it, reporting for the United Press International until she was 79, and quitting only after the Unification Church bought the wire service. She now works as a columnist for Hearst News Service.

"I still have goals," she told me after having to hang up mid sentence on our phone conversation to handle a breaking news story. "I want to be a good reporter. You know, you are only as good as your last story."

She once asked President Reagan, "How would you assess the credibility of your own administration in light of the prolonged deception of Congress and the public in terms of your secret dealings with Iran, the disinformation, the trading of Sakharov for Danilov?"

She grilled President Clinton, "Monica Lewinsky may have to appear before a grand jury. Under the circumstances, do you stand by your previous denials of any relationship with her, or that anyone encouraged her to lie?"

And yet, this legendary journalist told me, "I don't think I'm special at all. I don't think I've done anything outstanding." Well, she focused on what she wanted and broke the barriers. She went out there and did the job so well that by the time women like me showed up in the newsroom as reporters, we were able to go for the big stories as well. Finding your vision and living it takes more than that initial burst of inspiration. You have to decide what you want and commit to it. Don't do it to impress others. Do it to satisfy yourself.

We create the biggest optical illusions in life—seeing obstacles that might not really exist, or certainly aren't as difficult to surmount as we imagine. We live in a world that moves way too fast, making us impatient to see results. We come up with an idea, but don't follow through. Or, we cook up a plan, then think of an even better one before we've started work on the first. Then we distract ourselves from that one by messing with something else. Great ideas and great plans are absolutely worthless without action. You can have the clearest vision in the world, but you might as well close your eyes and stop dreaming if you aren't willing to do the work to make it happen.

One person can do so much. You can start a revolution. You can turn an idea into a conglomerate. You can start or destroy a political agenda. You can care for your children so they grow up to be decent human beings. You can honor your own self, realizing that you can do extraordinary things, whether it is making a difference in a corporate setting or in your community. "Ordinary" women do those things all the time, once they stop thinking of themselves as ordinary. Remember that there is only one difference between an ordinary woman and an extraordinary woman: The belief that she is ordinary.

A MOMENT WITH . . .
JANE GOODALL

"From the time I was eleven, my dream was to go to Africa, or at least some-where where there were lots of wild animals, and live with them. I thought I'd be like Mowgli in *Jungle Book* or Tarzan, and if I didn't hurt the animals, they wouldn't hurt me. So I never felt it required courage. It didn't seem that way. I don't think it does when you're that young. It was just a question of how I would get there.

"Fifty years ago, when I began dreaming of it, Africa was the 'Dark Continent.' We thought of poison arrows and cannibals cooking missionaries in pots, partly because nobody went off and did that kind of thing.

"The only time when being a female caused a difficulty was in the beginning, because the British administration of Tanganyika was absolutely shocked by the idea of a female going off into the bush. They thought I was amoral, but agreed I could go, provided I had a companion. My mother, who always supported me through my childhood dream, volunteered to come with me. She had always told me if I really wanted something and really worked hard and took advantage of opportunity, I would find a way."

It took courage for her. She had to uproot herself, come to Africa, live in the wild, see her daughter go off into what could have been danger, and spend nights on her own.

"When I got my first experience of wild Africa, it was the Serengeti plain. Louis Leakey took me on one of the early digs of fossil human remains. All of that part of Africa was totally unknown. There was no road or track or anything. It was wild Africa. All of the animals were there—the lions, the giraffes, the ostriches, the zebras, the rhinos. And we were on foot! It was the Africa of my dreams.

"I can still remember waking up and hearing the hyenas giggling, hearing the lions roaring and thinking, 'I'm actually in my dream. My dream is now my reality.' It was absolute magic.

"I can still smell the Serengeti. The excitement and the magic of it all seems as though it were just yesterday—all this time later—and I feel at home. Totally.

"Another amazing thing was getting into the forest and Tarzan's jungle—Mowgli's jungle. That was even more home to me. That was the truest, true of all the magics. Just to be in a forest with trees all around with vines and ferns and butterflies and monkeys.

"In the wild there are times when fear of the wild is a very good thing. I was certainly afraid of leopards in the night, of a water cobra that was brushed onto my foot by a wave. I felt fear when the chimps first started challenging me instead of running away.

"Africa has changed a lot. I get little glimpses of it when I go into the forest with the chimps, flashes of how it was and, for the chimps, still is. But going back is not the same because my responsibilities are so different. I still love it. I'm not the carefree young girl who was living her dream, finding excitement every day and learning to have new dreams. That is over, except in my mind, in my memory."

TWO

GAINING SELF-ESTEEM

ADMIT IT. IT'S BEEN A WHILE since you thought, "Gee, I really like who I am. I look great. I'm smart. I do a terrific job." No, we usually reserve our self-talk for episodes of self-flagellation when we harp on all the ways we fall short. Apparently, we prefer thinking, "How did I ever let myself get this fat?" or, "I'm looking old," or "I'll never be able to do that." We routinely criticize ourselves with never-ending streams of meanness that we would *never* inflict on anyone we know, not even a stranger or an enemy. We crave validation from others, but seldom acknowledge that the only validation that counts comes from within. And we put off liking ourselves, thinking that our self-esteem issues will vanish once we reach our goals and find success in the outside world. I didn't know how wrong that notion was until I talked with Kristine Fugal Hughes.

From a distance, she has it all. Fugal Hughes sits atop a $290 million-a-year vitamin company that she started with $150 and an idea. "What you see is what you get," she told me. "I got my hair cut in high school into a pixie cut. It's always been that way. I don't even put on enough pretense to curl my hair. I put on my mascara, put on my lipstick, then put on the clothes that fit me because I'm overweight, and I just go out into the world and do my best."

"Stop," I told her during our interview. "Let's talk about your weight."

The sigh was audible, and when she began speaking again, her voice cracked with emotion. Suddenly, this wasn't Kristine Fugal Hughes, chair of the board of Nature's Sunshine Products, the woman who rallied family members into a vitamin and herb business that literally began with them sitting around the dining room table, filling gelatin capsules with cayenne pepper. Or the mother of seven who never earned a college degree, who helped build the company into an international industry that distributes more than five hundred products with the help of 650,000 salespeople.

She's every one of us who pushes relentlessly toward our goals, racking up success after success, but still feels unworthy, never fully understanding our goodness, our contribution, our beauty. It was a powerful moment of revelation, one that led me to ask all of the women I interviewed about their self-esteem. They, much like the rest of us, described difficult self-esteem issues on two levels: physical and emotional.

Only a handful of the women I spoke with said they feel good about themselves and don't have a problem with their self-esteem or body image. Almost always, the question of body image was met with the same excruciating sigh that came from Fugal Hughes. Former Surgeon General Dr. Joycelyn Elders admitted, "Well, at this point, I only have two outfits that fit. It's hard to feel good about that." Frances McDormand, who won the best actress Oscar for *Fargo*, was asked whether her self-esteem matched that of her character, Marge Gunderson, the sheriff in the movie. Said she: "Fundamentally, no. No! But, I think having to live with low self-esteem makes you stronger. Your arsenal of weaponry has to be a little more elaborate."

Low self-esteem can be triggered by criticism or failure—or astonishingly—by flattery or success. If you ever feel you aren't smart enough or think you are not beautiful enough or are just plain not good enough, you've suffered from it. You won't give yourself the same breaks you'll give others, and you keep pounding on yourself because of it. More important—a lack of confidence in yourself manifests in your life in many ways.

Yale psychology professor, Marianne LaFrance, Ph.D., says that most women believe they have strengths in some areas, but that they end up focusing on the areas where they fall short, especially when it comes to the body beautiful. When *Psychology Today* polled four thousand readers about their body image in 1997, nearly 60 percent of the women said they didn't like their appearance and nearly two-thirds were dissatisfied with their weight. One in four women said they would be willing to trade more than three years of their lives for thinness.

Amazing.

But, there is a lesson here. No promotion, no raise, no award, no recognition, no relationship is going to fix what is broken inside of us. If high self-esteem is not the reward for achieving success, then we might as well give ourselves a break now.

I once interviewed a college professor who detailed her research on how individuals perceive their flaws. I asked her why she started looking at the subject and she grew uneasy. "Can't you tell?" she asked. No, I shrugged. "My lisp," she said. "You must hear my lisp." And, the truth was that until she brought it up, I hadn't noticed. She assumed that everybody noticed and that her very mild speech impediment was so remarkable that it was the most prominent attribute anybody noticed upon meeting her. What a load to bear, and it wasn't even real.

What's Going on Here?

The beauty magazines tell us our face isn't smooth enough; our teeth aren't white enough, straight enough or perfect enough; everything about our bodies is somehow inadequate; and there is not an acceptable spot on us. Our society is geared toward a perfect beauty ideal and we can't escape it. Because of these unrealistic beauty images being held up as the ideal, we think that who we are is not enough. Kim Vaz, a professor of women's studies at the University of South Florida, who specializes in feminist psychotherapy and women of color issues says, "We get messages that we fall short on a physical level. Then there is the intellectual level, where we question whether we are smart enough, know enough or are ready to handle the challenges in front of us." She believes that we question ourselves emotionally, too, wondering whether we are too pushy, too assertive, too strong, too weak.

"If you feel so intensely criticized deep within, it attacks your self-esteem," Vaz said. "Self-esteem is the engine that runs our minds and bodies. It's the engine that gets us through life. Just like it is important to keep your car properly oiled and checked, monitor your self-esteem and keep aware of the things that make you feel diminishment in yourself. It might be a situation, it might be a person who drains the energy out of you. Maybe you haven't found the right work environment, and that depletes you because you aren't given the opportunities or encouragement you deserve."

Many of us suffer from the "Dorothy Syndrome," she said, and like Dorothy in *The Wizard of Oz*, we don't realize what we have at home within ourselves until we realize our own beauty and power. "You have a whole lot of skills, but the cognitive distortions in your mind won't let you see how valuable the skills are that you possess. You have to go through a lot of changes in your life before you come to see, 'Gee, I've had that all along.' Maybe you have worked a dead-end job for a long time. You spend years traveling through Oz in the land of the Wicked Witch until you see the power was within you all along—but you couldn't access it. Maybe you meet somebody kind and benevolent, like Glinda, who says, 'I can't do anything for you except hold up this mirror and say, Look, you have this power within you.'"

That can be a powerful moment. Hopefully, seeing self-esteem as a universal problem will help you to hold up a mirror and put your self-esteem issues in their place. Imagine what it would be like if you could hear all of the negative messages people around you are telling themselves all day. Think about it. The noise would never stop, and the sound of all that negative energy would show you how tragic this self-esteem crisis is. What a sad, sad way for us to live.

Yet, it is ever present. Especially when you see it in someone like Faye Wattleton. Here is a woman who has been showered with some of the nation's most prestigious humanitarian and service awards, been featured in dozens of major national magazines and has continued to be a regular spokesperson on national television for women's issues. She exudes intelligence and is strikingly beautiful—so beautiful that *People* magazine listed her as one of the twenty-five most beautiful people in the world.

And still, Wattleton, who led Planned Parenthood for fourteen of the organization's most challenging years, is haunted by some of the same ghosts that vex us all. "I have a profound sense of inadequacy," she admits. She says that she doesn't see herself as beautiful. She knows she's intelligent, but says she doesn't always think she deserves her success. "I was not brought up to feel good about myself. You see someone onstage and think, 'Wow, wouldn't that be a great life?' But you don't often know the burden that person is carrying." She thinks she's her own worst enemy. "We have been conditioned to not think of ourselves as achievers," she says. "We don't escape the power of that conditioning by success. I was not programmed to think of myself as beautiful or smart or worthy of attention. I always strive to be better and to justify the goodness that people think is in me. But the self-doubt is there, and I wonder if I am a fraud and if I am as capable as people think. These are questions that still constantly burden me."

She knows she isn't the only one with such feelings. "Women who move on the edge of achievement are always dogged with these fears," she says. "Men don't have that. They are conditioned to expect to succeed. They believe it is their right." Yale's Marianne La France agrees there. Men carry the burden that they must succeed. Women carry the burden that they must succeed at being the traditional woman first, before trying to succeed at anything else.

"The idea that anybody can do it all is preposterous," says LaFrance. "Despite all the beliefs that a lot of modern marriages are egalitarian and have the assumption of shared child care and domestic efforts, women still do the majority, if not the totality, of domestic work, even if they are working fifty, sixty, seventy hours a week at a job. They are also supposed to be great moms, great hostesses, have the perfect house, perfect meals, perfect children, perfect hairdos, perfect bodies and perfect whatever. I don't think that's changed."

The good news is that you *don't* have to be perfect. You just have to learn to love your imperfections. There's a difference between wanting to be good—or great—at what you do, and wanting to be perfect. "Perfection is a terrible burden to be preoccupied with," LaFrance adds. "The trouble is, I think some women believe there is such a thing as perfection, and by definition, one will always fail if that is the goal. It cannot be achieved. Make peace with that by not aiming for perfection. Decide what your goals are, figure out how you are going to get there. Then quiet all the other messages down."

Let's cut to the sight of teenage supermodel Crystal McKinney, sans makeup, in front of the MTV camera. As the camera closes in on her, an astonishing reality is revealed. Her forehead is covered with pimples. She taunts the camera to come in even closer for a better look. WOW. Major acne. And then, she shares an incredible truth with the viewer: Those perfectly-toned, perfectly coifed, perfectly dressed models like herself are as imperfect as the rest of us. The perfect woman has zits. That is good news.

Accepting Your Uniqueness

Have you ever come into work, sat down and gotten this feeling that you are different, not like the others, not quite as "normal" as the rest of your peers? You are probably sitting right in the middle of a bunch of people who don't think they are as "normal" as you. Experts call this the "Misfit Complex," and it is exacerbated when you are good at what you do, when you have achieved some level of success and when you are standing out front. Those elements are isolating in a competitive environment.

Gayle Greer, who gave up her job as senior vice president at Time Warner Cable to plunge into her own Internet business venture, spent years battling her self-esteem. Her own feelings of being a misfit were magnified by the experience of being one of the very few females—and the only black female—in a senior management position in the whole cable industry as it developed. Most of the women she encountered were sitting behind desks as secretaries.

She was the only black person in the Time Warner corporate headquarters in Denver. "I didn't feel like a peer, and I didn't feel like a subordinate. I just always felt different, like there was something wrong with me," she said. Isolation is a killer. And, learn this one from Greer: The more you find yourself trying to fit in, the more you need to make sure you don't lose yourself. Greer said she regrets her never-ending quest for validation from people at work. Her personal reference points shifted until her work persona overpowered her individuality. "When I would say, 'I'm Gayle Greer,' it wasn't enough to stop. It was, 'I'm Gayle Greer, senior vice president of Time Warner.' One day, you look around and you have all the things you think you should have, and you still aren't there. You don't feel right."

She went into therapy and really went to work on herself. Looking back on it, she thinks her self-doubts and low self-esteem hurt her career because she never saw herself as others did, and missed out on opportunities to advance because she was afraid to show interest in them. She was too afraid she'd be rejected. Although Greer is now one of Colorado's most visible power brokers, serving on all the right boards, in all the right places, she still says, "I don't think of myself as a successful businesswoman. I don't think of myself as a successful anything."

Low self-esteem is so widespread among women that even top entertainment actors suffer from it. Rita Moreno, who won the Oscar in 1961 as best supporting actress for *West Side Story*, waged a torturous battle to build her self-esteem. She felt inferior to others and her fight to break out of stereotypical Latino roles for women convinced her she wasn't good enough. "I was an extremely insecure young woman, which was ironic because I looked to the rest of the world like I was always in charge. I was charming, cute, and I was sexy. I twitched my little hips around and rolled my little eyes. I was playing a role. Of course, the more you pretend, the worse it gets. You keep digging a deeper hole for yourself."

She said she felt like the whole world was looking at her and making fun of her. "I had a real fixation with mirrors from the time I was about sixteen," she said. "I remember being in a nightclub with a guy I had a crush on and there were mirrors all over the place. He said, 'Do you mind looking at me when I talk?' I was so scared that the next time I looked, I'd be ugly. I lacked a sense of identity." Finally, a friend sat her down and told her she needed to go to work on herself and get some therapy. It took seven years to get to the point where she liked herself. "When you leave therapy, you don't leave the demons behind," she says. "You simply learn how to control them."

Have people always been so hard on themselves, or is it just our generation? Psychologist Jackie James, of the Radcliffe College at Harvard University says it's us. "I don't think our parents thought self-esteem was what mattered, so they didn't take their self-esteem temperature every day," she said. "Ours is a generation of self-examination—much more than our parents' generation was. My parents were focused on having enough money, putting food on the table, being sure they could educate their children and making sure they could prepare their children to be self-sufficient. Ours is a generation of psychological self-help and professional help."

Rita Moreno points out something important. She lacked identity, and that's what many of us lack. If we felt whole and that we truly knew ourselves, we wouldn't have this sense of not knowing who we are and we wouldn't try and fill ourselves up with externals that can never satisfy us.

Nothing To Laugh At

Comedian Margaret Cho's self-esteem battle was paralyzing in its own way. The quick rise and fall of her television sitcom left her doubting everything about herself. To satisfy the producers' expectations that she slim down for the show, she embarked on a dangerous diet regimen that damaged her kidneys but didn't quell the barbs about her weight from the tabloids. The *Star* magazine still ran her picture under the headline, "Would you be caught dead in this outfit?" "It went back to a ballet recital I was in when I was eight years old," she says. "I was so proud my father came, but all I can remember him saying was, 'You were the fattest ballerina.' I felt inadequate."

After her show was cancelled in 1994, she bottomed out, consumed by her drug and alcohol addictions. She had to believe she was worth saving before she could begin her climb back up. A year after sobering up, she's one of the most successful women standup comics around. She says she's finally coming to embrace who she really is. "One day, I wondered what I would think if I was somebody at one of my shows watching me perform," she says. "I started to realize that, if I wasn't me, I would like me. That is such a wonderful thing to realize. That is true power."

Radcliffe's Professor James says we start losing our confidence if we don't feel good about ourselves *all* the time. Real self-esteem comes when you know you have flaws, and become comfortable with that fact because you also know you are always working to improve yourself. James has had her ups and downs, just like everybody else. One day, she might be riding high, appreciating her work. The next day, she might not get a grant, then dog herself with questions like, "What am I doing wrong? Why is this happening?" Instead of spiraling downward, she deals with those moments by acknowledging them for what they are—ups and downs, like everyone has in life.

The key to dealing with these issues is the ability to put negative experiences in perspective says Harvard psychology professor Ellen Langer. Some people learn, as children, that they are bad. They go through life taking any failure as proof of their lack of worth. "If one is brought up believing that, essentially, they are nice, they are good, they are caring, then when something goes wrong, the individual searches for situational explanations of why something went wrong, rather than questioning their basic worth," Langer said. But, if you don't have that kind of foundation, any bad experience can be internalized. "If you believe that at the core you are bad, all you need is one instance every so often to confirm that," she said. In other words, you might get it right ninety times out of a hundred, but you'll seize on your ten mistakes as proof you aren't worthy. "Self-esteem goes up and down in all people," says clinical psychologist Kathryn Jens of Denver. "But because of the entitlement principle men are socialized with, they just tend to blame the situation. They externalize the blame and say, 'That guy was a jerk' or whatever. Women internalize it. They question themselves."

Overcoming It

For someone who started working in cotton fields at age ten and rose to the highest ranks of organized labor as executive vice president of the AFL-CIO, it is surprising that Linda Chavez-Thompson would ever question herself. But, she does. She says sometimes she feels "stupid." She has no college degree—or even a high school diploma and that sometimes makes her feel inadequate. Chavez-Thompson found a way to preserve herself after dealing with a boss who used to try to intimidate her because of her lack of formal education. "I'd bounce back and say, 'I am smarter than that,' " she said. ". . . One of the problems so many women have is, we care what people think about us. That they talk about us. I have had so many bad things said about me, so many innuendoes. It really used to break my heart. Then I got a little tougher and a little tougher and a little tougher. Not that I don't care anymore. I care, but I don't let it stop me. Women have yet to learn how to get tough on the inside, how to have a harder shell. That is why it is so important to believe in what you are doing. If you really, truly believe in what you are doing, that gives you a lot of power. And gather good people around you. That helps you to be empowered to make changes."

Ease Up on Yourself

"There are so many ways in which we are so critical of ourselves," says Sarah Weddington, the attorney who won the landmark 1973 *Roe v. Wade* case in front of the U.S. Supreme Court. "There's an old story a nurse told me years ago. Women will be brought into the emergency room having been in an accident or shot or whatever, and they'll say, 'I'm sorry. I didn't have time to shave my legs this morning.' We are so quick to criticize ourselves. We all have those tapes in our heads, critical tapes, and we are the first to know what our faults are. We're always going to have those tapes. The key is to offset them. Make other voices louder." She believes that one way of doing that is calling in your personal support network. "When you are down on yourself, they say, 'Yeah, but think of how wonderful you are or what a good friend you are or how much you have done . . .' "

Psychologist Jens agrees that one of the single most important ways to empower yourself when you are feeling bad is to surround yourself with people who understand you and what you are going through. "There is a daily stress level that each of us carries with the daily digs and comments we get," she says. "Just going for it, we are under a barrage of flack. The way to withstand it is to have a strong support group that shares your reality." When women get isolated from their support base, they often don't have an understanding of why they are being disregarded, she said. "Criticism and insults tend to be taken personally," Jens said. "That erodes self-esteem."

That erosion is magnified if you dare buck the status quo and push for change. "People tend to shy away when they see somebody starting to get 'out there,'" she said. "They don't have courage to come forward to support you, and instead, you'll hear comments like, 'She's too far out there.' They start taking away their association, their claim to friendship with you because they don't want to wind up under attack too. So, you get scared, and without support, you tend to start personalizing more of what is happening. Like you have done something wrong. You start believing what everyone is saying, that you are getting too far 'out there.' That is why you have got to find your support community."

When You Talk to Yourself

Work sucked today. You sucked at work. Or maybe someone said something about you behind your back and it made you feel bad. Or, there's that ten pounds that crept on over the holidays. There's *always* an excuse to give yourself a hard time and start the process of self-loathing. Well, you can like yourself today or you can hate yourself today. You can be happy, or not. So much of how you feel in life is up to you. Have you ever noticed that once you start being mean to yourself, it gets worse and worse? Why not start being kind to yourself, instead? We're talking about *self*-esteem here. That means *you* have to take control of your *self*.

The first task is turning off your negative self-talk. When you catch yourself saying "I'm fat" or "I'm looking old" or "I'm not any good" or "I'm slipping," you have to consciously replace those negative messages with positive ones. Say, "I'm strong, I can handle it . . . I'm beautiful. I may not like this or that about how I look, but I can work at it and change it if I want."

If you're experiencing tough times, don't fill your head with thoughts like, "I have rotten luck," or "This isn't my year." Tell yourself, "Better days are coming . . . This won't last forever . . . There's always going to be some obstacle in life." Brainstorm ways to make your situation better. If there is nothing you can do, brainstorm ways to make it bearable.

One of our biggest challenges is taking charge of our negative thinking. Research has repeatedly proven that repetition of positive affirmations convinces the brain of their truth. The most powerful affirmations come from within. Look to your specific situation and find positive thoughts that will get you through it. If you're in the middle of a bad breakup, you might say "I am feeling stronger every day." Or, "This needed to happen. It's all for the best."

If you are having a hard time achieving a goal, do a little soul searching. Believe in yourself enough to keep fighting and say, "Well, I want this, it isn't going to be easy, but I'm up to the challenge. I'm stronger than this situation. I'll win." Whatever. It's not just affirmations—it's positive thinking.

Psychotherapist Vaz suggests starting your "reprogramming" by getting a tape player and either buying or checking out audiotapes that focus on improving self-esteem. "We think a certain way because we have been given a lot of ideas, a lot of knowledge from our families, church, the political system and the work world," she said. "All of our tapes basically come from the outside world. Changing those tapes involves a process of reconditioning. Substitute those old tapes with new ones that are more empowering."

There is something very validating knowing that other women—strong, successful women—are fighting the same demons we are fighting. It's liberating. It's priceless knowledge that you can use. Instead of expecting the "reward" for your angst to come once you have achieved your goals, claim your reward now. Give yourself permission to be hopeful about your life and about yourself. You are on a long journey, and you can feel good about it—or bad. You have to be strong enough to allow yourself to be imperfect and like yourself either because, or in spite of, those imperfections. Live. Love yourself.

You don't get to be anyone else, so you might as well make peace with who you are.

A MOMENT WITH . . .
LINDA CHAVEZ-THOMPSON,
executive vice president, AFL-CIO

"I started in the cotton fields when I was ten and went full time when I was fifteen. That was the year my dad made me stop going to school. He had some of those ideas that girls don't need an education. I remember I was out hoeing cotton in the field and was watching the bus pick up my brothers to take them to school. I cried for two weeks.

"I hated it in the cotton fields. You'd have nine-foot cotton sacks, long tubes, that you'd have to put your cotton in. Then you'd carry it over and they would pay you for the weight of the cotton. They gave me thirty cents an hour because I was a kid. The grown-ups got fifty cents.

"All you do is fill it, weigh it, unload it. Any sack could weigh between ninety and 120 pounds, so I was literally carrying my own weight. At twenty-five, I found out I had curvature of the spine.

"If you were hoeing, it was ten hours of whacking the weeds in the field, five days a week. Picking cotton was just eight hours a day. Given a choice, I would always choose hoeing. Always.

"I never knew what it was like to spend a summer doing nothing. I saw kids swimming, playing ball—having real summers. My sisters, my brothers and I all worked. We were a good team. My dad had standing orders for jobs from all the ranchers because we were diligent and had a good reputation. That kept us going. It gave us a little bit of self-esteem.

"I was alone a lot and I would dream that someday I was going to be somebody. I didn't know what, but I was going to be someone who was well-respected. My dream was to have a white-collar job. Like being a clerk at Sears. For me, that was being somebody.

"I wanted to be somebody, to do something. But I didn't know what. The opportunity came in 1967 when my uncle talked to a guy who needed a bilingual secretary. The secretary he had couldn't speak Spanish, but 75 percent of the workers were Mexican-Americans. He asked if I could type, and I said, 'Just a little.' But some of his workers came in and I talked with them in Spanish. That did it. I got the job.

"I couldn't believe I had actually made it into a white-collar job, purely by accident. Once I got there, I saw people who didn't understand English well who were getting union wages. They were doing backbreaking work, but they had good wages, a health insurance plan and good hours. We didn't have that when we worked on the farm.

"The most I ever remember my father getting paid was thirty dollars a week. He had a wife and eight kids. That was the 1950s, and as sharecroppers, we had a free house and utilities, with land to grow vegetables.

"I tried to convince my dad to join the union and let me find work for him. In 1968, my dad was fifty-four years old. I said, 'We can find you a job.' He said, 'But, I don't know how to read and write.' I said, 'Dad, you speak English, they'll tell you what to do.' We got him in.

"I will never forget the tears in his eyes when he got his first paycheck. He worked a forty-hour week and had earned more than he was earning in two months on the farm.

"I fell in love with organized labor."

THREE

DARING TO TAKE RISKS

A PETTY INSULT CHANGED JILL Gould's life forever. The mother of five was working as a secretary in a small town in Kansas when a man came into her office and told her, "You have an idiot's job." "I decided right then and there I was never going to be in a position again where somebody was going to call me an idiot," she said.

Gould took a chance and bet on herself. At age twenty-nine, she started college, went to medical school, and then went on to specialize and become one of the world's first women forensic pathologists. She ventured into politics, then gave that up to spend a year traveling around the world. After that, she went for a master's degree in public health so she could use her medical expertise in her world travels. Her latest e-mail comes from Bosnia, where she is investigating the deaths of the people left behind in mass graves. Had she not embraced risk, she'd still be sitting behind a secretary's desk. "Nothing comes to you if you just sit there and wait," she said. "You have to look for things yourself. Some of the things you try won't work. All you say then is, 'Oh, that one didn't work. I'll try something else.'"

Gould has two beautifully simple mantras:

1. If you aren't doing something, you're doing nothing.

2. Don't let security be your dangerous anchor.

The only things she truly regrets in life are the things she didn't try she says. "Sure there are a few things I look back at and wish I hadn't done, but they were always the building blocks, the teaching blocks. All you have to do is have the real desire. You can do anything you want."

Why Risk It?

Where would Jane Goodall be had she not dared to go to Africa to study? What if Ellen Goodman hadn't dared show her editor that first column? What would be the status of women in the U.S. Navy had Paula Couglin not told her superior she had been assaulted at the Tailhook convention in San Diego? What if oceanographer Sylvia Earle hadn't dared to go scuba diving that first time? How many of the protections gained by women and children would not have been won had Pat Schroeder not run for U.S. Congress in a race no one expected her to win? This list goes on and on, beginning with these pioneers and finding life within our own daily experiences. So much greatness begins with one small, bold move. Most of these women never imagined the success they would achieve. They built it, one risk at a time, often unaware of how very far they would go.

Remember: This is your moment. You can choose to live your life to the fullest and risk the unknown. Or, you can spend your life living indoors with the shades drawn. You can choose to eat only the healthiest foods, drive in the safest neighborhoods, save all your money for an emergency—it doesn't matter. You're still going to die. Just don't forget to live.

Here is a true fact: Men like risk more than women. Women fear risk because they fear making mistakes, says psychology professor Carol Dweck of Columbia University. "If you think mistakes measure you, risk is threatening," she said. "If you see risks as exciting opportunities to learn, then you are way ahead."

Women are more wary of risk because, as girls, we were taught not to act out and praised for our intelligence and good behavior. Boys were criticized when they acted out or messed up. But, they learned that criticism was a message about effort, and saw opportunities to improve things. We didn't learn that because we were too busy being good. We took criticism as a sign that we weren't intelligent or perfect. Girls tend to learn it is better to not risk failing than it is to try something and miss.

"Girls are the stars of grade school," Dweck says. "If life were one big grade school, girls would be the stars. But, the name of the game changes to reward risk-taking and resilience. That's where girls start losing their edge." When a woman is applying for a job and is asked if she can do something she knows little about, she'll say no, Dweck said. Men will say, "Sure," meaning "Sure, I can learn."

"Women feel insecure about things they don't already know," she says. "For them, having ability means already knowing something, as opposed to ability meaning you can learn it over time. So, women want to know in advance that they will be able to know everything." We lack the confidence of knowing we'll learn it over time. Before we can dare to learn to succeed, we have to conquer our fear of failing. Usually, the odds are much greater that we will succeed. And we must draw our own definitions of personal success and reward ourselves for our small victories. If you find yourself worrying about failing, think about it. Is that really going to happen? And, if you do fail, is it going to kill you? No! You'll just pick yourself up, dust yourself off, and try something else.

Trust Your Gut

Carly Fiorina has quite an interesting resume for a woman hailed as the most powerful businesswoman in the world. Among her credentials: Receptionist. Law school dropout. Teacher. Job jumper. She wouldn't be where she is— CEO of Hewlett-Packard, the thirteenth largest company on the Fortune 500—if she didn't have the guts to leap into the unknown. Like the other women interviewed for this book, Fiorina credits the ability to embrace risk as the most important ingredient for success. She ought to know.

In 1989, when deciding whether to transfer from the communications side of the AT&T Corp. to the technology side, everybody warned her off. What did she know about such things? This is a woman whose college majors were medieval history and philosophy. It wasn't the first time she was told not to do something, but this time *everybody* was against it, and strongly against it. "You have to make decisions yourself and accept the consequences," she says. "You can't let other people make the decisions, or shift the blame for them. When people would say I shouldn't do it, I'd end up saying, 'I appreciate your input, but I'm going to make this decision because . . . ' and usually the answer was because I'd find the change more challenging, more interesting."

The naysayers warned that "interesting" wouldn't matter if the move killed her career. To that, Fiorina would simply respond, "Well, if it does, it does." At first, it looked like the warnings were right. Her first six months were killers, causing her to doubt herself and wonder if she'd sabotaged her own career. "I remember this heavy conversation with my husband over Christmas saying, 'Frank, this was a huge mistake. I need to go figure out something else to do,'" she recalled. "You're not failing," he told her. "It's just hard." She doesn't remember the exact turning point, but she does remember it getting more fun. She said she noticed her work making a difference and having an impact on the people around her.

Fiorina says we shouldn't be so afraid of failure. Making mistakes can build a powerful self-confidence, one that only comes from failing and surviving. "Part of what that period taught me was that it does take time," she says. "Change takes time. Influencing people takes time. It takes persistence. You can't go rushing in and expect everything to be different in a month." That tough career decision is now what she calls, "the best thing I ever did."

She believes that the fear of failure may hold someone back but it shouldn't. "I like the high-wire act. I like the rush of having to stay concentrated in order to be successful. If things get easy, I get bored."

Your Risk Profile

Don't kick yourself if you aren't immediately ready to start jumping out of airplanes and taking extraordinary risks. Your appetite for risk is something that is greatly influenced by your personality, says Dr. Jackie James, a psychologist and professor at Radcliffe College. "One of the things I have studied a lot is motivation. There are people who are affiliative: They are usually low risk-takers. There are people who are power-oriented and they take huge risks. Then there are people who are achievement-oriented and their risk-taking is somewhere in the middle." She says that everyone is motivated differently by the need for power, achievement and affiliation with others but one of those needs is generally dominant. Where do you fit on the risk continuum?

How Much Risk Can You Stomach?

This test looks at six different areas of personality to see how much risk you are comfortable with.

First, look at the area you are being asked to evaluate. Then, look at the scale below and determine where you fit. Award yourself zero to four points for each risk, based on the scoring system here. When you have finished an individual category, total the points, then divide by the number of questions in the category. Go back to the scale below and see where you fall in that particular area.

SCORING YOUR APPETITE FOR RISK

0 POINTS

NO RISK. You hate risk. You don't like change, you don't like risk, you want things the way they are. You'd rather deal with what you know than take a chance at something different. You'll keep your money in low-interest accounts and stay out of the stock market.

1 POINT

LOW RISK. You are wary of risk. You're only willing to try if you are certain of a favorable result. You'll occasionally try something new, but only if you know, up front, that you have it cinched.

2 POINTS

MODERATE RISK. You aren't afraid of trying something new if its odds of success are more than 50 percent in your favor. You'll tiptoe into the danger zone, but you also will retreat if it looks too scary. If you're investing, you might try a little bit of risk, but you'll never chance the whole wad.

3 POINTS

HIGH RISK. You aren't afraid of risk. You know that you win some, you lose some. Generally, you'll try something as long as the chance of success isn't impossible. You'll take certain big risks because they come with big rewards.

4 POINTS

EXTREME RISK. You love risk, more than you should. Chances of success are less than 20 percent. You love bucking the odds. If you have a slim chance of pulling it off, you want to go for it. If you make it, it shocks everybody. If you like risking what you have when you have a lot to lose, you are on fire.

ASSERTIVE RISK

_____ General personal assertiveness

_____ Correcting gossip or misperceptions about you

_____ Addressing it when someone has wronged you in some way

_____ Asking for refunds

_____ Making an informal complaint

_____ Filing formal complaints or lawsuits

_____ Challenging a decision by going up to the next level or higher

_____ TOTAL ASSERTIVE POINTS (Divide by 7)

_____ ASSERTIVE RISK SCORE

PERSONAL RELATIONSHIPS

_____ Asking someone out on a date

_____ Interacting with strangers in cocktail party situations

_____ Telling someone who is interested in you that you don't want to go out anymore

_____ Getting married

_____ Ending a bad relationship

_____ Mixing finances with your significant other

_____ Buying a house with someone else

_____ Being open about your problems or concerns, sharing secrets

_____ TOTAL PERSONAL RISK POINTS (Divide by 8)
_____ PERSONAL RISK SCORE

RISKING BEING DIFFERENT

_____ Dressing and looking "different"

_____ Making a speech, singing solo in public, sharing your personal writings

_____ Publicly voicing disagreement with the majority

_____ Acting different and being noticed because of it

_____ Having a relationship that doesn't fit the "norm" (commuter, gay, bi-racial, etc.)

_____ TOTAL UNIQUE RISK POINTS (Divide by 4)
_____ UNIQUE RISK SCORE

FINANCIAL RISK

_____ Investing in stocks, money markets, bonds, etc.

_____ Riding out downturns in the market

_____ Buying a home

_____ Gambling

_____ Going into debt

_____ TOTAL MONEY POINTS (Divide by 5)
_____ MONEY RISK SCORE

WORK

_____ Seeking promotions

_____ Asking for raises

_____ Changing jobs

_____ Changing careers

_____ Responding to negatives on your performance review

_____ Taking the blame for a mistake

_____ Speaking out when you or others are being wrongly treated

_____ Speaking out when your company is being unethical

_____ Associating with the office "oddballs" or "troublemakers"

_____ TOTAL WORK RISK POINTS (Divide by 9)
_____ WORK RISK SCORE

LIVING

_____ Being adventurous in travel, sports and activities

_____ Relocating to an area where you don't have friends

_____ Trusting experimental or risky medical treatment

_____ Taking time for yourself, even when your family may resent it

_____ Smoking, drinking excessively, being overweight

_____ TOTAL LIFE RISK POINTS (Divide by 5)
_____ LIFE RISK SCORE

Where do you take risks? Note the scores for each category here and look back to the scoring key to see what kind of risk-taker you are.

Assertiveness_____
Personal Relationships_____
Being "different"_____
Finances_____
Work_____
Living_____

Are you surprised by those scores? Satisfied? Consider using the results as a guide to personal growth. For example, if the test made it clear that you avoid financial risk, maybe it's because you need to learn more about managing your money so it feels less foreign and intimidating. In that case, your first step could involve reading a book about investment strategy or taking an inventory of how much money you have and need, or making an appointment with a financial planner. Or, perhaps, the test indicated that you fear interpersonal conflict and refuse to stand up for yourself. Then, you might do confrontational role play with a friend whose assertiveness you admire, or practice saying "no" to unwanted requests or ask for help the next time you need it. Or, at a minimum, you'll say something the next time someone cuts in front of you in the grocery line. The point of the test is to show that no one is perfect and we all have room to grow. Use the information from this test to set realistic goals for change, then take action and enjoy the journey.

Embrace the Unknown

I interviewed oceanographer Sylvia Earle the day I was deciding whether or not I would chase my dream, leave my job and write this book full-time. She talked of risk, success and failure, redefining all of those concepts in a way that turned the interview into an awakening, rather than a question-and-answer session. I'd wanted her in this book because of her courage and her legendary status, but as we talked, I realized she belonged here because she knows how to live. And she changed my life forever.

Earle is the world's best-known female oceanographer, marine biologist and aquanaut, a woman who has lived a life defined by risk. She says she knows no other way of living. At age three, her family spent summer vacations on the Jersey shore. "That's where I first fell in love with the ocean," she says. "A big wave knocked me over, just tumbled me right over. I couldn't find the bottom for what seemed like a very, very long time. It was probably just a minute. But I finally found the bottom and I found air. I was exhilarated. It was very exciting and I jumped back in for more." That was her flash of inspiration.

By legend, Earle is now known as "Her Deepness." She is the undisputed queen of the depths, as the world's most accomplished woman oceanographer, marine biologist and aquanaut. In 1970, she led the first group of women aquanauts in the Tektite II expedition to live for two weeks in a submersible, fifty feet below the surface of the ocean near the Virgin Islands. She and the others became celebrities and were hailed in a ticker tape parade and a White House reception. Nine years later, she walked at the bottom of the sea at the lowest depth ever achieved by any human. For two hours, she walked alone at 1,250 feet below the surface, a record that still stands. "I feel driven. I don't think of what I do as something involving courage. It is not only what I want to do, it's what I must do," she said. "It's not even a choice. It's as if the road is out there in my head. Not that somebody has put it there. It's there. Opportunity is there. I have to know where I want to go in my own mind. It is hard for me to mentor someone else to do what I have done. What I try to do is cause people to have confidence in themselves to do what they want to do.

"Prepare in every way you can to take advantage of what comes in front of you. Whether your passion is to be a scientist, run a business, be a mom or anything else, give it everything you have. That is the pleasure. That is the fun. Every moment of every day is filled with life. I don't fear going to places where no one has been. It's exciting. It's a challenge. People are afraid of the unknown, I suppose. That's what causes people to be afraid, not just in terms of exploration. You fear an enemy mostly because of what you don't know. You are afraid of what they might do, not what they are doing. I fear ignorance."

When Earle says she knows about risk, she is often talking from her experience in business, when she started an engineering company for underwater exploration. That venture failed, but she said she doesn't have regrets. "I don't have a lot in the bank," she said. "In fact, when I started Deep Ocean Engineering, which really had the potential to be a very successful enterprise, I rolled the dice and lost. It put me substantially in the hole. I put my faith in people who were not worthy, who squandered the investment, and all these years later, I am still in debt for that. I mortgaged the house to finance the company and had poor judgment in terms of some of the people I had asked to serve on the board of directors. They did not serve well. I finally left the company, but I still have the debt."

You'd think she would be smarting from that one. Not Earle. "I don't feel bitter," she says. "I feel enlightened. Boy, did I learn a lot about what to do and, in some cases, what not to do. I learned there comes a time when you need to let go. I regret that I didn't have better judgment of some of the people I surrounded myself with, including some who were lifelong friends. I feel disappointment and I feel sadness that they have taken this wonderful opportunity and have not made the best of it. But, I got the best of it. I got the education. They can't take away what I put in my brain and they can't take away history."

Sylvia Earle knows who she is. She understands that she is comfortable being a risk-taker. She also understands that most people are not. "Many people resist risk and are only comfortable with the security of knowing, when they go to sleep at night, what the next day is going to be like. That's comforting. It's secure. And, living like that is a choice they are free to make. I recognize the importance most people place on having structure in their lives," she says. "Not having structure can be disconcerting. They should not try to do what I do if structure brings them peace and comfort. Risk is a choice. It is the only way to test your potential. Weigh the odds and understand potential obstacles, then decide where to go," she said.

That's why she chooses to take risks that satisfy her soul now, rather than waiting for some other day. "Most people choose a pattern for living by getting a job and trying to hold on to it for dear life because that is security and at a certain age, they can retire and then do 'what they really want to do,' which is relax or play golf. Well, I've always done what I wanted to do. It's riskier, but people pay a lot of money to go out on an expedition and do what I do. I do it as a part of my work. I love it. I have a good friend who is an engineer and develops submersibles. He said, 'I never worked a day in my life.' He worked very hard, but it was such a pleasure. That's how it's been for me."

And in the time since I listened to Earle's advice, that's how it's been for me, too. The risk can be enormous, but the payoff can be bliss. It's a matter of embracing the possibility in life and accepting the fact that change is inevitable. Choose change, rather than letting it happen mindlessly. Maybe you're just tired of your job. Or, your boss is a condescending jerk. Maybe you've gone as far as you're going to go with your current employer or maybe you just don't feel challenged. Or, maybe you want to make more money. In any case, if these doldrums are prolonged and you keep getting up each morning and doing the same thing while rationalizing that it could be worse at another job, you are likely in a rut. Here are ten more telltale signs:

1. You aren't having fun

2. You aren't challenged

3. You enjoy your job less and less

4. You don't ever feel like talking about your work with your friends and family

5. You are smarter than your bosses

6. You keep reminding yourself of the good attributes of your job, and they all have to do with "golden handcuffs"—good pay, benefits and time off

7. You can predict your future and it looks exactly like your present

8. People say, "Are you *still* working there?"

9. You are jealous whenever someone "climbs over the wall" and quits

10. You feel "stuck"

The good thing about status quo is it's so damned comfortable. If you've done something a hundred times, you feel pretty competent. If you've never done it, you aren't so sure. But, that's also the bad thing about status quo.

Getting Out of a Rut

Most of us know a little about getting bored at work. Too often, our bosses are more than happy to remind us that we should be grateful to even have jobs. It is so important that you always, always know your marketability and worth, so you don't fall into a rut because you are convinced you can't do better.

Most of us aren't lucky enough to have a continuous stream of head-hunters calling to beg us for our resumes. That means we have to have the guts to go out there on our own. It is so much easier to stay in a rotten job than it is to quit, and even though inertia may be boring, it is generally a safe place to waste time. But, if you suspect that your future will look a lot like your present, it's time to consider another path. I once worked as a reporter in a newsroom where everyone felt frustrated and unappreciated. Some felt abused by long hours and tyrannical managers. We were all in ruts. Me, the guy across from me, the woman next to him. It wasn't any fun, but none of us had the courage to leave since the job market was tight and our bosses made it clear we were ever-so-lucky to work at such a good paper. Once, a manager showed us a computer printout they kept that tracked and rated the hundreds of applicants waiting in line for one of us to leave.

But, one day, a coworker picked up her purse, walked over to the city desk and told our boss she was leaving for lunch. She went to lunch and never came back. Instead, she marched off into the great unknown, leaving the rest of us to stew in our own inertia. (I have since named this the "Going to Lunch" option. It's my favorite work-related fantasy.) Most of us assumed she'd really done a number on herself because, who would want to hire someone who walked off the job without giving notice and without even quitting? Surely, she would have to spend years on unemployment before finally taking a completely undesirable job just so she could survive. We knew we were much better off, having done nothing.

But, it wasn't long before that woman landed a more prestigious and better-paying job than the one she'd abandoned. And there we sat, still waiting for opportunity to come get us. I lasted another one and one-half years. One day, I updated my resume, to have it "just in case." A few days later, I wrote a cover letter. A week later, I actually mailed it all out. I even sent it to a newspaper that I thought wouldn't give me a second look. One month later, I was working there at that great newspaper, in a much better job with a much better paycheck in a much better city. Moral: You have to take a chance.

Contrast that with a third reporter at the bad paper who never had the guts to leave. Deep down, she was sure things would get better and she would be appreciated and treated with respect. More than a decade has passed, and she's still sitting at the same terminal in the same room being unappreciated, underpaid and mistreated. The rest of us have gone on to new challenges and success, have had new adventures and are making much more money. No guts, no glory.

Always have an updated resume, "just in case." It's amazing how many people remain stuck in bad situations because they fear the ordeal of typing up a new resume. Well, thank God for the computer age. There are hundreds of templates out there, and all you need to do is come up with a few specifics. Give yourself a few hours or even a full day to update the credentials on your resume. Then, write a cover letter, just for practice, just in case. Although you should individualize every letter sent to potential employers, you should always have a stock approach ready, talking up your main assets.

Then, take a chance and mail it all out. Be bold! Send it to places where you know you might get hired and to places you think wouldn't give you a second look. Why? Because the workplace is filled with surprises. Too many people miss out because they assume certain opportunities are out of their grasp. That can be a false assumption. You don't know what options await you until you test your limits. Besides, a good word processor makes it all too easy to crank out a batch of good cover letters. Taking a shot at the seemingly impossible costs just two minutes of time and a postage stamp.

When taking a plunge into the unknown, I often think of a woman I encountered working at the grocery store. After more than twenty years of marriage to a verbally and physically abusive man, she finally had the guts to walk out. She'd never worked in her life. "Six weeks ago, I was living in a

$250,000 house," she said. "Now, I'm making sandwiches for minimum wage. You know what? I have never felt better." She had to know that the perils of the unknown had to be better than the certainty of continued violence. She had to know that she was worth taking the chance. That woman had to fight for her life. And there so many of us sit, so worried about taking chances because we have secure jobs with three or four weeks of paid vacation, two personal days, good insurance and big, fat 401(k) plans.

We aren't going to bottom out. Smart women survive. We take chances, knowing that we've succeeded in the past and will succeed in the future. Odds are, we can get even better jobs with even better benefits. If you sense that you've fallen into a rut, look around you. Is your situation going to improve on its own? Is your boss on his or her way out? Or, could he or she be promoted and become even *more* powerful? If it's possible that good times are coming, what's the time frame? If you are going to suffer indefinitely, you have to look inside yourself and ask why you are unable to take action on your own behalf. Don't you deserve better? Whether it's dumping a bad boss or a lousy husband, you don't get a heck of a lot of time here on this earth. You know how fast the years go by, so why lose them being mired in a rut?

Make Your Own Choices

We've spent a long time looking at the danger of inertia because it is a significant obstacle to taking healthy risks. It is not, however, the only one. Some women also are waiting for someone else to open the door. They feel someone else must grant them permission to take a chance, to be daring.

Kathrine Switzer, a running legend and motivational speaker, frequently mingles with women who offer excuses for their fear of trying. "I had a discussion with a woman the other day who said, 'I can't do that. They won't let me.' I said, 'Who is *they*?' She kept trying to articulate the 'they.' It came down to men. I said, 'Why are you asking permission of them? Just do it,' " Switzer said.

"I think a lot of women are raised to think they have to keep asking for permission to do things. They don't realize that they don't need permission. They can just do it. It takes a lot of courage to do it because we are raised to ask permission. If you don't take the chance, you don't reap the rewards. Woody Allen said 80 percent of his success was that he just showed up," says Switzer, credited with being the first woman to compete in an organized marathon. "Sometimes, by just showing up, you get what you are after. It's having the courage to try it, the courage to take the chance."

Many of us are waiting for the perfect moment to make our move. We think, as soon as all of our ducks are in a row, then we can finally do it. Call it the curse of perfectionism, if you like. Whatever you call it, know that it's a fantasy and a delaying tactic. In fact, television newswoman Cokie Roberts warns that if you wait until you think you've covered every base, you'll never accomplish anything. "Anything I do for the first time is scary, whether it is anchoring *Nightline* or throwing my daughter's wedding. What works for me is to just go do it," she said. Forget planning for all the possibilities.

"I feel that way about life," Roberts said. "That it isn't worth a lot of agonizing about and it's certainly not worth a lot of planning. These young women who say, 'First I'm going to get married, then get the job, then have the children . . . ' Well, probably not. It won't work that way. Life will happen to you. Things will happen to change your life's view while you are busy planning. The best thing is to just do it. Get up, put one foot in front of the other and don't be afraid to take new challenges, even if they are scary, because it is going to be interesting. And, you learn something."

She has a great point. Dreams are dreams. Plans are plans. Whatever you expect to happen is the only thing that won't. Just knowing that gives us incredible freedom. Instead of worrying about staying on course and keeping to our plans, all we have to do is ask ourselves what we are learning along the way, and if we are having enough fun.

Indecisiveness is another critical obstacle to change. "One reason people have trouble making decisions has to do with regret," says Rachel Croson, professor of business at the Wharton School of Business at the University of Pennsylvania. "They say, 'Look, I have to make this decision, but if I make the wrong one, I'm going to regret it a lot. So, I'm going to avoid it and keep collecting information and keep collecting information and not make a decision.'"

The problem is that the decision-making process gets tougher as the stakes get higher. High stakes require high commitment. Choosing what brand of corn flakes to buy doesn't require much of a personal investment. But choosing a job or a life partner does. "For some people, every decision is like that," said Croson, who has done research on the subject. "For others, they think 'I make the wrong decision, so what?'" One way to make the process easier is to do research. If you are deciding whether to commit to a new boss, find out about the person, about the company. Find out why the previous employee left. See how happy other employees are there. Then, start talking about the decision with other people. Their input may help you clarify your thinking.

Don't just make a list of the "pros" and "cons." List as many possible scenarios as you can think of, then decide what's good and bad about each one. How strongly do you feel about them? Give each one a positive or negative impact score of 1 to 10, with 10 being the strongest. Some issues are like "trump" cards that are worth more than all others. If something is *extremely* negative or positive, pay close attention to it. Still nervous? Run through this checklist the next time you're facing a tough decision.

Decision Making for the Decision Wary

1. Ask yourself what you are trying to achieve.

2. Act quickly on decisions that can be changed, more slowly on those that are permanent.

3. What are the alternatives? What are the possible outcomes of each alternative? (Ask yourself, "If I do this, what will likely happen? Then what? And then what?") Plot out the different alternatives on paper. Note the pros and cons. Give weight to each one on a scale of one to ten. Then, evaluate each possibility for its likelihood of happening on a scale of one to ten. Do the math to determine what's best for you.

4. Brainstorm possibilities with other people.

5. Ask yourself what, deep down, you really want to do.

6. Determine whether you are giving too much weight to your fears. Are they realistic? Are they holding you back? Think about how you would act in this situation if you weren't afraid.

7. Don't overly minimize your decision. Decisions are like dominos. One affects the next. At the same time, don't fear decisions. One decision will not ruin your entire life.

8. Don't let decisions pile up.

9. Timing is everything, and think about timing before you start agonizing. A good decision at the wrong time is as harmful as a bad decision at the right time.

10. Pay attention to your gut. If you are unusually apprehensive, anxious or stressed, you may be on the wrong course. Does it feel right? Use your brain to calculate the particulars and your heart to see how it all fits for you.

11. You can always do nothing. Just remember, that's a decision in itself.

12. Involve others in the decision, especially if they are affected by it. That gives them "ownership" and helps them commit to making it work.

13. Make your decision. Live with it. Don't spend the next week or month or year or lifetime beating yourself up because you think you should have tried something else.

14. If you really made a mistake, cut your losses. Decide what to do to fix it. If you still can't make up your mind, go with your gut. Make sure you aren't psyching yourself out with fear and do what feels right.

What's Stopping You?

At some point, you must ask yourself: What is holding me back? Generally, it's fear. But, what is there *really* to fear? If you are afraid of failing, you need to ask yourself what are the real odds that you will bottom out. Is failing at something going to kill you? Force you to live homeless on the streets? Or, will you just learn something that will help you later on?

It's also difficult to conquer a fear of success. Psychologists have long documented the "impostor" complex in women, when we think we don't deserve the success we've attained. We wonder what other people would think if they really knew how ill-prepared we are for our jobs. When you catch yourself getting all negative, realize that others aren't any better prepared for these challenges than you are. They are doing their own dance, making themselves look more knowledgeable, more able and more confident than they might really be. You may fear taking chances because risk can wipe away your security. Security can be a regular paycheck or the familiar faces of bosses and coworkers. It can be the knowledge that you aren't the last hired so you won't be the first fired. But, before you let security coax you into the safety net of predictability, ask yourself how much security you really have. Sure, your employer likes you, but won't your next employer like you, too?

Embracing risk means embracing change. That can make you feel unsafe and on edge. But, be confident that, in time, your new challenge will become as old as the one you're living right now. And, at that point, you'll have to ask yourself again, what's stopping you from moving forward? "People who are brave are scared," said Aida Alvarez, who led the Small Business Administration during the Clinton years and watched as thousands of women fled the corporate world to start their own businesses. "If they weren't scared, they wouldn't need to be brave. When you take a risk, you can fail. I don't care how successful you are. You feel that. I feel that every day. . . . But, if you don't make mistakes, you are not taking risks. If you are not taking risks, you are not learning."

Every bold attempt makes you stronger for the next challenge. There will always be reasons, pro and con, shaping your decision to go for it or to wait it out; just take care that the deciding factor isn't really fear masquerading as something else. You may be frozen in the fear that what you've got is as good as it gets. You may wonder whether you will trade a bad situation for one that is even worse. Walking away may seem to be an admission of failure. Or, you might convince yourself that things will get better if you just wait. Don't fool yourself into inaction. Respond to this fear with faith that you are tough enough to field every curve life throws your way.

Remind yourself that any new challenge is not going to be a struggle every day for the rest of your life. The first time you run ten miles, it's a killer. The twentieth time, it's routine. That's how it is with any new challenge. Every challenge becomes easier as the unknown becomes known. You become more confident. Your self-esteem rises. Soon, it'll all be routine and you will start questioning whether you have fallen into another rut and need a new challenge.

Another good thing to know is that the more you try, the less you'll fear trying. Once you leave a job and discover how employable you are, you'll be more open to make another move. And another and another. Once you go for a promotion and get it, you won't be as timid trying for the next advancement. You have options. It is a big, beautiful world out there. Whenever you catch yourself feeling bored or trapped, throw off the blinders and start brainstorming. Think about all the possibilities that exist for you. What are your wildest dreams? Where would you like to go? What would you like to do? Who would you like to meet? And, what's the risk? Is it big enough to stop you? Or is it time to take your foot off the brake?

From now on, you don't have to feel "stuck" with bad bosses or companies. You don't have to buy it when people tell you to be grateful for an unfulfilling job or bad relationship. That's their line. It doesn't have to be yours. You are in business for yourself. Nobody but you controls you or your future. Keep that power for yourself. Once you recognize that power and decide to use it, the possibilities truly are endless. Change is scary at first.

But, over time, it becomes the most invigorating part of the adventure. What a relief to know that you are the one who makes your own rules!

Challenge yourself every day of your life, not to exhaust yourself by working too hard or dog yourself with ambition. The point of each new challenge is to feel the exhilaration of taking charge of your life. And to enjoy the deepening self-appreciation as you become aware of new talents, capabilities and resolve. Every time you catch yourself making excuses for putting up with the status quo, remember forensic pathologist Jill Gould. Remember the mantras:

1. If you aren't doing something, you're doing nothing.

2. Don't let security be your dangerous anchor.

Surprise yourself.

A MOMENT WITH . . .
AIDA ALVAREZ,
Former Director of the Small Business Administration

"When I was thirty-four, I was a reporter working for the ten o'clock news on Channel 5 in New York. It was in 1982 and I was in El Salvador on assignment. There was an election going on in the middle of the civil war. My assignment was to cover the rebel side of the story. I needed to enter El Salvador on the northwest side, which was under control of the guerrillas, and this was during the height of a huge offensive.

"I was met at the unofficial border in Honduras by a group of six rebels. The next thing I knew, I was hiking through the countryside and the mountains. It was dangerous. I traveled into the different encampments, and there I was, in the dead of night with these rebels, people I had met for the first time, in a part of the world I had never been. We'd see people in stretchers because of the fighting going on. That moment was a real epiphany.

"I realized I was risking my life, my physical existence—for a news story. That was when I realized that, if I could risk my life for a story, I could take any risk. There wasn't anything I couldn't bear to do.

"I had been thinking about going into public service, but everytime I thought about it, I kept saying, 'How can I step out of the media? What would I do about the people who watched me every night—including my parents?' In my mind, I had all the reasons not to take the risk until I found myself there in El Salvador with the rebels.

"I realized then that I could certainly change careers, walk away from the TV camera and embark into the unknown. Nothing could happen to me that was any more serious than losing my life in El Salvador.

"It was very liberating. I realized life was a rich opportunity and I could do something different.

"I saw true courage there. Being brave can be a very complex matter. It was really a lesson about, again, following your instincts and not being afraid to take risk. You have to realize that, most of the time when you take a risk and follow your instincts, you have probably made the right decision.

"In the end, you win out."

CLAIMING YOUR TURF

CARLY FIORINA, THE LAW SCHOOL dropout who'd done time as a teacher and receptionist, stared at her picture on the cover of *Fortune* magazine and felt the same way any one of us would have felt. The magazine proclaimed her "The most powerful woman in American business." The queen of new turf. She laughed and said, "In a completely feminine reaction, my initial thought was, 'Thank God it's an okay picture.'"

Fiorina is a woman who claims turf, but she does it on her own terms. We sure saw that when the CEO steered Hewlett-Packard's difficult merger with Compaq. Fiorina learned early to stay centered. When she entered the business world in 1980, "Dress for Success" was the buzz and women wore masculine skirt-suits with puffy bow ties. "The message for me was that you could not be feminine and get ahead," she said. "I remember a lot of discussion about it with women. There were arguments. I would say that, if I had to be something other than what I was comfortable with being in order to be successful in a corporation, then the price of success was too high."

You have dreams and ambitions, but if you are reading this book, you are probably asking yourself some critical questions. Are you doing what you were meant to be doing? You will obviously have to make some self-sacrifice, but will you be able to travel your path without sacrificing your true "self"?

"Never sell your soul because nobody can pay you back," Fiorina said. "Ever. To me, being your whole self, your true self is as much a part of success as anything else. I am who I am. I have my own style and it has freed me to bring my whole person to work. Not only does it make it a lot more fun, but it has helped make me successful. I sometimes hear people say they are a different person at home than they are at work. I feel bad for them. The workplace isn't getting who they are. And both the workplace and the person are missing something. If you can't be yourself at work, find a different workplace. If you feel you are constrained or are selling your soul or leaving a part of yourself behind, then you aren't performing to your potential and should go somewhere else." Fiorina's point is golden. Success is born out of what is authentic inside of you. Honor that. Be who you were meant to be—not who you were told you should be and not who you think it would be nice to be like. You are all you've got.

Being Heard

Once you have your vision, the next challenge is to find your voice. Too often I hear women describing their struggle to be understood by others. They complain of being perceived as too weak, too strong, too bitchy, too pliable—too much of what they aren't. Who better to train us on making our point but Ellen Goodman, one of the most accomplished women columnists in America? Goodman says things many of us wouldn't dare say because she knows how to make a point without screwing it up.

She started her career at *Newsweek*, before the Civil Rights Act of 1964, when it was still legal to blatantly discriminate against women. She was only allowed to work as a researcher—not a writer. She says that was the way things were. She remembers "Being a researcher was seen as a good job for a woman. But, all of a sudden we were saying, 'The way things are is not right.' That's a hard thing to hear. You are asking people to look again at what they already know."

She moved on to the *Boston Globe* where she worked for an editor who was sensitive to the sweeping social upheaval that came along with the civil rights and antiwar movements. She started writing columns once a week in 1971, then wrote them full-time in 1974. Goodman has been at the *Boston Globe* since 1967 and is now an associate editor. She won the Pulitzer Prize for Distinguished Commentary in 1980. Her syndicated column first started in six papers, then was in fifty by the end of her first year. She is now published in more than four hundred newspapers.

She believes that you have to make your point by leading others through the merits of your case, and showing how you reached your conclusions. You won't win skeptics over by force-feeding them your point of view. "You have to bring other people through the argument, so it's not you saying, 'This is what I think, asshole,'" she says. "You have to bring them through the argument to show respect for the opposition. You also have to show how your mind is working so they will run with you, even if they don't come to the same conclusion." She says she frequently hears from people who say, "I usually disagree with you but . . ." or from readers who say they disagree with her but respect her reasoning. Others tell her she wrote what they were thinking.

So much of success comes down to good communication skills, and especially in the work environment, it is important to articulate your ideas well so they will be heard. How many times have you felt frustrated by bosses or colleagues who don't listen or don't understand what you are saying? Goodman learned to make her case by arguing with her father, and those lessons will help the rest of us. "You have to have evidence," she said. "You have to do the reporting—whether you are a reporter or not. Some of it is knowing what you are talking about and believing you know what you are talking about. I think women have a harder time at this. Women are often accused of speaking emotionally, like that's a bad thing. Very often, the reporting is in the honesty of the emotional experience. You have a reaction to something."

"Know in your gut what's right," she said. "Don't get talked out of it by someone else you think has marshaled an argument that is not true. Don't build your position around 'I just think' or, 'That's just the way I feel.'" She believes that when you do that, you lose the argument. Instead, ask yourself "What's wrong with this story? What do I see going on here? There's something wrong going on here." Then, you can argue it intellectually without giving up your feeling.

"I don't tell people what to think. I tell them what I think," she said. "A lot of people, particularly women, are too busy trying to be popular or too worried about what the reaction is going to be to just say what they think. You have to say what you think, even if you feel it's risky. What's the worst thing that can happen? It's not cancer. That doesn't mean you hit somebody over the head with an ax. But say what you think so other people can hear it. You just do it and the world doesn't fall down on you." If you lose the first time, come back at it again. She urges, "Don't shut up if you have lost the first time! Pick your moments and pick your voice and do it again. You're not going to win the first time out and if you get defeated or if you run off feeling rejected the first time or the second time or the fourteenth time, find another way to do it. Find another way to be persuasive, or find another way around it." Her job has taught her that repeatedly. She can't expect to write one column on abortion rights and have it solve the issue forever. Instead, she writes it when it comes up, again and again.

Part of her success is her tone. She's not shrill. She laughed about that when I brought it up. "I've said, 'In my old age, I'm going to get shrill,' " she chuckled. "Shrillness doesn't work. You have to ask what you want. What is your goal? Do you want to make your point, do you want people to listen to you, or do you want to vent? If you want to vent, go home, get into the shower and scream. If you want to have a public argument in which people will actually listen to you, get a grip. Pay attention to what the other person is saying, and as you are speaking, feel comfortable arguing back. It takes time."

Know You are in It for the Right Reason

If Nobel Peace Prize winner Jody Williams thinks she's right, she fights. "I believe I'm right with every cell in my body, and I will do whatever I think is necessary to achieve what I am focused on," says Williams, who won the prize for leading the International Campaign to Ban Land Mines. "I don't believe that 'means to an end' bull. I just don't see obstacles. I've been told that I take no prisoners, and I take that as a compliment."

She does that by tapping into a sense of justice that was born out of two experiences in her childhood. Williams has a deaf brother who developed schizophrenia in adolescence. She grew up protecting him, acting as his "voice." Eventually, that translated into becoming the voice of those who couldn't defend themselves. Then came the fourth grade. Williams lived in Brattleboro, Vermont, and was a quiet, good kid. She'd vacuum, help Mom around the house and do what she was supposed to do. She remembers a boy in her fourth-grade class who was the class stud. Blond hair, blue eyes and the biggest boy in the room. Another classmate was a complete geek. He had big ears, thick glasses and couldn't do anything right.

One day at recess, the stud wouldn't let the geek play. That set Williams off. The geeky boy couldn't speak up for himself, and even though she was terrified, Williams defended him. "Every time you do the right thing, it becomes easier," she said. That lesson carried Williams to the forefront of the movement against deadly land mines, which resulted in a treaty to ban land mines being ratified into international law. The more you claim your turf, the more you will accomplish.

Making It Happen

Dr. Bernadine Healy has had to fight her own turf battles in an arena that blatantly disregarded women. She once led the cardiologist who leads the American Red Cross but gained great notice in 1991 when she put women's health issues on the scientific map as head of the National Institutes of Health. She reformed research forever, requiring all studies funded by the NIH to include men *and* women. She won $625 million worth of research into diseases affecting women. Until Healy's fight, medical research was almost completely focused on male anatomy and physiology. Scientists assumed, wrongly, that whatever conclusions they reached about men would be the same for all of womankind.

For years, she'd known different. But, Healy had a determined approach to getting things done. "You can't just walk in and give orders. Find your place. Your place is what you choose it to be. If somebody wants to push you out of your place, stand tough. Be firm. If they don't like the fact that you are where you are, don't even compute that. Always know where your friends are and where your enemies are. Know what people think of you, who you can trust. But, don't be consumed by it. Keep it in your peripheral vision and focus straight ahead." Despite the politics that ended her time at The Red Cross, Healy remains emboldened. "The most important things that I have done that were lasting and had purpose were the most difficult to achieve and the most controversial at the time," she said.

That's tough when bucking up against barriers and that is why it is so important to keep from becoming intimidated. Try new things. And, as you move along, don't rely on past accomplishments to define you. "What matters is what you are doing now," she said. "When you take on something new, perhaps a new job, perhaps a new cause, it doesn't matter what you've done in the past. You have no laurels to rest upon. You use that past experience for the betterment of the next task, the next challenge. Never be afraid to move on. I have never been intimidated in my life. Things have made me cautious and a little scared, but not to the point that I wouldn't take them on."

I was struck by an extremely powerful bit of advice Healy passed on to me just as we were ending our conversation. "Remember," she said, "-

wherever you go, you can never do anything by yourself, alone. You have to institutionalize what you are trying to accomplish. If you want to make a difference, you have to make sure that things change outside of yourself and if you get hit by the proverbial milk truck tomorrow, there is something left behind. Always create the infrastructure so it can carry on without you. Make sure your mission is clear. Make sure your goals are clear. Otherwise, you are a firefly. Just a piece of light that disappears."

Share the Light

Too often, leaders become seduced by the attention they get for being in the lead, and they forget to bring other leaders up with them. If you truly believe in what you are doing, it is vital to share the moment with others. That is the whole point of this book. To pass on what other women know and have experienced. I once watched Switzerland's first woman president, Ruth Dreifuss, interact with a delegation of American women leaders who specialize in everything from business to government to the military to activism. She looked to them as she ended the meeting and told them firmly, "Don't lose your power. Give it to others."

That message is crucial. If we fight only for ourselves and our own goals, they die with us. The stronger we make others, the stronger our vision becomes. Think back on your career to those managers who were so threatened by other talent that they chose to surround themselves with "yes" people and brownnosers. What could they have accomplished had they embraced others who were as talented—or more talented, as smart—or even smarter than themselves? Leadership is not about being the brightest or most visible. It's about getting the job done. Whether your objective is to change the world or run an office, share your power and you will find your true strength.

The thing to remember is that, as women, we've been socialized to defer. Truly, you can't instantly erase such a long history of being kept in the background, and despite the gains we have made, we still are among the first women to exert our power as individuals in the workplace and political structure. So, if there are times when you feel a little shaky as you step for-ward to claim your turf, realize that's all part of growing into your full power. Stephanie Allen, a national workplace consultant and author, remembers watching one of her women mentors preparing to go into battle. "She was going to just lay it on them this one particular day," she said. "Her hands were trembling. I said, 'Are you OK?' And she said, 'I'm just going through my normal scared-shitless stuff. I'm frightened. This always happens, but there is a point where I put it aside and I'm ready to go.'" The issue has to be more important than your own personal fear, Allen said. Do the job. Get it done.

"You have to learn to confront in order to prove your point," said Allen, who trains women how to be formidable in her consulting practice. "Push for the truth, be resolute and driven to pursue whatever it is that you think has to be done so no one thinks there is a soft underbelly they can get to. Make sure they know they have to deal with you." She teaches women to see confrontation as a good thing. "If you think you have to be nice or you will risk damaging relationships, then you have to reframe how you see confrontation," she said. "Confrontation is part of being an authentic person of integrity. You can't maintain integrity if you can't fight your battles when you need to. And it's not a scene. It's not about pounding on the table and yelling. It's about pursuing the truth in a tough-minded way. It's about the conviction that you are right." And of course, there are points in your life when you have to be uncompromising. That doesn't mean everybody is going to like it—or you. But, you have to be clear about what you are after. "I've never been accused of being shrill, but I have been accused of being a bitch," Allen said. "It took a long time to realize that's a badge of honor. People don't want to mess with you if you are formidable, which they call being a bitch. It takes time to learn these skills," she said. "Don't start off with the major battles, but rather, with smaller challenges like dealing with someone who is giving you trouble with a bill. You learn not to be bitchy because getting nasty with people doesn't pay. Be nonnegotiable. Say, 'I'm sorry about x-y-z, but your advertisement said this, and I expect you to take care of it.' Hang in there until you get what you want."

Going into Battle

We wouldn't send troops into war without ammo, so don't let yourself go into battle without facts. Many of the women interviewed for this book emphasized how critical it is for you to back up arguments with solid data and facts. That boosts your credibility and makes it more difficult for adversaries to tear you down. "Try not to go into a battle unprepared," Allen said. "What I learned to do was boil down my war to three points. Never more than three, always more than one. One, they can eat you alive by just making that the issue. And people can't remember more than three."

Allen writes down her points in concise language so she always remembers what she is after. "Practice this with the things in your life that are unimportant, like a trivial argument with your husband," she suggests. Women find themselves alone in many work environments, or their numbers are so slim that they feel isolated. Allen has experienced that from many of the corporate boards she's served on, and says she's overcome the feeling of being "the odd man out" by building alliances. "I also think you have to establish a niche that is yours alone, one they cannot do without," she said. "When I got on this wonderful old boys' board at the hospital, I made ethics my empire. They had no interest in ethics, but see it as an appropriate, good thing we do, and they are glad I do it because they don't want to."

Mastering tough office politics is a matter of mastering relationships. Politics are all about friendship. Women are masters of friendships. Be quite deliberate with it. Don't make friends out of people you dislike, but make allies out of them. Share some common agenda in trying to get things done. Don't feel you have to brown-nose your way to the top. Savvy people know when you are doing that. You may be embarrassing yourself more than helping your career. Allen believes that you have to be genuine and do authentic useful things that are helpful to them. Figure out what other peoples' turfs and agendas are, and do that on two levels. Figure out if their agenda helps or hinders the organization, and how their agenda helps or hinders what you are doing. Alliances are everything. "Do not be caught by surprise," Allen said. "It is handy to get a male ally because I don't think like a guy, I don't have all the scuttlebutt. I don't know who is in a business deal together, who hates each other. Guys know all that. It's important to find a male ally who will tell you all the male relationships."

Another tactic is to self-promote, no matter how much you hate doing it. Men consider it normal to claim their place on top of the mountain, but women feel awkward about it. Weren't we told not to brag about ourselves? We were. And the legacy of that socialization has been costly to us as we have tried to move up in the business world. I've always found it tough to self-promote because I've always found it so distasteful when watching others do it. When I catch others in the act of self-promotion, I'll often roll my eyes and laugh at how transparent they are, rather than appreciating their efforts at ensuring their advancement. For too long, I assumed that other people would notice that I was doing a good job. Allen says that is a mistake.

"Think of yourself as a set of skills or accomplishments that your boss and the people you work with should know so they can be sure you are put in jobs where those skills can be used," she said. If you don't put out the word about what you are good at, they're never going to put you in the place where you can do the best job. "It's about saying who you are and where you want to go, because if your agenda fits where the company wants to go, they will say, 'Oh, Steph wants to do that. Let's let her do that,'" she said. "It is one less thing to figure out. And it's a good idea to find out where they want to go, their careers, their skills, so you can say, 'Cindy knows how to do that. She's perfect for that.' You get this back-and-forth caring for one another. I find that much more helpful and less dangerous than people think."

If you don't self-promote, others will always underestimate you. They will assume you are not tough enough for a leadership job. "All the competent people on earth work like hell," she said. "What makes you so different?" If you think your good work should speak for itself, remember, they aren't looking at your work. They're looking at *their* work. You don't want to turn people off with self-promotion, but you can find excuses to say things like, "That's what I was doing when I was fund-raising as a senior person," or "This is what I learned," or "This is how I know Fred," or "I found this supplier that was good." "You are the one who needs to fill in the blanks about your credibility," Allen says. The main thing is that you have to figure out what are the positive things you can do to help people and the organization. "If people perceive you are just out for yourself, forget it."

Protecting Your Turf Is a Whole Other Battle . . .

Of course, once you get your piece of the turf, you still have to fight to keep it. Kristine Fugal Hughes, chairman of the board of Nature's Sunshine Products, has learned that lesson over and over again. Even though she and her husband own the largest chunk of stock, she has to fight to keep her turf. "From the very beginning, I've had to deal with the woman issue," she said. "If I didn't have the stock ownership, I'm not sure I would still be here. I've been a survivor, and tenacious. I've been through a lot of battles, and I don't give up because I love the company. If I have to go, it will be by force, and that won't happen because the field people love me so much and I've got the ownership. But, as chairman, I have had to deal with some strong CEOs. Interestingly enough, they have gone and I have stayed. Many of the men who thought they knew so much are long gone."

She summarizes the main problem she's had to overcome, "Men can't stand strong personalities." The great thing is that she's learned to play the game her own way. "I ask questions," she says. " 'Well, what about this? What about that?' If push comes to shove, I am tough and can do it. But, to get along with the men in this company, I have to just kind of stay in the background. I get my agenda done by telling them my opinion, and I think they respect me enough that they listen to me. But I never try to be tougher than them. That doesn't work." It astounded me that the founder of the vitamin empire would have to play politics with her own business. She doesn't like that reality, but she lives with it. Instead of amassing power by force, she gets it by earning the respect of the thousands of people in the field who sell her products. Their support gives her the power to influence.

"A man once told me to never go into a meeting unless my ducks are lined up and I know the outcome of the meeting in advance," she said. "Well, that's foreign to me. I'm impulsive. I say what I think and I'm not a political animal. I wish I were. I have to depend on peoples' goodwill. I have to connect with them. . . . The one thing they say about me is that I'm sincere. There's no phoniness. I connect with our salespeople and we look at each other and we are the same. We're honest. What you see is what you get. In order for this company to grow, we just have to find more people like that. We're not the kind of people who are slick. I really think that one day we are going to be judged. The judge isn't going to say, 'How did you run Nature's Sunshine?' It's going to be, 'How did you treat others?' I try to be very aware of that." Her story is a reminder that, even when our dreams come true, there is always something else to worry about. Despite those worries, stay true to your center.

Claim Your Turf

1. *Know where everyone stands and what motivates them.* Listen well and recall with precision.

2. *Speak up when you have ideas.* Send memos documenting them. Then, act on them. Ideas are plentiful. Action counts. Say something when you see a coworker stealing someone else's idea, like, "Chris, that's just what Ellen suggested earlier, and you're right, it's a great idea. How can we help her with it?"

3. *Even if you are the most brilliant person in the office, don't overwhelm everybody* with a hundred suggestions as soon as you start your job. It doesn't matter how good the suggestions are, you'll make everybody sick.

4. *Accept credit.* Don't shrug off your successes or attribute them to luck or the help of good coworkers.

5. *Work for the team.* As a team player, you will seem less of an individual threat. If you want to trust others, they need to trust you.

6. *Be good at what you do and don't be humble!* Keep notes on your performance. Be able to show what you have accomplished, and how. Don't throw this in your boss's face, but use it to show your value.

7. *If you make a habit of helping promote others, they'll generally help promote you.*

8. *When someone compliments your work, accept the kudos!* Never minimize it with an "Oh, it was nothing." Practice at accepting kind words, then learn to say, "Hey, I want to show you what I've done here . . ."

9. *Own up to your mistakes, then move on.* Don't make the same mistake again.

10. *Learn the difference between being aggressive and assertive.* There's a fine line. Assertiveness is standing firm in your position. Aggressiveness is shoving it down someone's throat and leveling personal attacks.

11. *Keep your word.* Do what you promise to do, when you promise to do it.

12. *Align yourself with the people who make it happen.* If you work in a company with satellite offices, try to locate near the power base. In a meeting, sit next to the power center. Volunteer for committees and assignments that make you a player.

13. *If you sense a coworker or boss is threatened by you, diffuse it.* Ask that person for input to show you value his or her opinion. Flattery is powerful, as long as it's genuine. Stay on the high road so others will notice that you never say bad things about the person who trashes you behind your back. Eventually, they'll wonder what is the matter with your coworker.

14. *Help get your boss promoted.* When people move up, they like to surround themselves with people who they trust who they are certain will perform.

15. *You don't take power, it has to be given to you.* People who work for you must work *with* you. Earn your power through strong leadership, competence and hard work.

A MOMENT WITH . . .

KATHRYN SULLIVAN,

First American Woman to Walk in Space

"I was running down this path as fast as my feet and my brain could take me. It's like drinking from a fire hose. I tended to stay very high-energy, completely thrown into it. Overtraining, overpreparing, overcapability was not a risk. Underpreparing was.

"I enjoyed every part of it. Designating roles, consulting, operational planning, and rehearsals. They'd launched twelve shuttles before, but had they launched this particular cargo? No. Had they done this mission before or checked off those steps? No. This is not like being handed the manual for your new personal computer and being quizzed at the steps. This is like being handed blank pages. 'Your next assignment is to launch a Hubble Telescope. We've never done it, there it is in California and here are some blank pages. Go launch the telescope.' Somebody had to sit down and write the title, 'Hubble Telescope Deployment.' Step one. This book had not been written.

"The day of the launch is actually in the hands of other people. Your job is to be in your seat. From the flight crew's point, there are very few actions prior to liftoff. It is literally a handful of switch throws. Your job starts at T-zero at liftoff.

"It's not personal time, it's not vacation time and it's sure not daydreaming time. It's busy and highly focused.

"We had a satellite to deploy and engineering experiments and a package of eight different earth science experiments and a half-dozen smaller experiments inside the cockpit. None of us were the principle investigators. We were there as proxies for a pretty big array of scientific and engineering teams. Our role was to take their work and do right by it. This was not time to be staring out the window. We had the professional futures of other folks and a lot of federal money placed in trust in our hands.

"The space suit is a miniaturized spaceship that happens to be formed by the shape of your body. Head outside without it and you die. Head outside with a bad one and you can die. So you are paying very good attention to that as you get it rigged and you are going out. If you do it wrong, you can dump all the air out of the spacecraft, and then you've killed the crew. We had an intense time line with a choreographed set of things to do, and we had trained to keep it very tight.

"While we were out there, Bob Crippen, our commander on that flight, called out to us and made us look away from the task so we would know this was not a (training) repetition in the safety tank. It was the real deal.

"There was a planet over our shoulders.

"He made us pause to absorb the reality, and I'm so glad he did. We could well have gone back in the airlock and said, 'Was that the (training) tank or was that for real?'

"I don't think hanging off the handrail of the spaceship in a space suit changes a person's core philosophy or values or spiritual views. I don't think being two hundred miles above the Earth is something that struck me to being closer or farther from the powers that be. I often get that question, 'Up there, do you feel closer to God?' I think you feel closer to God holding the hand of someone in great pain who needs you. I feel closer watching a baby cry. There are thousands of ways. Traveling two hundred miles anywhere doesn't put you farther or closer to anything. What I cherish is all the ways it stretched and taught and grew and educated and shaped and refined me."

FIVE

Taking the Lead

W HEN AIDA ALVAREZ WAS TWELVE, she learned about leadership in a brawl. One of her classmates anointed herself boss of the school and formed a gang. She bullied everybody around her, getting other girls to give her their homework or hand over their money. "I never gave in to that, and finally, she figured the only way to get at me was to call me names that were ugly, names that put me down for being Puerto Rican," said Alvarez, who led the Small Business Administration for much of the past decade. "That was the straw that broke the camel's back."

The next thing Alvarez knew, she was in the middle of a big brawl, outside a fire station yards away from the school. All the other girls yelled and cheered them on. When it was over, Alvarez dusted herself off and walked away. "I was embarrassed that it had happened. I didn't think there was any particular winner," she said.

The next day in school, a lot of girls approached her and told her they'd heard she had won the fight. Some of the girls who came up to her were even members of the other girl's gang, and they wanted to know if *she* would become their new gang leader. Alvarez said no, even though she admits now that she was secretly pleased. "It taught me a big lesson about what people look for in leaders," she said. "I realized then that when you step up to a challenge and are not afraid to fight, you win just because you took the challenge. In that case, I was challenging somebody who was bullying people around. If you aren't willing to risk losing, you are never going to win. You've got to be able to face your challenges, even if it means losing. And, sometimes when you think you have lost, you've won. Other people admire the fact that you have taken the challenge, so you've actually had a moral victory."

You don't have to be a "born leader," but rather, you do have to give birth to the passion that allows you to lead. Opportunities for leadership show up in every pocket of your life, whether it's at work, concerning a political issue or even at home. How much you choose to embrace those opportunities depends on you. Not everyone hears the calling. Not everyone likes to defy the status quo. But those who expect a few tough battles should be ready to act. Creating change can be an excruciating process, and along the way it is likely that you'll have at least one moment when you question whether it's worth all the stress, or wonder whether you even have a chance. You have to believe in yourself enough to go at it again, after every rejection or loss. With every risk you take as a leader, you build your confidence. If you follow your instincts, do a good job and gravitate toward people who will strengthen you, you will thrive in the lead and inspire others to follow along.

Do the Work

Jody Williams was a staff of one when she began the land mine project, fighting the deadly legacy of war that continued to ravage populations throughout the world long after the battles ended. She grew her project to include nearly 1,300 independent, nongovernmental organizations in eighty countries. Talk about a woman who knows the power of individual leadership. Williams won the Nobel Peace Prize for her work in 1997. "What makes you a leader? You do the job," she says. "It wasn't that I needed to be the leader, it's just that I was. The others who have emerged have done so, not by appointment, but because they do the work. Because they do the work, people go to them. One and one is two. There is nothing magical about it. . . . It's a hard job. You have to develop a plan and do all of the little things to be sure that the plan actually bears fruit. But, you have to do the work. I don't just develop the plan. I am my own secretary. I have never had staff. I am everything."

In five years, Williams's grassroots crusade went from nothing to removing a weapon from the militaries of the world, a weapon that has been used by nearly every army of the world since the U.S. Civil War. She says of her efforts, "It is a model for other people, to show that ordinary people can achieve extraordinary things." She's often asked how she's been able to be effective in such a male-dominated arena like arms control. "I know I am a woman, obviously, but that's not how I face the world," she said. "I face the world as a competent human being. For men of fragile male ego, it is difficult. But, if they have a problem that I am in a woman's body, that's their problem. I talk to everyone the same—presidents, nonpresidents. I don't care. If one is consistent that way, eventually people don't see you as a man or a woman. They just see you as a strong, competent person."

A leader.

Lead from Behind

If you want glory and adulation, get a publicist. If you want to get things done, don't make recognition your reward. Satisfaction is a reward in itself. Share victories with those around you, and give them the power to lead and succeed, as well. Leadership has always been so natural to Betty Williams, who won the Nobel Peace Prize for organizing the women of Northern Ireland to begin the peace movement there. "Lead from behind," she said. "That's where the true leadership is. Consult with the people you are leading, listen to them and categorize their opinions. In true leadership, you wait until everybody else has spoken. If what you say is all you, you are doing it all wrong. True leadership comes from directing and example. You should only be a directional operator." She recited the words of famous anthropologist, Margaret Meade: "Never doubt that a committed group of people, however small they may be can change the world. Indeed, it's the only thing that ever has."

In life, there are leaders and there are bosses. Leaders lead and bosses boss. Good leaders are not threatened by ideas from people above or below them in the hierarchy, but rather, they find new ideas invigorating. They invite others to give input and feel a shared ownership of their goals. They coach their people, and motivate them to give their best performance. Leaders work as members of the team, knowing that, without a team, there is no one to lead. They say "Let's do this," not "I expect." They praise people publicly, criticize privately. They own their own mistakes, admitting when they are wrong. Leaders are human! They are as human and imperfect as everybody else, and they aren't afraid of that. When others mess up, they focus on fixing the problem, rather than rebuking the person. They share the glory of every success.

Then, there are the bosses who boss. Why is it that some bosses isolate themselves in their power circle without seeking ideas or feedback from the real people they were counting on to implement their vision? This creates a horribly unhealthy environment, one dogged by the shortcomings of the "us/them" philosophy. It creates an environment where the leaders have trouble firing up the followers.

If you keep your eyes open, you will see that scenario play out in party politics, government, academias, management, science, sports and every other discipline. Some people stand up front and act like the rest of us should follow behind them, just because they tell us to. They think they are too good to involve others in their plans. What's the threat of asking others for help and input?

I once worked at a newspaper that was fighting one of the nation's fiercest newspaper wars. Our editors had a top-down mentality, because they were the only ones allowed to have ideas, and we were the ones who were to do as we were told. They never once sought input from staffers, even though we were out on the streets interacting directly with readers, and when employees offered suggestions, we were shut up or ridiculed. We went three years without a staff meeting. Their arrogance was fatal: circulation plummeted, and eventually the newspaper surrendered to its competition, agreeing to a joint operating agreement. I can't help but wonder what would have happened if the people in management would have been able to put their egos aside to lead from behind.

Share the lead. Why limit your power to your own limits, when you can expand it by bringing in others who are just as concerned as you? I learned a lot in a recent conversation with archconservative Phyllis Schlafly, who has been given credit for defeating the Equal Rights Amendment, which would have guaranteed equal treatment, regardless of gender. I may hate her politics, but Schlafly has proven repeatedly that she knows how to lead and organize. As she explains, "One thing I am particularly good at is getting along with women. That is not easy. I think you have to be straightforward, aboveboard and honest. I don't ask anybody to do anything that I am not willing to do myself. Don't talk about them behind their backs. Tell the same story to everybody. If you don't do that, the organization breaks apart. It takes sides."

The ERA passed Congress in 1972, but fell three states short of getting ratified by the thirty-eight states needed in order to be added to the Constitution. That was largely due to Schlafly, who began by challenging one hundred other women to become leaders in her Eagle Forum. "And, they did. I gave them the model. I gave them the tools and they became leaders and self-starters," she says. "That is what we have in our organization. We don't have a bunch of peons who do what they are told. We have developed women leaders who are very capable of electing candidates, lobbying a bill through the legislature, talking to their Congressman and speaking to the media."

What she gave these women was guidance on how to go about their game plan. She worked to develop a reputation for being able to back up anything she said. "They were never left in the lurch," she said. "If you are in leadership, you have to learn to get along with people. You have to have a record of reliability, of consistency, of predictability. All of my Eagles know how I will behave in a given set of circumstances. I'm completely predictable. They would know how I would react to legislation, or how I would debate situations."

So much management is leadership, and leadership is mentoring. As you step up to the challenge of pushing against the status quo, it is so important that you mentor others, so they can expand the impact of your leadership. Do this by identifying those with leadership qualities, and including them in strategizing and carrying out your plans. This doesn't mean you create an environment where everyone is boss and no one does the work, but it means you inspire others to invest a little of their own passion by doing more than what is expected of them. Reward them with praise and gratitude. Share the moment.

As you encounter those inevitable moments of difficulty, seek out your own mentors. Often, they are women and men who have pushed for change in the same arena—or others. They know how hard it is to face criticism for refusing to follow blindly on a course that needs change. They've fought their own battles, and learned from them. Tap into that experience. Ask for help. Say, "I need a little support here." And, you'll get it. I have recruited total strangers to be in my group of mentors by calling them and saying, "My name is Fawn Germer, I'm banging my head against the wall trying to accomplish x and y, and I was hoping you would be able to meet for lunch sometime soon. I need mentoring." I have never been refused, and in the process have expanded my support network with influential, passionate people who know that part of the duty of a good leader is to teach others.

The Right Stuff

So much of your success as a leader depends on your attitude and the attitude you inspire in others. Realize that anything significant is going to come with some fairly ugly moments that may cause you to question what you are doing and who you have chosen to do it with. Remember what your mother told you? Say "I can," not "I can't." It's a fact of leadership that a negative attitude can kill the most positive of objectives. Most leaders have overcome overwhelming odds and faced tough opposition. They've had to believe when it seemed like there was no reason to hope. Believing in your vision—even when you think the time has come to give up—will keep you on course.

IT ISN'T GOING TO BE EASY! If it were easy to lead people and change the status quo, everybody would be leading and nobody would be following. Too many people are afraid to stand up for what they believe. At least you know what you want. Just realize you are likely to go through some trying moments that will cause you to question what you are doing and why. Be bold, move forward and know that, in time, you'll get there.

Wilma Mankiller learned that lesson when she entered politics and ran for deputy chief of the Cherokee Nation in 1983. She knew she'd have to have political rallies to get her message out, so she staged one and put the word out on the radio and in the newspaper. When her big moment came, five people showed, and three of them were relatives. She remembers, "There had been no women principle chiefs or deputy chiefs, and the resistance I found was not subtle. I was running for election, which is different from evolving into the vice presidency of a bank. That's more buttoned down. This was a very public attempt on my part to become a leader, and the opposition was verbalized very openly." Rather than give up, she pushed even harder, succeeding in that dream and soon after, becoming the first woman to lead the Cherokee Nation as its chief. She is forever etched in women's history for her courage.

During the campaign, Mankiller was making her way in a conservative area in eastern Oklahoma and expected her politics to be an issue. She'd been involved in many causes that others might label as liberal or even radical. But, that wasn't what her detractors seized upon. It was her gender, and she refused to engage. She continued to hammer on her message, hitting the issues of health care, housing and the future of the tribe. When others would raise the issue of her gender, she'd just come right back to those issues that mattered. The lesson: Define your message and stay with it, despite attempts by others to push you off course or define you differently.

Mankiller won and took over as principal chief of the Cherokee Nation in 1985. At first, it was clear she was not welcome in leadership. Once the men lined their chairs at a long table, leaving no room or chair for her. Mankiller just pulled one up and sat down, ignoring the slight. That was her strategy all along. To just keep moving forward. She cared so much about the issues that she overcame a battle with low self-esteem that kept her from speaking out. Her passion drove her in everything— from her will to protect the environment to her hopes for rejuvenating her tribe. "When I came into office, I had done work that had not been traditional work for women. I'd been in charge of community development. We built water systems and housing. So, I could talk with the men about the hourly cost of a backhoe. I had supervised carpenters and electricians, and I could talk on their level. They didn't feel entirely uncomfortable with me. We had some things in common."

One small town near where Mankiller was raised was violent and dangerous. She went to the people who lived there to find a way for them to rebuild their community—enlisting them as volunteers to build new houses and find constructive ways they could interact with each other. While naysayers on the outside told her she was wasting her time and shouldn't even go there after dark, Mankiller and her husband, Charlie Soap, plowed ahead. That community built new homes, rehabilitated old ones and constructed a community water system.

The project was a huge success and showed the power and effect of her vision and message. With more than 140,000 tribal members and an annual budget of more than $75 million, Mankiller's job was very much like that of a CEO. But, it was even more demanding since she oversaw more than 1,200 employees spread over 7,000 square miles.

She led the tribe until 1995, when she became sidelined by health problems. Throughout her life, she has faced unbelievable adversity, surviving a terrible car accident that forced her to undergo dozens of operations, a neuromuscular disease and a kidney transplant. Of her adversities, she says, "The biggest challenge in my life has been to try to continue with my life and my work while dealing with an unbelievable array of health issues. I've dealt with that the same way I dealt with the opposition I had because I was a woman. It's a problem, I acknowledge it and I try to deal with it the best way I know how, and then move on. Just like I don't let my energy be siphoned off into questions of whether women should be in leadership, I won't let my energy be siphoned off by a question of health. I can control my mind when I don't control my body. I can do what I can to keep myself well and continue on. It's really a choice. You can dwell on hard or bad things if you want. You don't have to." She continues to work hard in tribal politics, campaigning nonstop for the candidates who continue fighting for the same ideals. Mankiller's ability to lead is owed to her determination and hard work. Her past experience of doing nontraditional women's work helped her implement change when she could make a difference. And most important, her passion was her motivation.

Producing Results

You have the inspiration and motivation business down pat? Great. What do you have to show for it? Great leaders know what they are after and if they are on course. They have planned out a strategy to achieve their objectives and the results are measurable. Vision is critical, but it is nothing if it can't be translated into action and results.

Timetables help you to know where you'd like to be. Be flexible in this area, because things rarely happen as planned. What is important is that you know what you expect to accomplish, and have some general timing goals that you can aim toward. Get organized, and plan out as much as you can so that you begin your day knowing what you need to be doing to move you toward your goals. That is critical. If you have a good "to do" list, it is so much easier to stay on course. You will know where every day fits into the big picture of what you are trying to accomplish, and you won't be tempted to waste time.

You should regularly evaluate your progress to see what you have accomplished, and more important, what you have learned. Along the way, you will pick up ideas that will help you fine-tune or completely overhaul your plan. Don't be rigid in your vision and refine it as you learn.

As you start to see your ideas or leadership work, remember what you did right, and what you need to change the next time. If you are having problems moving forward, evaluate what is going on. Pull in other people and ask them to help you brainstorm new possibilities. Just because your plan may have been flawed, it doesn't mean you need to give up on your vision. Just play with it a little.

A MOMENT WITH . . .

JUDITH HEUMANN

First, she was kept out of public schools. Judith Heumann fought back until she became the highest-ranking disabled person in government as the assistant secretary of education during the Clinton Administration.

"There is handicapism, there is sexism. I experience the same forms of discrimination that other women do, plus what I experience because of my disability.

"People still don't know how to relate to me as a disabled woman. Issues are frequently trivialized, and I sense there is this significant feeling that, if I could only not be disabled, I wouldn't be disabled. It's difficult being a woman in this country, but the truth of the matter is the vast majority of women don't fantasize about being men. They fantasize about changing the world so they can be women. I fantasize about making this world accessible so I can get around, get into peoples' homes.

"To me, being in a wheelchair is not what's strange. I like going down the street in my wheelchair. I like the speed I can have. I don't want to be somebody else. I don't think people really understand that, but it's very sincere.

"Progress doesn't happen quickly. We are dealing with the systemic, historic devaluation of disabled people. I'm working so hard and then something happens that I describe as being put back 'in my place.'

"My self-esteem varies at different parts of the day. Sometimes, I'll be in a situation where I feel very strong, centered, on message. Then I'll go someplace a short time later where a person ignores me and talks only to the person I am with. I feel one minute like a high-level political appointee, and then I feel like a child. All within a minute. That is difficult to have happen.

"When people are in power networks, they will socialize together, play tennis or golf together. I can't do those types of things, so I don't get asked. I don't get invited over to peoples' houses for receptions because so many houses are not accessible. I just don't get invited to those things. I'm not a social climber at all. But, from a professional perspective, the ability to meet people you need to know to help make changes in policy and other things is somewhat hampered.

"We have moved forward to gain greater civil rights, to remove barriers that will allow people greater opportunities to participate in society on an equal level. The Americans with Disabilities Act (ADA) and other events give us a stronger sense of dignity and self-respect and, I think, allow us a stronger sense of self-will to move forward.

"On the other hand, we all know that pieces of legislation in and of themselves do not end discrimination. What it lets you know is that now, the battle is really beginning in earnest.

"There are still millions of disabled children and adults who are being denied the ability to live and work within the community to the fullest extent. I still can't get on an airplane and use a bathroom because the law doesn't require that. I can't visit the homes of friends because nothing requires private housing to be accessible. I still know that the odds are I will not be given the same equal opportunity when I apply for some jobs. And I know a large percentage of the populace still doesn't accept those of us with disabilities as being equal to them.

"It's very important for you to look within yourself at what your biases are. What buttons are pushed, and why they are pushed. What are you doing in your everyday life to help disabled people to come into the community? Do you look for disabled people to hire? Do you view the issues affecting disabled people the same way they feel about the issues affecting other minorities? Do you even see us as a minority?

"Do you feel vulnerable because you could become like us?"

PERSPECTIVE

PLAYING WITH THE
OLD BOYS' CLUB

I**T'S THAT CLUSTER OF GUYS** over there. They don't know they're in a club. They don't think much about it when they get together for golf or beers and don't include you or the women in the office. They aren't trying to hurt anybody's feelings when they tell jokes that we might find insulting, because they truly don't think the jokes are offensive. It's just the way things have always been. We call it the "Old Boys' Club," and they say they're just "hangin' out with the guys."

Before we get accused of overreacting, we need to think about this for a moment. What some of us see as a nefarious clique meant to hold women back may just be the remnants of the Old World Order. We get ticked off because, in the midst of all that male bonding, opportunities and relationships can emerge that we, as women, are not privy to. It's quite simple. If Joe, as boss, spends his spare time yucking it up with Randy and Ed and George, why would he look first to Mary or Sue or some other "outsider" as material for promotion? Their associations give them easy access to promote themselves, their careers and their ideas. Despite all the access women have achieved, the "Old Boys' Club" is still a reality that affects our ability to be effective.

Tina Proctor's quail hunting story serves as a good example. For three years, she was the grants coordinator for the U.S. Fish and Wildlife Service and chaired a committee that met in Phoenix every year. She was the only woman in the group and when she'd get together with the others, she had the feeling that she wasn't "in" on something, and that everything had already been agreed to in advance. One day, she ran into one of her committee members who told her that the reason they always met in Phoenix was because some of them liked to go quail hunting.

What an "Aha!" moment for her. "That was the moment when I saw that I was left out of the loop and there wasn't any way I could get into that loop without going quail hunting, which I wasn't about to do," she said. "I don't even want to go quail hunting! It's a cultural thing and I am not able to have the connection with them that they are able to have with each other through bonding in the hunting experience." I asked why she didn't just move the meeting, considering she's in charge. "Move it? Then they'd go fly fishing. They would find another outdoor activity that would exclude me."

She *knows* the guys weren't trying to slight her and is certain there was nothing purposeful in their actions. But she does believe that their hunting outing is a masculine event that she doesn't fit into and doesn't want to fit into. She's handled the problem by spending more time on the telephone with the members of her group so she has her own individual connection with them and knows what they are thinking and where the group will head.

The first rule of playing with an "Old Boys' Club" is this: Don't try to be an old boy. You aren't one. You can't be. You don't want to be. You're a woman! Be yourself. Instead of lamenting the way things are, develop your own strategy, as Susan Butcher did, as one of the first women to compete in the grueling 1,049-mile Iditarod Sled Dog Race from Anchorage to Nome, Alaska.

When she started competing in 1978, she was joining a man's world, and she knew it. She thought that to win, she'd have to do what they did. "I wasn't trying to prove that women were any better than men. I don't think any one sex is better. I think we are both very different and capable of anything. There is this very macho mind-game playing that they do—a lot of lying to each other and bravado. They lie about how their team looks or what their plans are or how they are running their race. They either act cocky like they have a better chance of winning than they actually do or they act really humble when they actually have an incredible chance of winning. I have watched them win using this mind game."

So, she tried it their way, but it didn't work. She remembers, "I couldn't play it and I finally went to not playing mind games. I just had the best possible team I could have, and I was honest about my chances. They'd ask a question and I'd be 100 percent truthful. That was confusing to them." They thought she was lying, and figured she was trying to psyche them out with some sort of mind game. "They didn't get my ways any more than I got theirs," she said. She says that she was always aware of the boys' club and that she would be excluded. She wouldn't be asked to join the campfire or was told to go away and was even called rude names that could only be directed at women. She says it was even done by people who, one-on-one, were her friends. But, around a bunch of men, they would turn around and backstab her. It was pretty painful and difficult to compete in a man's realm.

Studies show that if you ask women whether they have been victims of sex discrimination, they tend to say no. But, if you ask whether women are discriminated against in general, they'll say yes. "There's been a lot of research on that," said Alice Eagly, a psychologist and professor of psychology at Northwestern University. "That's for a number of reasons. In part, it's who you think of when you make a comparison. If I ask you how women are doing, you use men in comparison. If I ask you, you might use another woman. You might think, 'Well, I'm doing so much better than other women.'" She says that kind of comparison protects us from thinking of ourselves as victims. If we look around and see we've done as well or better than other women, we might tell ourselves we're doing fine.

Eagly also says that women can't be effective by behaving or managing like men because the people around them won't accept it. "People have these stereotypical expectations that are not always appropriate. Women who just stick to their jobs and don't deliver kindness and nurturing behavior are seen as competitive and cold. People don't want or expect or like women to behave in what is essentially a more masculine style. We judge women like that very harshly, and we shouldn't. We should think, 'Oh, if a man did that same thing in that role, would we say anything? We probably wouldn't say he's bitchy.'"

So if we can't be in the "Good Old Boys' Club," and we can't even emulate its members, what can we do? Well, we can make our own club, suggests Ruth Dreifuss, the first woman to be president of Switzerland. Imagine what it was like for Dreifuss, leading in a country that didn't even let women vote until 1971! Yet, women quickly gained ground there, and now have a greater presence in government than women here in the United States. I asked Dreifuss how we should deal with being in a situation where we are the obvious minority. Her suggestion: "The first necessity is to find a club of 'Good Old Women.' This will be an important step to avoid the monopoly of power. We did it. We made progress in that. Men had places where they met—the military, sports clubs—and it was a one-gender society." What Dreifuss and the other women did was band together. Who was there to mentor them? There wasn't anybody. Instead, they mentored each other. "We had many opportunities to work together," she said. ". . . there was more networking than mentoring. Mentoring is in vogue now that we have women in responsible positions. The first generation has to network."

It is critical to develop two strong networks: one professional, the other personal. The professional network is filled with mentors and allies who help you get your mission accomplished. Your personal network is right there by your side when things get ugly. These are the women with whom you can vent emotions and feelings. Don't assume that you need to know somebody in order to get to know the "right people." You don't. It is amazingly simple to put together a high-power professional network by joining professional organizations or directly contacting people and asking for a quick meeting or lunch because you are trying to accomplish something and need some assistance or advice. Before you go, know what you are after. You want a professional relationship with this person; you want access; you want him or her to like you and want to help you and invest in your success; and you don't want to come off as a fawning, helpless brownnoser.

It's not uncommon to hear women complaining about missing networking opportunities on the greens, at golf games they were not invited to attend. But while there may be action there, it's not the only place to make your mark. "I don't golf," said Carly Fiorina, CEO of Hewlett-Packard. "It's an example of my doing it my own way. Everyone says, 'You have to play golf.' Sorry, I don't want to take the time to learn it, and I don't want to make the time to play it. I do not believe deals get cut on the golf course. They may have been in a different time. It's still a good way to develop relationships that can lubricate the wheels of business. Relationships are certainly important to business, and I have spent time developing them in other ways."

Still, she has to schmooze. In Fiorina's technology industry, the decisions clients make are high-stakes. The amount of money spent is huge and the cost of taking a wrong turn is substantial. She says that people make those kinds of decisions not just with their heads but with their guts, and having connections beyond the workplace is important. "Relationships are everything," Fiorina said. It's not a matter of getting a membership into an Old Boys' Club, but rather, a matter of getting to know and relate to its members.

Dreifuss agrees. "Networking is a necessity because we don't have the same advantage that those 'members' have. The difficulty is that women are often not met well, often have less information of what is going on and fewer opportunities on which kinds of jobs are available." Sources within your network can help tremendously.

Dreifuss sympathizes with those women who still struggle to be heard, especially when their voices are dismissed for being too bold or boisterous. It may be hard to get the validation you need to know you are doing the right thing. Even when your network is in place, there will be times when you feel isolated. Just keep moving forward, because you are blazing a trail. "You will not lose your identity or what makes you unique when you fight to be at the same place as the others," she said. "Don't fear losing something. Find your deep 'me' in the place where you are not welcome."

What she said hits the core of the battle because there will be times when we exert ourselves and find ourselves being criticized, ostracized or even terrorized for what we know we've got to do. Her point is sound—that we can continue on when we are true to who we are, when we act from a genuine calling.

Use the Good Old Women's club as a starting point, she said, but once you get your chance, work with men, too. "A brain is formed by both hemispheres," Dreifuss said. "Let us use both to be smart. Power can be monopolized, but it is ridiculous to have different opportunities for men and women."

Being Tough Enough

Every time I hit a rough spot, I like to remind myself that it could be so much worse. Imagine what it was like for Linda Chavez-Thompson, the executive vice president of the AFL-CIO. Here was a woman intruding in union business—in a state like Texas. Her tactic? Being a strong woman. "It was a man's world when I started out in this movement, and believe me, the men in this movement made sure I knew it," she remembers. "When you are in Texas, you have to learn how to operate with the guys. Are you tough enough? Can you handle the remarks? Can you handle the attitude, the arrogance? There were many rough spots on my career road that left me wondering what the hell I was doing. I wondered if it was worth it."

She found herself doing what many women have had to do as they've made their way in male-dominated fields. She maneuvered carefully and in a way that was *her* way. "I had ideas. If the idea came from me, my union brothers were not willing to grab on to it until they thought it came from my boss," she said. "I'd hear myself saying, 'My boss said . . .' so they would listen." Ouch. They were always trying to get her to know her place. If she wanted to run as a union officer, they wanted her to settle for being secretary. "I'd say, 'I will be president. I will be secretary-treasurer, but I will not be recording secretary.' Then, the next time, they'd say I should be the recording secretary again. I'd say, 'Nope. I'm running for vice president.'" So she ran and she won.

She believes that a woman has to combine a certain amount of aggressiveness with know-how in order to get the job done. "I don't ask women to take a step back from men. So often they say men feel threatened by us. I say, 'Do a good job.' Just go out there and get it done, and if someone gets in the way, don't cry." The problem is that we have to do a very tricky dance. "If we are too feminine, we're not seen as doing the job and we don't appear to take charge," notes psychologist Eagly. "But, if you come on strong, the way a man might, people don't like it or tolerate it as much from a woman as a man," she said. "There are no easy answers. I think successful women who do well in these roles do manage some mix of the behaviors that keep people assured they are women. Sometimes, that's by feminine or verbal behavior, or maybe it's by more cooperation or a participative approach in their management styles."

We have to watch the tone of our voice. We have to be direct, but not too direct. Assertive, but not overly aggressive. We have to smile, but not giggle. Hopefully, we are all beyond playing dumb, whining, over-apologizing and backing off because we are intimidated. "It's a gender stereotype operating here," Eagly says. "I think women develop a compromising style. That may be a large factor in their coping."

That kind of adaptation was a way of life for Kathryn Sullivan when she was in NASA's first class of women astronauts. Thirty-five astronauts were in the class, and only six were women. "It's a pretty rough-and-tumble crowd, hard-charging, hard-teasing," she said. "Everyone jostles and teases and elbows all around the circle. That's the nature of the group culture of that sort of operational environment. Was there sexist or gender-related teasing? It's the kind of climate where if there is a crack in the armor, they were going to drive a semi-truck through it." There were sexist cracks and every other kind of remark too. Instead of letting the dynamic destroy her, she accepted and dealt with it, succeeding at NASA and becoming the first American woman to walk in space. "It was what it was. It wasn't going to bother me," Sullivan said. "I bet if I searched, I could think of some people who were trying to hold me back, but I was either too blind or too stubborn or too intently focused on what I was doing for that to register," she said. "You don't have to react to all of these things that hold you back. It sometimes works very well to blow right by them."

The fact that these experiences are so universal to these trailblazing women is rather comforting. They've been there and we aren't imagining these problems because others see them as well. We have no choice but to deal with them, whether it's up in space or in the hockey arena.

Cammi Granato, captain of the U.S. Women's Olympic Hockey Team says, "Women don't get the luxury men get to learn and grow into something. That's not a new concept for me, being in a male-dominated field. I had to buck up and say, 'This is going to pass. I'm going to get better, I'm going to take it a day at a time.' You can't get mad at everything. You have to expect certain things to happen, but you shouldn't expect to be treated unfairly. You should expect to be treated equally. You have to prove yourself, a lot more than a male who is equally talented would have to prove himself. You have to be patient and persevere and show them your talent. But eventually, they will see it."

I've often said that half of what I have learned in life, I learned on the seat of my bicycle, riding in the Rockies. I've learned not to worry about the clouds until it starts to rain, because sometimes the rain never comes. I've learned to watch my back, because someone else might be trying to run me off the road. And, I have learned that when a man falls behind a woman, he will *kill* himself to get back in front. That is a true fact. I remember passing a forty-something man while climbing Wolf Creek Pass in Southwest Colorado. I wasn't rushing at all, but just tooling around and enjoying the scenery. I didn't pass him to show him I was stronger or better than him, I just passed him because I was moving faster. But, about three-tenths of a mile from the top, that guy came back around me, literally groaning in agony as he hyperventilated toward the 10,850-foot summit. He didn't care about getting to the top. All he cared about was getting to the top *ahead of me,* a complete stranger who he would never see again. I, of course, found that hilarious, and painlessly glided right past him again, without breaking a sweat. I have watched this happen again and again. Men don't have the same reaction when being passed by men. It's women. It bugs many of them more when we get ahead.

So, I asked women's basketball champion Teresa Edwards about competing with men on the court. What she describes sounds a lot like the usual dynamics of a routine day at work. "Men think that anytime they are challenged by women, it is questioning their manhood," she said. "To this day, men have trouble with being beaten by women. Even if they never played organized basketball, in their mind, there is still no way a female is going to beat them. That's incredible to me."

Hmmm. What's the difference between how a man and a woman loses? "I don't think they (men) deal with losing very well," she said. "When they aren't able to achieve the level they want to achieve, it haunts them for a long time. Women move on or find another way to get where we are trying to go. When I play a man, I don't try to strip his male pride. I want him to know that we, as women, are capable of beating men, but it doesn't have to be a male-female thing. It can just be between me, Teresa, and whoever else it is. I say jokingly, 'I'll make sure to leave you with your manhood. But, I am going to win this game.'" She always laughs as she says it, and says warning them ahead of time makes a loss easier to take. Plus, that lighter atmosphere makes them less likely to push and shove and be rough on the court because they are angry that they are behind and getting desperate to win. "I just take the game and go. They get a kick out of it." Women don't have to be men, she said. "Our bodies and our minds are different," she said. "That's been proven time and time again. Strength is not in the size of your muscles. I think God made men stronger physically. I agree with that. I don't think I should get in the weight room and try to be stronger than a man. I should get in the weight room and be as strong as I can be."

Exactly. Imagine the stress you'd be able to unload if you could stop focusing on what other people are doing and start focusing on yourself. Think about that man cycling on Wolf Creek Pass. Why didn't he just focus on cycling as strong as he could? That way, he could have enjoyed the scenery and made the moment his, rather than mine. Think of how often you or your coworkers get wrapped up in what some office rival is doing at work. He or she may be the most productive person in the office, but when you set your sites on "beating" that person, you are competing against the standard that person is setting, not your own. Men don't need to compete against women, and women don't need to compete against men. Imagine what peace we would know if we'd just compete against ourselves.

What About the Guys Who are Hopeless?

"There are three things you can do with bad guys," said gender-in-the-work-place consultant Stephanie Allen. "Kill them, ignore them or leave them." Well, at least you get a few choices.

"If you're going to kill them, you need to go after them with a group of people—not just you," she said. "You can ignore them by insulating yourself from their behavior in every way you can, from smiling sweetly to saying things like, 'Well, he must have his objectives. I just don't understand them,' or, 'He's my boss, there's not much I can do about it.' Don't let it get on you." The other option is to go ahead and fire them. Leave. Send out your resume. Get another job. Do something.

One person who has spent a career swimming in a sea of sexist men is comedian Margaret Cho. "The world of stand-up comedy is a very sexist and racist world," she said. "It's almost all men, and I don't have their respect. I get respect from the audience, but in the world I live in, women are so looked down upon. It's really backward and infuriating."

Cho said it doesn't matter whether she is a headliner at 275 or 300 shows a year, outdrawing most of her male counterparts. "Comedy is a boys' club. They get very resentful at our presence," she said. "I have learned now to just turn my back on it because it doesn't matter. It doesn't bother me because I can be just as successful monetarily as a male comic, and surpass most of them anyway."

She takes her energy from her audiences. But, within the back rooms, green rooms and dressing rooms of comedy, the standards change when it comes to earning respect from her male peers. She recalls one incident at a club in Washington, D.C., where the dressing room walls were covered with photographs of different comics. "My picture was defaced with graffiti that said I'm fat and I'm not funny," she said. "Nothing had been written on anybody else's picture, and there weren't many women's pictures in there." She'd seen the graffiti on the picture a couple of years earlier when she played the club and remembers feeling absolutely destroyed by what she saw. But she thought she had to suck it up. "Now I know to deflect it," Cho said. "The real strength is not ignoring something like that. It's standing up and saying, 'This is not acceptable.' I've learned to do that now, but before, I didn't want to appear bothered by it or weak."

This time she went back and told the club managers that if the photo-graph wasn't removed, she wasn't performing. "I said I wasn't going on stage and they'd have to tell the audience and refund all the money," she said. "It was a sold-out crowd. Within the hour, all the graffiti was painted over."

When It's Enough to Make You Cry

You can paint over the graffiti, but you can't always cover up the hurt. Everytime I bring up the subject of women crying at work, I get a reaction. Why do we have to have hormones that make us so sensitive? "My big problem is keeping myself from crying," said Cokie Roberts, of ABC News. "I fail more than I succeed. When I get mad, I cry. We lose dignity when we do that. People expect us to be stronger than that. My mother thinks it is so terrible— a good girl doesn't cry because you don't impose your feelings on other people."

Businesswoman Kristine Fugal Hughes can relate. "Do I ever cry at work? Ha! Yes. I go down the hall with red eyes once every three months," she said. "I do cry easily. Of course I try to hold it in, but it comes out." So many women confront this problem. We're women! We've got different hormones, different emotions, different socialization, so we are more prone to sharing our tears. The problem is, men often equate tears with weakness. Even women have different opinions on this issue. Linda Chavez-Thompson says, "That's the last thing you want a man to see is you crying because your feelings are hurt or because somebody said something nasty about you. Go home and cry."

In more than two hundred interviews with consultants, academics and professionals, only a handful said crying is appropriate at work. One businessman told me, "The workplace is a business atmosphere. It requires rational thinking and efficient action. Which of these does crying fit into? Neither. Crying is emotional and impedes both rational thinking and efficient action. Don't cry, unless you want some man to feel sorry for you or another woman to coddle you. Then, the perception of 'empowered' goes right out the window. Of course, if you just got a call that your dad died, everybody will understand and will appreciate your human side."

I hate thinking about this subject because it brings me back to the one time it happened to me. I casually left the newsroom and headed for a conference room in the back of the building before I let go of the tears. My boss saw me leave and followed to offer support. But, the uncomfortable expression on his face told me I'd just crossed the line from "professionwoman" into "helpless female." He was an enlightened man, and compassionate. But from then on, I felt a shift in our relationship.

Consider how your office environment reacts to emotions before you get emotional, suggests Barbara Distler, a staff psychologist at the University of Illinois at Chicago and a clinician in private practice. "It's important to understand your work environment and the consequences crying might have," Distler said. "Think of these things in advance, know how your office environment deals with people having feelings, because if there comes a time when you feel upset, you'll know if it is better to release your feelings or try to hold them in."

So, if you don't want to lose it in front of other people, and they don't want to see you lose it, what should you do? Breathe deeply. Exhaling can release some of your anxiety. If you can, excuse yourself and head to the bathroom or a quiet place where you can calm down and regain composure. If there's no way to exit gracefully, just excuse yourself and bolt. You can say there is something in your eye, or that you have to use the rest room. You can check your beeper and excuse yourself, or, look at your watch and say the same. Anything. Get out of there, calm down and relax.

Distler suggests you focus on an image that is reassuring. Think of something you enjoyed recently, or something someone said that made you feel good. "Sometimes, going and getting a drink of water can help because it actually steadies the body," she said. If you do cry, consider bringing up what happened once you've gotten through the tough moment. Show the person you have bounced back, that the emotional moment did not last forever, did not affect your ability to be professional and did not change your productivity. "Some people might find it important to address this very directly," Distler said. "Something like, 'You know, yesterday I got very upset about this. I want to mention it briefly because I hope it doesn't cause any awkwardness between us.' You aren't pretending that it didn't happen. You are showing you moved on from it. It also gives the other person the opportunity to say something about it." Finally, if your job is making you tear up too often, it's time to question whether you are in the right job.

Living with the Way Things Are

The thing about the "Old Boys' Club" is that you really can't talk about it without someone labeling you as a male-bashing, angry woman. The question is, why shouldn't we talk about this "club" if it impedes our success? Remember, the median income of women as a whole is still just 73 cents on the dollar compared to men, even though the law has required equal pay since 1963. The old guard insists that parity isn't going to come until women move through that so-called "pipeline" to the top, gaining education and experience. But, who can say this problem does not exist when women hold only eleven percent of the 6,120 board seats in Fortune 500 companies, and only two women are CEOs in the Fortune 500? How can we justify the reality that only six women lead companies in the largest 1,000 companies in this country?

Some women actually are shattering the glass ceiling, but they are doing it one at a time. We've got to get off what is now being called the "sticky floor." Catalyst, a research organization that looks at women in business, surveyed women executives about what holds women back from upper management. The top three answers were: (1) Male stereotyping and preconceptions of women; (2) Exclusion from informal networks of communication; and (3) Lack of significant general management and line experience. Looks like numbers one and two fall into the category of "Playing with an Old Boys' Club."

It's going to take a long, long time before we get half of the CEO jobs, half of the seats on Fortune 500 boards and equal pay for equal work. But, in the meantime, we get to be women. We get to enjoy our connection to each other and celebrate our awareness and feelings. This is a tough journey, but it is a shared moment in our history that we can either lament or embrace. When it starts to hurt, do what women do best: Connect with one another. Give support and you will get it back, and be thankful that you can experience this depth of friendship because it is powerful. With this kind of connection, it really doesn't matter who gets all of the marbles at the end of the game. We win, either way. I remember the first time I had lunch with Jacqueline St. Joan, then a controversial Denver judge who had been at the forefront of the domestic violence movement there. This was before I had my feminist "awakening." I told her, "Well, I figure men make more money, have more opportunities to advance and generally get to rule the world. And, if the choice is being a man and having all of that or being a woman, I'd rather be a woman." She looked at me like I was out of my mind, and eventually, I also thought that idea was a little nuts. Now I am starting to wonder.

I look at Teresa Edwards, who has been called the "female Michael Jordan," who pioneered the American Basketball League and won gold medals at five Olympic games. Michael Jordan was paid more for one game than Edwards made in a couple of years, but she didn't let herself become consumed by bitterness. Instead, she found other rewards. "We get so much less in terms of the dollar figures, yet we give so much more in terms of passion," she said. "Personally, I get what I need. I can't really worry what everyone else is getting. I'm going to fulfill my desires when I go out and perform. I think we get more balance out of life." It's not about money or power, but rather, who we are. "It's not a man's world anymore," she said. "It's our world. All of our world."

A MOMENT WITH . . .

HELEN THOMAS

Legendary Reporter

"When I came here, I could belong to the White House Correspondents' Association. The dues were two dollars a year. The whole reason that association had a reason to be was to give a dinner in honor of the president of the United States once a year and present him with a gift. When I started covering the White House, I could pay my dues and belong, but I couldn't go to the dinner because I was a woman.

"After Kennedy was inaugurated, we didn't have time to muster our forces to fight this because the inauguration was in January and the dinner was in February. But the next year, there were five of us and we really put our foot down. I went to Pierre Salinger and said, 'You've got to tell President Kennedy he should absolutely not go to a dinner in his honor if the women members of the press can't attend.' And, Kennedy agreed. So, for the first time we were able to attend the White House correspondents' dinner.

"We've had to break down every door, separately.

"There was the National Press Club. We were never allowed to join. If we went into the club, we had to be taken by a man or we had to be the wife of somebody. But the heads of state would come to Washington and there would be one appearance before the press, usually at the National Press Club. Well, we couldn't go. In 1956, Liz Carpenter made a deal with the Press Club, since her husband was a member. Then newswomen could be in the balcony, overlooking the ballroom where the luncheons were held. We didn't have to wear veils, but we had to be in the balcony and we were escorted out immediately after the speeches.

"Well, when Khruschev was coming, we said we were going to hear him as much as any male reporter. Every press club in town fired off cables to Moscow inviting him to appear before their group, as we did at the Women's National Press Club. The Russians came back to the state department with all of these invitations and said, 'What do we do?' The state department said, 'Of course you will go to the National Press Club.' And we said, 'Of course he will not because we have to be at that luncheon.'

"We really raised hell. As a result, there was a big meeting at the state department and we had a showdown fight. They backed down and agreed to allow thirty women reporters to actually sit on the floor of the National Press Club ballroom and eat lunch.

"Because I was head of the Women's National Press Club, I got to sit at the head table with Khruschev and the other luminaries of the National Press Club. This was when Khruschev made his tremendous and scary speech, 'We will bury you . . .'

"I didn't think my being there was any great breakthrough. I thought I was where I should be. There should have been a lot more of us on the floor at that luncheon. I didn't feel defiance or any great victory. Just that this was where we should be, covering this story.

"We weren't allowed again until 1971 when they were down on their finances. That's when they first opened the door to membership for women."

SEVEN

WOMAN VS. WOMAN

How come other women can be such bitches?
That is the number one question I get asked. It's one thing for a man to get nasty and competitive, but for a woman to put down another woman? One of *us*? Why does that hurt so much more? Part of the problem is that women are supposed to be solid emotionally and socially, while at the same time being compassionate and nurturing. It is widely thought that one of the reasons women haven't succeeded or moved ahead as much as men is because women in power-positions don't support the women below them.

Workplace consultant Sarah Banda Purvis said she regularly hears from women frustrated with other women. "One of the most common e-mails I get is from women complaining about women at their level or more senior who are not supportive," said Banda Purvis. "They complain that other women are cutthroat and backstabbing."

It doesn't just bother us that women compete, it's the *way* women compete says Judith Briles, the author of nearly twenty books and a specialist in woman vs. woman conflict. Women tend to resort to underhanded behavior more frequently than men she says. Briles, who has done a number of surveys on sabotage, says backstabbing and gossip hurts even more when women are the perpetrators because we think we are being betrayed by friends. "The assumption is that we have been the underdog for many years and that we are all in it together," she said. "When someone does something that is undermining to you, you take it personally. You think, 'She was my friend. How could she do that?' "

Why don't all women help other women? One reason is that, as a whole, we are still being left behind when it comes to opportunities at work. We may have come a long way, but we haven't caught up to our male counterparts. "Because there are so few opportunities in these settings, women are vying for that same small slice of the pie," Purvis said. "There is that feeling that, 'There's not much here. If I help her, she'll get the slice of the pie and I'll be left with nothing.' " So, we feel even more competitive toward other women than we do with men.

There is a myth in our culture that women should always be supportive of each other. Women aren't "supposed" to be cutthroat and brutal says Marianne LaFrance, psychologist and professor of psychology and gender studies at Yale University. "But, women can also be very competitive. It's denying our full essence to say we can't be competitive. The reason it stands out is that women are supposed to be very good at relationships. The assumption is that, if we are good at relationships, we shouldn't be competitive. God forbid we compete with each other," LaFrance said. "But, women *do* compete with each other. Competition is a fact of life. It just bothers us more when women are competitive." But there is a difference between being healthily competitive and sabotaging other women.

It really eats at me when a woman who has made it actually sets out to create an environment where she is the only woman of power. I once watched a woman get promoted into upper management and then systematically demote or destroy the careers of every woman coming up behind her who posed a professional threat. It was bizarre. You'd think her boss might have realized that she only focused her discontent toward other strong women, but he either didn't notice or didn't care.

However, this kind of situation is not unusual. Margaret Beckett, who leads England's House of Commons, stunned me when I brought up the subject of Margaret Thatcher. I'd always imagined Britain's first woman prime minister to be a pioneer. Well, yes, she was a pioneer during her eleven

> "This kind of conflict exists when women feel powerless. It happens with minorities, too. When you are somehow oppressed, it causes what I call the 'crab in the bucket' effect. If a crab tries to crawl out, the others try to pull it back in the trap. They are somehow feeling inadequate in themselves and are threatened by you."
>
> —Stephanie Allen, consultant specializing in retention and advancement of executive women

years in charge, but not for the cause of other women. "I saw very little of Margaret Thatcher over the years," Beckett told me. "She wasn't a woman who had much to do with other women politicians. And, unfortunately, she had very little sense of humor. She wasn't someone you tended to get in conversation with."

Is this the same Thatcher who was hailed for transcending the gender barrier? The woman who amazed so many of us with her force and presence? "All of those years, she had just one woman in her cabinet, and there were women of her own party who were equal to the men she had appointed—in fact, in some cases, better," Beckett said. "I can't decide whether she didn't think other women could do what she had done or whether she just didn't want the competition. Most of us felt she didn't want the competition. There was a lesson in that." Beckett said the women who served in government banded together to help each other. "When I got here, there were twenty or thirty women, maybe less, of a total 659," she said. As Beckett moved on to become a senior member of her party, she said she tried to be helpful and encouraging to other women.

Beckett's description of Thatcher fits closely with the old definition of "queen bee" behavior. "The queen bee is a woman who made it in a man's world and beat him in his own system," said Jean Isberg Stafford, a consultant and executive coach who speaks nationally on the topic. "Her position is, 'I did it, you should, too. I'm not helping you because nobody helped me.'" The good news is that this is becoming less of a problem. We don't hear that term as much as we used to, which is likely because more women are in high places, and are unable to hog all the female success out there for themselves.

Certainly, there are men who exhibit queen bee behavior too. But, Isberg Stafford points out that women historically have been divided. A hundred years ago—even as recently as fifty years ago—women lived in separate houses and tended to their individual families. They didn't get together every day. They worked independently and were on their own. They didn't participate in team sports. "It used to be that we didn't get a lot of help learning to play with women," she said. "I think there was something lacking in our training, in that regard. We got in the corporate world and there weren't a lot of us to work together, either."

For now, we seem more focused on our individual success. But, is that such a bad thing? "Women *are* competitive! That should be said. They want the goods. They want to get the interview, they want the book, they want to be the chair. They are willing to fight for it, and I don't think that's so terrible," said psychology professor Jackie James, of Radcliffe College at Harvard. But, why does it feel so terrible? James laughed when I asked that. "Maybe it bothers us because we think women are supposed to say, 'Be my guest,' or, 'You take it.' That's the female servitude we are socialized into."

She definitely has a point there. Women have traditionally been taught to put their feelings second to others and be the ones who make the big sacrifices in relationships to make things "work." Women have been the ones to say, "Your feelings matter more than mine," then sacrifice a piece of themselves to make it all better. Sometimes, we wonder why other women don't put *our* feelings first, like Mom did. So, let's stop expecting others to sacrifice things that we wouldn't want to sacrifice for ourselves. James suggests that instead of worrying about what someone else is doing, work on your own competitiveness. "Unfortunately, one person is going to get the job, and if you want it, you've got to be competitive," she said. "Accepting that may be harder for us."

Many of us think the woman who goes all the way and gets all the marbles has an obligation to mentor other women so they have the same opportunities. But, that "obligation" is a flawed concept, said Carly Fiorina, CEO of Hewlett-Packard. "Women will say many times that men ought to focus on their talents, their skills and not the rest," said Fiorina. "Women need to do the same thing. That means they shouldn't necessarily feel they have to support a woman who isn't capable just because she is a woman. They have to accept that sometimes a woman isn't getting ahead—not because she's a woman—but because she's not qualified."

The Catfight

For some reason, watching two women go at it to see who's boss has captured the fancy of the masses ever since Anne Baxter took on Bette Davis in *All About Eve*. Remember that very public moment when Deborah Norville unseated America's sweetheart host Jane Pauley on NBC's *Today*? Four months after Norville became the morning news anchor at *Today*, Pauley was dumped from the show. The media *loved* it! The viewers came to despise Norville for unseating our perfect Jane, the ratings went into freefall and finally, Norville left *Today* to go on maternity leave—never to come back to NBC.

That whole scene might have made for interesting drama in the media, but it plays out every day in the office. "What happens is that men often unintentionally pit women against each other," said Harvard psychology professor Ellen Langer. "I think some women have an awareness that the game doesn't have to be played the way they are playing it, and that conflict is distressing."

Broadcast icon Cokie Roberts has seen that up close, but said she's lucky to have escaped the worst catfights among the best known women television anchors. We've all seen the gossip columnists pitting Diane Sawyer against Barbara Walters against Connie Chung against Katie Couric or whomever. "I'm really removed from the rivalries you hear about with other women," Roberts said. "As one of my bosses said to me, 'You have a schtict.' He meant, I have knowledge. I'm not a superstar in the superstar strata where everybody is fighting with each other or purported to be fighting with each other." Still, she knows some people relish in watching big-name women battle for the camera's eye. "It's always, 'Look at the girls go at it,'" she said. "They do try to play you off against each other. I assume, at some point, this will change."

Fighting Back

How many times have you remained silent when you felt someone was doing a number on you? None of us especially likes confrontation and few of us actively engage in it. You might think you are taking the high road. Or, you might think that stirring it up will only make it worse. "Your silence condones whatever the behavior was," said Judith Briles, the sabotage expert. "The mere silence of it signals that it was no big deal, or it's okay. It is critical to vocalize when you disapprove of someone's activities or behaviors." One difference between men and women is that men aren't afraid to confront someone. Women don't do that directly. Instead, we might go to a friend or other coworker and say, "Do you know what Georgia did?" And this is not directly handling the problem. "What they are doing is seeking empathy, sympathy or support in their feelings of being hurt, betrayed or pissed off," Briles said. "Then you get a domino effect. Suzy tells Nancy, who tells Jessica, and there is this steamroller rolling that can create an extraordinarily toxic environment." Why don't we just deal with the problem directly? We're afraid to confront. We were raised to be nice, share our toys, wait our turn, be gracious and avoid conflict. We all know the truth of what she's saying. When someone does something duplicitous or underhanded, we're mute.

It doesn't mean you have to confront every little thing. Choose your battles. Decide whether the situation is important, likely to escalate, and what you have to lose. If it is significant, don't wait weeks or months to deal with it. Prepare your argument. Briles says the first step is to come up with your set of bullet points and issues that need to be addressed—before you begin the confrontation. Know what your concerns are, what your evidence is. "The most common thing that will happen is that they will deny whatever the activity was," she said. "They'll say you misinterpreted it or did not see it correctly." It is best to have actually seen the behavior yourself, rather than rely on secondhand information.

When you are ready, arrange to meet in neutral territory. Her turf may intimidate you; your turf will threaten her. Go for a walk, go out for a cup of coffee, get lunch. Then, be very specific and direct in your language. Briles has it all scripted out for you in her book, *Woman to Woman 2000: Becoming Sabotage Savvy in the New Millennium*. Use this conversation guide by filling in the blanks.

When you_____ (action)

I felt_____ (reaction)

Because_____ (looks, sounds, feels like)

Was it your intent to_____ (Remain silent here when it comes time for the response. Don't answer your own question.)

In the future, I prefer that you_____ (action)

Consequences_____ (what you'll do)

An example: "When you went over my head to Ed to get approval for your project, I felt left out of the loop because you hadn't told me anything or included me in the process. It looks and feels like you didn't want my participation. Was that your intent? In the future, I prefer you come to me first, because, if you don't, I'll have to assume you are deliberately trying to do an end run around me, and we'll have to come up with a written plan for communicating your efforts to me directly."

Yikes! Can you imagine the courage it would take to confront something like that, head-on? You bet! But imagine the results. You can bet that next time this person isn't going to go to Ed without going to you first.

One tool journalists, lawyers and psychologists use to get results is silence. When the confrontee gives you an answer you don't like, just sit there. People can't stand silence, and feel they *must* fill the void. The more they talk, the more they start to hang themselves. Silence is such a force in a tense conversation, and it is best used with a confident expression that makes the confrontee think that you aren't showing all of your cards. And, remember, listen for silence, as well. I *love* it when somebody tries to turn silence back on me. I'll just sit there, smiling. I don't care if it goes on for ten minutes. The person becomes so uncomfortable that *he* or *she* starts blathering. Finally, try to come up with some sort of constructive result from your confrontation. If at all possible, end on a positive note, saying, "I'm glad we talked," or, "I feel better about things."

At some point, we have to look at our role in all of this. It's really easy to write a chapter about the problem with "other women," but at some point we have to ask ourselves if we might be part of the problem. We all take turns being competitive, manipulative and egocentric. Even if we see ourselves as honorable and kind, others might not. The mere force of our personalities and talents, combined with the pressures of an intense work environment, can cause others to see us as more threatening and driven than we think we are.

Maybe we should listen to the likes of my good friend Carolyn Little, who always seems to be the most popular person in the house. *Everybody* loves her at work because she is so easy to get along with, so helpful and so much fun. One day, as I mentioned that I might benefit from some of her tact and diplomatic skills, she blurted out, "I just manipulate people with kindness."

Carolyn? Manipulating? She said she likes the term "manipulating with kindness" because it seems like an oxymoron. It's funny, but it's right on the mark. "I think the word *manipulation* has a negative stigma attached to it because of all this psychobabble," she said. "I would argue that manipulation can be defined as a way to create the best out of any given situation. You can manipulate something in a good way or in a bad way. I would never do it with malicious intent." Her basic philosophy is that you can't lose by being nice to others.

"Your kindness has to be genuine. It has to come across as genuine. It can't be sugary-sweet, or condescending, or laced with selfish motives," she said. "People will read right through you. So, in order to effectively manipulate with kindness you have to find some way to feel that kindness in your heart toward the other person." She laid out the three possible scenarios of conflict:

1. *Being nice to somebody who is being mean to you.* "You steal all the thunder out of their meanness and you steal all the satisfaction they get from being mean to you."

2. *Being nice to somebody who is indifferent.* "They'll be nicer to you—probably without even realizing it."

3. *Being nice to somebody who is already nice.* "That's the easy one."

Maybe being "nice" is not a new concept for you, but some of us have gotten a little cynical in our relationships, so this kind of information is especially valuable. "Being nice entails respecting other people as people," Little said. "You don't have to keep score all the time about who is winning in the conversation, who is winning the meeting—whatever."

Little things make a big difference she said. Going out of your way to be nice, whether it is to let someone cut in line for the copy machine or passing on an article of interest, can be appreciated by the people around you. Part of her secret is finding something she can like about every person. "You figure out what you have in common, what makes you connect with this person," she said. "Whether you do it because you have to or because you want to, you figure out what they respond to in you, then you emphasize that with them." So, after all of that traditional socialization telling us to "be nice," here we go again. However, this concept of "manipulating with kindness" has an intellectual component to it, and I like it. It's a start.

What does it say about us when so much conflict is generated amongst ourselves? When women find other women to be the "enemy"? Here we are, enjoying more clout, access and success than any generation of women before us, and some of us are turning on each other! The only reason we are able to take advantage of the opportunities we now have is because of the stamina and success of other women who came before us. I'm sure they dealt with their share of backbiting too. But now that we recognize that this issue bothers us so much, why don't we do something about it? If we'd address it when it comes up, and be mindful of our own actions toward other women, our ability to reach our individual potential would grow and the legacy we give to the next generation would be even richer. Why would we want to limit what we give to the next generation by being nasty or petty? And, why would we want to put those kinds of limits on ourselves?

Dealing with Women

- *Don't single out other women for extra scrutiny or competition.*

- *The high road is not always a silent path.* When someone does you wrong, say something. What's the worst thing that will happen? He or she might talk behind your back, which he or she is probably doing already.

- *Don't be a victim.*

- *Support other women, rather than singling them out for competition.* You don't have to prove you are more intelligent, sharper, faster or more productive than the women around you.

- *There's enough success out there for everyone.* Celebrate the achievements of others, rather than resenting them. There's more than one prize out there to be had.

A MOMENT WITH . . .
PAULA COUGHLIN

She forever changed the U.S. Navy after coming forward in the Tailhook assault.

"I once read an article in the *Washington Post* weekend supplement and they had me on the cover. It read, 'Paula Coughlin, The Woman Who Changed the Navy.'

"That was in 1992. I didn't believe it. I looked at that cover and thought, 'That's not anybody I know.' But I think I did change the Navy. There have been so many women out there in every branch of service who have just been taken advantage of and abused and harassed and beaten and assaulted. They had no recourse. Now, if nothing else, they have recourse. The government may say it has zero tolerance and have steps and procedures for those women to make complaints, but if something goes wrong and all of that just turns into lip service, that's the Navy's biggest fear. It will be on *60 Minutes*. People will lose their jobs. It's going to blow apart.

"That's how I changed the Navy. I've instilled a little fear.

"I resigned in 1994. My quality of life had diminished well beyond what a reasonable person should endure. There was tremendous pressure from people around me saying 'Don't quit.' 'Don't resign.' 'Don't let them beat you.'

"Was I a quitter? I had to reconcile it in my own head. I was having physical manifestations of stress. I had an ulcer. I was suicidal at times. I wasn't allowed to fly. Finally, I thought enough years of that had gone by.

"My healing process was in abeyance until I got out of the Navy. Every day was a bad experience, over and over again. I think that's what happens to any woman in a workplace that is a hostile environment. You don't heal until you get out of that environment or until the person creating that hostile environment is gone.

"Once the civil trial started, we knew we were going to win. All of the discovery was over, and I was right and they were wrong. When the trial was over, I was tremendously relieved. Finally, some real validation. I was awarded $6.95 million. It was unreal. I didn't see half of it, but it meant moving to a new town and buying a house and starting a new life. I am happily married with a baby. I teach fitness and yoga and I have a dog. My life has gone on. I don't think my job is done. I don't want to think I peaked at age 30. I'm just looking for the right situation and the right cause.

"I still have bad Navy dreams, mostly about flying. But I have dreams about being in the Navy, about being with Navy people, about being stuck in a Navy uniform and not being able to get out of the Navy. It's that feeling of being captured. I can't get away.

"The Tailhook experience still comes back. I had construction guys here the other day, and one of the guys said, 'Dang, this is a nice house. Where did you get your money?'

"I said, 'Somebody died.'

"I left it at that."

EIGHT

PERSEVERING, REGARDLESS

I HAVE A FRIEND WHO has a great idea for a new career about every two months. One week, she's an inventor who has arranged with a manufacturer to create a household product that sure sounds like a winner to me. A few months later, she's finishing course work to teach her to run her own public relations firm and already has designed her own snazzy Web site and business cards. A month after that, she's decided to use all of the computer equipment and office space she bought for the P.R. firm to create her own graphic design business. She could have succeeded with any one of those endeavors if she had a single ounce of follow-through, but she doesn't. What she has is an initial explosive burst of energy that helps her create, strategize and get moving at a frenetic pace, followed by a paralyzing lack of interest. She lacks patience and stamina. She even makes fun of her whimsical approach to her careers saying how lucky she is that she is not the sole source of income in her household.

What is sad about this story is how she deprives herself of the success she most certainly could achieve if she would just keep her eyes trained on any one of her dreams and keep going. It's one thing to have vision, and another to have follow-through. One without the other is a straight shot to failure. You have to be willing to persevere.

Everytime I hear the word *perseverance*, I think of some newspaper or television story about a remarkably driven or committed person pulling off the impossible. Superhuman effort, which leads to extraordinary results. But that's not what we're talking about here. We're talking about the kind of perseverance that you need to stay on your path and move toward realizing your vision—despite the difficulties you encounter by just being out there trying. True perseverance is an everyday experience. It's a way of life, whether you are trying to slay dragons in the workforce or at home. You persevere from day to day, regardless of whether you are coping with a new boss or new job or professional burnout or a mate at home who doesn't make matters easier. Perseverance gets you up in the morning for another round. At a distance, it may look like other people have it easier than you do, that they don't have the same kinds of clashes with bosses or coworkers that you might have, or that they seem to get things handed to them. By now, I've come to realize that *everybody* has struggles. Some cope with them better than others, and some advertise their difficulties while others don't.

What makes the day-to-day challenge easier is the knowledge that you are traveling on your own chosen path—you are doing what you want to do, and knowing that gives you a certain degree of satisfaction, despite difficulties. If you aren't doing what you were meant to do, it *is* much harder to put up with the ordinary b.s. you encounter in life. You won't get the personal enrichment out of your daily experience, because a paycheck and health insurance isn't enough to fulfill your soul.

We all have many choices in life. Some of us choose to excel, while others choose to be average or below average. The important consideration here is that *you* choose to do what you want to do with your life, testing the limits you feel comfortable testing and knowing that there are two things standing in your way: (1) Your negative thinking and (2) The fact that life isn't always fair and doesn't always give you what you want, when you want it.

The women in this book have convinced me that it is so much easier to succeed when you are passionate about your course. That's an easy lesson. The hard lesson is this: Just because you love what you are doing and are committed to your dream, it doesn't mean there is going to be this huge confluence of luck and good fortune to help you pull it off. *You* have to make it happen. That means you have to believe in your goal and yourself again and again and again and again, despite experiences that leave you questioning yourself. If you don't believe in yourself enough to fight for your dream, no one else is going to do it for you.

Your self-talk is everything. If you tell yourself, "I can do this, it's just a little hard right now," you can have the strength you need to keep at it. But, if you tell yourself that you are encountering trouble because you must be on the wrong path and certain to fail, well, you'll probably fail. Maybe you are encountering difficulty because you are being tested to make sure that this is the *right* path for you. I have chosen the stories in this chapter because they speak to perseverance on a personal level. These women had their vision and they had to fight to make it real because nobody was going to make it real for them.

Television producer Mary-Ellis Bunim struggled to make her vision reality. Bunim left behind her career as a producer on the nation's top-rated soaps (*Search for Tomorrow, As the World Turns* and *Santa Barbara*) to join with news documentary producer Jon Murray to create an edgy new production company that would, one day, revolutionize modern television. Bunim-Murray essentially created the reality television genre that so dominates the television industry today. MTV's *Real World* and its sister show, *Road Rules,* are the Bunim-Murray productions that led to shows like *Survivor* and *Big Brother*. But selling their vision involved a process filled with uncertainty.

From the beginning, it was tough. They sublet a small conference room from another company and filled it with a table, two dining room chairs, one word processor, an IBM Selectric typewriter and two telephone lines that never, ever rang. "We'd walk a half mile a day to go somewhere for lunch—just to use up the time. We'd budget five dollars a lunch," she remembers. "Then, we'd take turns with what we'd do in the afternoon. He liked golf and I liked tennis, so one day he'd golf and I'd stare at the phone, the next day I'd play tennis and he'd stare at the phone until it started to ring. People don't realize how much tenacity it takes to get anything done or get anywhere. They think, 'All I need to do is have a good idea and the world will be at my feet.'"

Well, you can sit around and wait for someone else to notice how great you are, but odds are it's not going to happen. You have to be the one to make things happen until you get what you are after. "You have to take charge," Bunim said. Just because you are smart and have good ideas, you can't assume that other people will recognize it and reward you. "It's up to the individual to carve their own path and have their own vision. No one knows what twists and turns will come along—and they shouldn't. That would be boring," she said.

In Bunim's case, the twists and turns involved MTV. The young network wanted to branch out beyond airing music videos and wanted to produce some sort of an original drama, but it didn't want to spend the kind of money it would take to produce a series with actors. Bunim and Murray came up with the *Real World* concept, bringing together a handful of culturally and racially diverse young people to live under one roof. Bunim's instincts with soap opera helped her to cast the kind of people where tension would create a natural story line. Murray's knowledge of the documentary genre helped them chronicle what happened in the house.

"I didn't realize it would take off until we were halfway through the pilot," she said. "It was extremely experimental. But, once she saw all those people working back in the control room watching, mesmerized as they watched the people we'd put together in that New York loft for a weekend, we realized it was going to work. We looked around and everyone was absolutely frozen solid, listening to every word out of those kids' mouths. We had cast for diversity and cast interesting people. Immediately, they stripped off their clothes and got into the hot tub. Then we thought, 'Hmmm, these are good conversations, there's good sharing and there is a lot of sexual tension in the group.' We thought, 'This is going to fly.' "

After that *Real World* pilot was sent to MTV, Bunim and Murray were put to an especially excruciating test. MTV had nine months to decide whether it wanted the show or not. Bunim took a consulting job that entailed a weekly commute to New York from California, but feared she'd have to take a regular job with a boss who would tell her what to do, when to do it and where to be when she was doing it. "I was living on a plane, just to pay the bills," she said. "It was the most miserable time I can think of, having to take a job because I was so desperate to pay the bills," she said. "Yet, I didn't want to give up on this dream." The day before MTV's option was up, the call came. MTV wanted *Real World*. Bunim's perseverance paid off, big time.

Learning To Enjoy the Ride

My first full-time reporting job paid peanuts and required me to work three day shifts and two nights, mostly covering the stories nobody else wanted. I had so little expendable cash that when my paycheck came on Thursday, a friend and I would celebrate with a "payday dinner" at Quincy's steak house, where we would each order the kiddie burger and salad bar for $2.49. Damn, those were the good old days. I knew what I was after so I worked feverishly to make it happen. I had a great time. Older reporters (the ones way up there in their 30s) would tease me and call me the "Doe-eyed Fawn." It didn't matter if an editor ripped apart something I wrote or a reader called in to complain. I was learning my craft. I worked so many extra hours that one coworker joked, "You are here all the time because your life is meaningless and you have nothing else." That didn't matter to me, because what I had was my dream, and I was living it. If only we could maintain that same sense of optimism now. Wouldn't it be great to still be able to get as much out of the process of persevering as we get out of the end result of reaching our goal? Why do we have to be so quick to retreat? You know that anything you have earned after hardship is worth so much more to your soul than something that came easily. But, we are so impatient that we assume one or two tough moments are signs that we are on the wrong path. Why can't we re-create some of that naïve faith we had in the old days when we were still learning?

Before winning an Academy Award as best actress for *Fargo*, Frances McDormand struggled like the rest of us, auditioning for parts that would turn into great opportunities—for other people. "For me, it was hard not to think of it as constant rejection," McDormand said. But she endured it by reminding herself that rejection of her acting skills was not a rejection of her as a human being. As she persisted, she discovered how important it was to put stress in its place. If she went into an audition showing how much she needed and wanted a particular part, directors didn't want her. She had to learn not to let the ups and downs of the process make her desperate.

If getting what you want isn't easy, have faith. McDormand was passed over for plenty of roles, but every few months, something would come through. She'd get another role that would keep her going until she did hit the big time. She won herself an Academy Award for best actress in *Fargo*, and other nominations for her performances in *Mississippi Burning* and *Almost Famous*. She was also nominated for a Tony Award.

It's hard to imagine that great actress struggling to pursue her dream, but she did. We all do. If you find yourself beginning to wear down, take care of yourself by pampering yourself with some free time or a bubble bath or a massage or a good workout. Don't let your struggle consume all of your time or energy because you will lose your edge and stop enjoying the pleasure that comes from pursuing your calling. Instead, step back, see what you can do to make yourself feel better about the present moment, then do something wonderful for yourself. Reward yourself for having the guts to stick with what you are doing, and come to enjoy the craziness and unpredictability of the process.

After you have de-stressed a little and cleared your mind, start looking at what it is that is causing you to struggle. Are there ways to better prioritize what you are doing? In your heart, do you feel that Plan A is not working? Then it might be time to start thinking about Plan B, a different way to Plan A. And, if so, what is Plan B? This is not a moment to contemplate quitting, but rather, to fine tune your strategy. Instead of looking at what you are doing from an "all or nothing" perspective that places too much emphasis on your original plan, take another look at your vision. Aren't there other ways to achieve the same or similar end results? What do you need to do to make it happen?

If, in the back of your mind, you are entertaining the possibility that you will quit, do yourself a favor. Put that thought away until you have exhausted all of the potential of your dream. Wait until you know you have taken it as far as you can take it—then think about quitting. Sometimes, you are only a moment away from success, but you can't see it yet.

> "Even in the hardest times, I've never said, 'I don't want to do this anymore.' I know if I say something like that to myself, it will go into a downward spiral. So, I ask myself, 'How do I get through this? Am I going to just get through this and just maintain or am I going to get through this and go well beyond?'"
>
> —Ret. Gen. Claudia Kennedy, the first three-star general in the U.S. Army

The Longest Marathon

Kathrine Switzer's story has a lot to do with running, but more to do with stamina. She was a teenager when she started jogging, and back in the 1960s, women didn't run. She says that back then, "People thought that any woman who could do anything in sports was going to have big legs, grow a mustache and turn into a lesbian. As if anybody cares nowadays. But, in those days, it was important for a woman to be feminine. I didn't see why a woman couldn't be feminine *and* run."

In college, she defied the skepticism of her friend and training partner, Arnie Briggs, and readied herself to be the first woman to officially run an organized marathon—the Boston Marathon. Race organizers assumed she was a man when they saw the registration form that read "K. V. Switzer."

Her marathon took place on a snowy, sleety New England day. Dressed in a warm-up suit, few people noticed her gender. But, about four miles in, photographers spotted her and zoomed in. When the race director saw that—gasp!—a woman was running in his race, he took off after her. What followed, all captured on film, was what turned her moment into unforgettable history for all women athletes. "I wasn't going very fast, and he grabbed me by the shoulders and threw me back, screaming at me, 'GET THE HELL OUT OF THE RACE!'" She jumped out of his grasp as Briggs shouted, "Leave her alone, she's trained! She's trained!" "I burst into tears," she said. "The guy was terrifying. He was very, very aggressive. Big Tom, my ex–all-American football player boyfriend, threw a cross-body block against the official and sent him into the air—right out of the race. There's this amazing series of photographs of girl being attacked by official, girl being saved by burly boyfriend."

After that, Switzer continued running the marathon. "I was emotionally exhausted. I felt, for a split second, like just going home. But then I said, 'No way. I've trained too hard for this.' If I'd stepped off, they'd have said, 'See, women do that all the time. It gets tough and they quit.' I would have finished that race if it were fifty miles." She finished in 4:20, which "wasn't terrific." But, she finished. "I was determined when I finished that I was going to be a better athlete and change things so women had more opportunities in running and sports," she said.

Switzer went on to run thirty-five marathons and would later prove instrumental in the drive to have the women's marathon become an official event in the Olympics. She now works as program director for Avon Running, coordinating running and other athletic events for Avon worldwide. "I was proud to show a woman could do these exceptional things," she said. "When I ran Boston, the idea was not to show the world that a woman could do it. The idea was to show myself I could do it."

She eventually went on to win the New York Marathon with a time of 2:51, and championed the cause to get women officially into marathon and long-distance running. In 1972, women could officially run marathons. "The marathon used to be the most arduous, difficult, romantic event there was," she said. "The triathlon wasn't even heard of in the 1970s. Women are now doing endurance events that last six to ten days. I was just happy to be a part of breaking apart the whole notion that women are weak and passive. We think it's exploded now, but that's nothing to what's coming. Women's capacity for endurance and stamina is unknown."

The question of perseverance isn't whether we are tough enough to run the long course, but rather, whether we can face whatever tries to stop us along the way. The challenges are considerable, and even when we think we have made it, something inevitably happens to remind us that we are still in the process of creating ourselves. Switzer talks about a woman's capacity for endurance and stamina, but in most of our endeavors, those qualities are as emotional as they are physical.

Look at Connie Stevens, the blond-haired, blue-eyed, singer, actress and dancer who some in Hollywood called "The Face." Her story tells of the kind of psychological endurance we all should have because she is a master of reinventing herself. She is now the CEO of her own cosmetics and skin-care empire, Forever Spring.

She had no choice but to brainstorm alternatives to her life in show business when Las Vegas no longer wanted her as a headliner and her business manager died, leaving her with nothing in the bank. She worried how she would support herself and her two daughters. "I learned I am very resilient," she said. Stevens realized she had to do something to generate income, and used her celebrity to market skin-care products on Home Shopping Network, which was just starting out. "I worked my ass off," she said. "I saw the potential of a new media, and I didn't see any downside to it. I went with it and rolled the dice." She started selling off her real estate, piece by piece, to keep up with expenses. Naysayers were everywhere, warning her not to mess with big business because she wouldn't be up to the challenge. "There were many mean-spirited people who said I'd fall flat on my face and lose everything, and they said that I wasn't very smart. That's right. They said, 'You aren't smart enough.' " She didn't believe it, even though those words hurt. "I believe everybody can do anything," she said. "So, when people said those things, I became more determined to prove them wrong." Her business has turned into a skin-care, makeup and hair-care company with more than four hundred products and more than three million customers. Not bad for someone who wasn't "smart enough."

There will be times when you will start to lose energy and wonder whether it's worth the effort it will take to keep going. You might fantasize about how much easier your life would be if you would take a less stressful and more predictable path. If you don't have a good support network cheering you on, you might begin to doubt whether you are even capable of pulling it off. These are the moments when you must remind yourself of why you chose this journey in the first place. Whether the end result of this struggle is outrageous success or nothing at all, you will gain so much personal power from taking charge of your life and having the fortitude to stick it out.

I know a remarkably talented young woman who spent over five thousand dollars to cut a CD, *and never sent it out to a single radio station or agent.* As if some telemarketer was going to randomly call her at home and say, "By the way, do you have any CDs we might be able to distribute?" I kept wondering why she would choose to sit on so many boxes of beautifully recorded CDs that no one would ever hear. Finally, it hit me. What if people heard the music and didn't like it? At least, this way, she didn't have to endure the embarrassment. Imagine if she'd focused on what would have happened if the listener's reactions were positive.

I'll say this again: Vision is nothing without follow-through. Along the way, you will be repeatedly tested to see whether you have what it takes to succeed on your terms. The difference between success and failure often comes down to your ability to stick with your plan, make adjustments to make it work, and remain devoted to what inspired you in the first place. There are too many excuses for quitting, and it's your job not to listen to them.

Judith Heumann sure didn't. Heumann, who suffered from polio when she was eighteen months old, tired of being told she didn't belong. She's spent her life getting around in a wheelchair—but that never stopped her from living well. Before you take in her story of remarkable perseverance, understand that the woman who fought so hard to have a chance to participate in the work world eventually became a top government official who forever changed the rights of the disabled. She was the Clinton Administration's most visible advocate for the rights of the disabled while serving as assistant secretary of education for the Office of Special Education and Rehabilitative Services.

Heumann grew up in New York and was very integrated into the neighborhood. "My mother took me to school when I was five years old, like any mother of a five-year-old would do, but the people at the school said I couldn't go," she began. "They said I was a fire hazard because of my wheelchair. I remember the message that gave me. That there was something wrong with me." Her friends would come home after school and they'd play together, go to Brownies, to Hebrew school and just about everything else. "I did everything they did, except during the school hours, I wasn't in school," she said. "People who knew me didn't treat me any different. But the people who didn't know me did treat me different. There were people who only saw my wheelchair."

In the middle of the fourth grade, she was finally allowed to go to a class where disabled students were segregated from the others. It was in a school far from her neighborhood and she recalls that there was very limited learning going on for this "special education." "But, it was the first time I got to meet other disabled people," she said. "I could spend large amounts of time with them. They didn't look at me different, didn't treat me different and I didn't treat them any different. It was like a family. I love my biological family, but there was something special I had there with the others."

She went to high school classes with students who were not disabled and she struggled because she didn't have the same kind of academic prepping the others did. She'd never taken a test before, and she feared them. But, she kept going, and then moved on to college, where she continued to grow more aware that the disabled needed a voice.

One weekend, somebody knocked on her door and said she was going out with a couple of couples, and mentioned that one of the guys' dates hadn't shown up. "Then I was asked if I knew anybody who would go out with him," she said. "I could not believe it. . . . It was, again, this invisible thing. People think disabled people are asexual."

She became more political, and would talk about problems and solutions with disabled friends. "It was very important for us to realize that our disability was not the problem," she said. "What was wrong was what was going on around us, and the problems were both structural and attitudinal. You can't force someone to change their attitude, but you can force changes that open up the doors of opportunity—even if the people you are with are not accepting of you as an individual."

When she graduated college, she had to sue the New York City Board of Education so she could be licensed to teach. They wouldn't license her because of her disability. "I was publicly acknowledging that I had been discriminated against. I was not being a victim around it. I was saying, 'I believe this is wrong and I'm going to fight for a remedy.' This was very public, and not only that, it was a fight I could lose. There was a real risk that I could have gone to court and the court could have ruled against me. But, that was okay. I felt that no matter what happened, it was important to try to get this one to go the right way."

That case generated tremendous discussion on discrimination of the disabled, and attracted media coverage for a year. When it was over, Heumann had won. "It was a Sampson and Goliath kind of thing and made me recognize that if you believe in something and you fight hard enough, you can make things better than they were before," she said. And, she did. Heumann has been at the forefront of the disabilities rights movement, having helped develop the Americans with Disabilities Act and other groundbreaking legislation to expand the rights of the disabled. Despite all of the obstacles in her way, Heumann did not quit. She had the guts to stay in the battle, no matter how much resistance she found. That's perseverance.

Often our own worst obstacle is the emotion of fear. Ski instructors will tell you that the trick to skiing advanced black diamond runs is to stop thinking about what you are doing and just do it. If you look down over a steep drop, you'll get scared and fall down. Don't think; just do, they will advise. We think too much about how hard something is, how steep the drop might be and how bad it will feel if we fall. Instead, we should lunge forward and just get it done.

When you have a rough day, tell yourself "Yeah, this was a tough one. At least I'm doing what I want to be doing." (If you aren't, maybe you need to re-evaluate.) When you think you can't stand any more, step out of the fray and look at the process. Remember, our achievements mean so much more to us when we have to fight to make them happen.

Recently, I went to Switzerland to discuss women's issues and was floored by two things. The first was that Swiss women did not get the right to vote until 1971. The second thing that impressed me was how rapidly Swiss women moved forward to claim their place, once they had the chance. Less than three decades after gaining voting privileges, women dominate a third of the House of Representatives, nearly a fourth of the Senate—and one has even served as president of Switzerland. There is a saying that "The Swiss may get up late, but they run very fast." Certainly, female political involvement there shows they are running a lot faster than we are, largely due to perseverance and endurance. When they find themselves pushing for something controversial, "We often need a second go and a third go," explained political leader Rosemary Simmen, who currently chairs the federal commission on foreigners and has held pivotal positions in Swiss government. I found that notion curious, seeing how American women so often become invisible after losing a big battle. Three times, Switzerland has voted against giving women paid maternity leaves, yet the momentum remains for another try. "Lick your wounds and start fresh," Simmen said. "You have to have one or two leaders roll up their sleeves and say, 'Now we start again.'" Ruth Dreifuss, the first woman to lead Switzerland as president, said there are certain advantages and disadvantages to every battle coming down to a vote on the ballot like their democracy requires. "You have to accept several failures before the idea spreads for the civilization," she said. "Reaching a consensus is a matter of endurance."

Whether the obstacles you encounter are blocking your way or the way of many others, it is so important to learn that lesson. Anything worth having isn't going to come easily. Don't listen to negative people, and don't listen to your own pessimistic thinking. Always tell yourself you can take one more step and another, if you must. Keep moving until you get there.

Life tests us. Sometimes things happen that force us to see how much we want what we say we want. Sometimes we have to get pretty banged up and bloodied before we get it, and too often, it's easier to say, "It's not worth it" and just give up. That's always an option. Just put it off until you can't go another inch. If it were so easy to reach our goals, wouldn't everybody be at the top? Along the way, there are so many dropping-off points where we can quit, lose interest or procrastinate.

Reward yourself every time you pick yourself up after a setback. See how that plays into your own growth. You might have to swing and miss a dozen times before you get your hit. But, know in your heart that you will get your hit. If you hang in there long enough, it's going to happen. If you suffer setbacks and rejections along the way, realize that in many challenges, you only have to score once. If you have sent your resume out to twenty firms and they all come back negative, find twenty others. All you need is one. And, the more you get used to standing up when you've been knocked down, the easier it gets. You'll know that, in time, things do have a way of working out.

There are a million excuses to quit, but you only have to pass once. Keep going.

When the Going Gets Tough

- Calm down. Remember, it's *not supposed* to be easy. If what you want is worth having, you are going to have to fight for it.
- You can't anticipate every possible challenge or obstacle. Expect difficulty, and be ready to be creative to overcome it.
- Count on your support group. Have your cheering squad around you to rev you up when you feel worn down.
- Don't over-analyze or over-negatize. The more you focus on the troubles you are experiencing, the more power those difficulties will have over you.
- Know what you've got to do, then do it. Focus on the task, not the degree of difficulty.
- Celebrate small achievements along the way so you know you are building to a bigger victory.
- You don't have to win the first time out. Or the second. Sooner or later, you'll get your victory.

A MOMENT WITH . . .

RITA MORENO

The only woman to win the Oscar, Tony, Grammy, Emmy and Golden Globe

"I lived *West Side Story* except I didn't belong to a gang. This was the ghetto. We were living in Harlem. I got called all of those nasty names: Spic, Gold Tooth, Garlic Mouth—like they used in *West Side Story*.

"When you are young, you absorb everything. If you are told often enough that you have no value, you believe it. All of that stuff accumulates. Sooner or later, it comes to the surface.

"My mom befriended a young Spanish dancer who saw me dancing in the house. I was only about five and she said, 'You know what? Rosita ought to take dance class.' So my mom sent me to her dance teacher, who was Rita Hayworth's uncle. A talent scout saw me in a recital and told my mother, 'I think Rosita has a future in movies.' When Louie B. Mayer came to town, he signed me up.

"Ahh, yes, it sounds so easy. It got harder.

"I was in Hollywood three or four years when they dropped my option. I had aspirations. I was thinking Chekhov, they were thinking Conchita Lolita. I was 'just a Latino,' and every role had to have an accent. It was very depressing.

"I was an extremely insecure young woman, which was ironic because it looked like I was always in charge. The more you pretend, the worse it gets. When I was twenty-four, a friend saw me on a talk show pretending to be somebody—frantically pretending. He told me, 'You really need help.'

"I was in therapy for about seven years, on and off.

"When I was told my work on *West Side Story* had been a nomination-worthy performance, I looked at them like they were mad. But, I won an Academy Award in 1961. When my name was called, I was truly stunned. You know why? There was Judy Garland, sick in a hospital room with a camera and lights, waiting for the announcement. I was sure Judy would win. But at the time the Academy had voted, Judy wasn't sick.

"I remember thinking, 'If I win, I am not going to run up to the stage like everyone else. I'm going to walk with dignity.' Everyone rushes because they want to get there when there is still applause. I don't care. I'm walking, not running. And, I'm not going to thank God or my mother. It's so hypocritical to take out those lists and say, 'I couldn't have done it without all these people.' I hate cheap sentiment. That's the street part of me.

"When my name was called, Spanish Harlem went crazy. To this day, I'm still the only Hispanic woman to win.

"I ran into the wings and started to cry, right into the arms of Joan Crawford who grabbed me because she knew a photo op when she saw it. She kept clutching me to her, hiding my face in her manly bosom saying, 'Aw, there, there, Dear.' I didn't even know her. The photographers were saying, 'Can we please see Rita's face?' They had to unclench her.

"At this age, you work less. More often than not, you are somebody's mother, which doesn't mean a hell of a lot in terms of a substantial role. Things may get better, but the best roles will still go to the younger people because younger people are writing the scripts. There is always work in theater. And there's more work in television. I've been doing a series on HBO for six years, *Oz*. You want to talk about nontraditional casting? I play a nun in contemporary clothes who is a psychotherapy and drug counselor in a maximum-security prison.

"People tell me I look good these days. I look good because I feel good. I know people who are older than I am who are twenty-five. I just came up from the gym an hour ago. I work out. I think it's important. I don't dance much in my big concert shows anymore because my knees are shot.

"It's all about attitude. To me, age is just a number."

NINE

TURNING CRITICISM
INTO OPPORTUNITY

W HAT MAKES YOU THINK I CAN'T TAKE CRITICISM?????"
Uhhhh, gee. I dunno. We remember a kind word for five
minutes and hang onto a criticism for the rest of our lives. Forgive the
overgeneralization, but you know it's true. Living with criticism isn't easy,
but the strong women in this book have managed to deal with it and use it
to better themselves. It's not a matter of learning to ignore the words of our
critics, but rather, to *evaluate* them and put them into the proper perspective. If the criticism is valid, respond to it. If it's not, let it go. Criticism can
be constructive, or destructive.

Legendary Congresswoman Patricia Schroeder faced the destructive
brand from the moment she reached Congress in 1972. Male editorial
writers were horrified by her essence. They hated her politics, they hated
that she dared go to Congress while having small children at home—they
even hated her looks. "There was nothing I could do right," Schroeder
remembers. "I was too flip. I was too cute. I smiled too much. What was I
doing to my family? What was I doing to my husband? What did I really
want? It was like, if I got up and breathed air, it was wrong. I realized this was
a society in transition. Tragically, they were the ones in power and there was
nothing I could do about it." She described the editorials as a nasty diatribe
that wouldn't stop. The columns would say, "And then she . . . And *then*

she . . . And THEN she . . ." Over the years, Schroeder has absorbed enormous criticism from colleagues and constituents who have attacked everything from her politics to her hair. The trick, Schroeder says, is to "blast on through." Write off those people who are hopeless critics because you'll never satisfy them. If you spend your time worrying about it, you'll lose your momentum. "In that kind of situation, you keep going. You just keep going. You have to work twice as hard. You just have to say, 'I will go crazy if I try to answer these guys.' You have to get up every morning and decide what you're about. And if people accept it, fine. And if they don't, you can go back to having a much easier life doing something else."

The greatest irony here is that today, as I write this, there is a big article in the Denver paper criticizing Schroeder's successor, Congresswoman Diana DeGette. What's the problem with DeGette? She's not enough like Schroeder, the article says. Strong women attract strong backlash Schroeder says. That means the criticism will come, regardless of whether it is just, and no matter where you sit in the hierarchy.

Gen. Claudia Kennedy certainly suffered her share of criticism as she rose to be the U.S. Army's first female general. Shortly before she retired in 2000, she filed a sexual harassment complaint that made international headlines. She endured blistering criticism until the Army substantiated the case. But she had learned much earlier how to deal with negativity. "I don't let anyone else judge me, which means I don't absorb the flattery, the compliments or the praise, but I also don't absorb the criticism and the things that are very negative from others," Kennedy said. "I have to judge myself."

Some criticism is worthwhile. All of it must be listened to and evaluated, but that doesn't mean you have to internalize it. "If you encounter criticism, just remember people don't take time to get you straightened out unless you are worth straightening out," Kennedy said. "So, when you get criticized, you have to remember someone thinks you are worth assisting. I've certainly found that to be true."

Making Criticism a Positive Force

The worst part of criticism is that—choke—it *can* be true. Right there in front of us, it's the proof we aren't perfect. If it helps us to make improvements, criticism can be a great tool. But, learning from criticism can be work.

Dr. Nancy Dickey, the first woman to break the gender barrier and become president of the American Medical Association, says it is *still* tough for her to swallow criticism, but she constantly works at it. "There are always detractors," explained Dickey. "Someone will tell you you're too short to play basketball, too dumb to be a lawyer. You have to go home and say, 'Is there any truth to that?' You have to process all the information and then decide how much weight you are going to give to your critics."

It takes an overt effort to develop a harder shell. You have to be certain enough to know your goodness even though you are dealing with negative reviews. "It's a one-person pep rally, if you will," Dickey said. "I don't take criticism terribly well but I think I take it much better than I did twenty-five years ago. One of the things you learn to do is hear the criticism, try not to be defensive or counterattack, then go back home where it is quiet and pull the criticism out and say, 'How much validity is there to this? Should I take it to heart?' If you can learn to delay that, you won't distort everything in your head." She believes that it is important to recognize that sometimes your critics are responding because they feel threatened by you, which is why they want to put barriers in your way. She advises maintaining external composure and to later evaluate everything internally. She also suggests practicing humorous responses and just practicing responses in general.

Constructive Criticism

The bad thing about constructive criticism is that it is still criticism, and who likes to be criticized? I don't. If we could train ourselves to be more open to such guidance, it wouldn't seem so insulting. The smartest way to avoid criticism is to actively seek input from the people around you that you trust. That turns it into information that is far less threatening.

I used to teach journalism to college students and for the longest time I assumed that each student knew that if, for example, all of his or her papers had C's on them, he or she was getting a C in the class. The only students who would ever inquire about their grades during the term were the two students getting A's. The ones who were in danger of failing never asked.

On a human level, that is very understandable. Why invite someone to stand in front of you and tell you how average or below-average you are performing? Curiously, when I would ask them what they thought they were getting, they always guessed high or low. Proof that, if you don't seek input, you really don't know where you are.

122 Hard Won Wisdom

Sure, asking how you can improve does suggest you don't think you are performing perfectly, but no one performs perfectly. Wouldn't you want to do the best possible work instead of guessing what is expected of you? And, why wait until you get a bad annual evaluation from a boss when you could avoid it by seeking constructive guidance ahead of time? Besides, the boss will most likely see that you are actively participating in your job and will see it as a good thing that you are interested in your performance.

I started giving my students progress updates throughout the semester so they would know what they had to do to get a good grade. And, guess what? The grades did go up. That taught me something: People do better work with input.

If you don't ask about your performance, you will never know what it will take to make improvements. Good grief, don't wait until you get a written performance evaluation in your personnel file to know how you are doing. If you are getting the right input, *nothing* on your evaluation should surprise you. Plus, you can fix the situation before it turns into a problem. Check in. Listen. Seek feedback.

Just make sure you do this without making yourself sound like an insecure, neurotic pest. When you are sick, you don't check your temperature every ten minutes, and you shouldn't check your performance temperature too frequently, either, because you might lose your edge. Focus on doing good work, rather than what someone might think of the work you do. But, check in periodically so you know if you are doing what you should. Before asking how you are doing, try to evaluate your performance for yourself. How do you think you are doing?

When you are ready for input of a supervisor or trusted colleague, ask simple questions, like, "Hey, is this what you want me to do on this assignment?" Or, "Have any suggestions on what we might do to make the next project better?" When you get an answer, don't get defensive. Remember, you are seeking input to help you do better work. Stay cool and objective so you can hear what is said, and ask what steps you might take to deal with the matter. Take notes, and when you go over them later, think of action steps that will help you address the situation. Check these notes every so often to make sure you are on track.

Basketball superstar Teresa Edwards said she can't perform her best on a team without knowing everybody else's strengths and weaknesses and playing to them. "Acknowledge your weaknesses," she said. "Work on them. The one person who thinks they don't have weaknesses will hurt your team before the person who has weaknesses." The hard part, for her, was getting others to know their own weaknesses so they could grow past them.

When the criticism is unjust, call your critic on it—in a nonthreatening way. Ask for specific examples. If none are forthcoming, say you are a little confused and would appreciate specifics. If you continually get feedback that is negative and hurtful, stop asking. Your critic may be on a power trip and might be more interested in keeping you down than boosting you up. You don't need to line up for a beating. At some point, you need to question if you are working in an unhealthy environment. Don't make an internal tape recording of the criticism you receive. Hear the input, evaluate it, use it. It doesn't make you any less of a person. It's just a performance measure. Move on.

Because some people are so awkward at giving criticism, it can be difficult to tell whether their remarks are well-meaning or just mean. Someone may give you the impression you are the lowest form of life on earth, hopeless in your endeavors. What is really going on? Is your critic trying to be mean, or, in a tough sort of way, helpful? Before you slide into a depression, take a little time to explore your critic's motives. Have you seen this kind of criticism come from this person before? It may be that you aren't the problem at all, but your critic is having a bad day, and taking it out on you. You need to figure out how to handle the matter. If you decide to confront it, do it without sounding like a victim. Just state your case, then move on. After you've calmed down, dissect what happened throughout the ordeal. Put personality issues aside and consider the specifics of the actual criticism. Was any of it valid? What can you learn from it? The conflict is seldom as bad as you'll make it seem in your head, and it is important to always remember that.

If the criticism is not true or accurate, you need to decide what you are going to do about it. Ignoring it can mean you don't dispute what was said, and can make the situation get even worse. Confronting it will at least put your critic on notice to be cautious about leveling more false criticism at you. Finally, if you still feel bad about it, write your critic a letter and really let him or her have it. Say every nasty thought that ever entered your head about the person. Be as mean as you can. Gift yourself with a good vent, and sound as defensive and angry as you want. Then, and this is the *most* important part, **tear it, toss it or burn it.** What an empowering solution for those moments when you feel completely powerless.

Destructive Criticism

You know what destructive criticism is. Jabs. Barbs. Nasty little cracks meant to cut you down. This kind of criticism can be manipulative or blameful. It can be used to make you feel guilty or put you in "your place." Whatever. Those who dish such criticism in your direction have one objective: To hurt you. And, no matter how tough your shell, it hurts. It hurts because, somewhere deep inside, you might not consider the source, you might not question the motivation, you just assume it's true and that there is something wrong with you.

As ill-meaning as this type of criticism may be, it is important to look at it and determine what is really being said. Is there any truth to it? Is the critic venting in a mean-spirited way because he or she has suppressed feelings for too long? Sometimes, destructive criticism is born of truth. As painful as the words are, take a little time to get a little distance from the words, then look at the message.

That's what Margaret Beckett does. As leader of England's House of Commons, she'd better have thick skin. From where she sits, the politics are brutal and unforgiving. Where else can you see elected officials publicly lambaste, chastise, skewer and bloody their nation's leaders in such mocking, rude and disrespectful ways? So vicious are the confrontations that they air on television—here in America.

But, for Beckett, it's not entertaining at all. Half the remarks are personal, judgmental and false, but that doesn't matter when hundreds are screaming at her without giving her a moment for air. "Anybody who is criticized feels sore about it," she said. "I don't know if it is worse if it is true or untrue. Either criticism hurts. But, my motto has always been, 'Don't let the bastards know they have gotten to you.' The absolute key thing is that, however you do it, you have to somehow find a way to come to terms with it. I find a lot of people in politics who have become bitter and have allowed their resentments and bitterness to fester. Ultimately, it is them that it destroys." At first, you have to be visibly tough. Then, you have to be open enough to use criticism in a positive way.

She said she questions what she can do to remedy the situation. Then she asks herself if she's going to take action. "Sometimes the answer is 'No, I'm not,'" she said. There is always that option of letting it go. But, before you make that determination, you really need to look at what was said and decide whether there is something to be learned from it. If so, how can you deal with it without internalizing anger or hurt feelings that have naturally arisen? There's no way to do this immediately after being attacked, but it is always important to look at what was said and see if you can use it to make yourself even stronger. You can take a destructive event and use it constructively.

From a distance, it is easy to say, "Keep your cool during an attack." I know that's not always easy. When somebody is coming at you full force, it's normal to want to defend yourself—or worse, hurt back. Once you are the target of a verbal assault, you might feel an uncomfortable shift in a power balance that might have existed in your relationship. Don't allow that. Just because someone has unkind things to say about you, it doesn't mean those words are valid.

And, don't overreact. Defending yourself makes you seem vulnerable. Don't attack back. That is often a matter of stooping as low as the person who started it. Better yet, leave 'em guessing. You can say, "Thanks for your input," turn on your heels and walk off. You can bet that will leave your critic guessing.

You can also say, "I respect your opinion so much, this is something I really need to pay attention to." Say it with a straight face as you walk off. The person won't know how to react at all. Are you being serious? Sarcastic? What? You can always kill with kindness. For example, an employee tells you that you are a horrible manager. Deep down you would rather say, "Well, I wouldn't have such a hard time managing if you weren't such a lazy moron." But, it's best to keep such wonderful thoughts to yourself. Just smile, then say, "I really appreciate your thinking enough to share your thoughts with me. Thank you so much." Your attacker will be speechless.

When you have a little distance from the conversation, think why the person made the remark. If it was made to hurt your feelings, ask yourself why that person wants to hurt you. It may be because he or she feels threatened or is jealous. Then again, it might be because the person is having trouble meeting expectations and wants to blame you for the problem. Okay, if that's the case, what can you do as a manager to help that person do better and feel more secure?

It's so important to be conscious about how you deal with criticism. Work at not taking it personally. Sometimes people vent because they are frustrated with the way things are, not the way *you* are.

What if the Criticism is Unjust *and* Public?

Joycelyn Elders knows all about public and unjust criticism. It started as soon as she was nominated for surgeon general. It didn't matter how much she had achieved as a medical doctor, academic, scholar for the National Institutes of Health—or as state health director in Arkansas. She was an outspoken African American woman whose presence was forceful.

"People said I wasn't qualified. I wasn't this, I wasn't that," she remembers. "They felt no black woman from Arkansas could ever be qualified to be the surgeon general. Most people didn't even know that I was a doctor. They'd call me 'Miss Elders.' They figured the best I could be was a nurse. But, I am a pediatric endocrinologist. There weren't many doctors around that had more training than I did."

Still, the barbs were endless, right in front of the national media. She wondered how people could criticize her when they didn't even know who she was. "People are ignorant," she said. "They don't have enough knowledge and they criticize you. Why get upset with someone who is ignorant? You can correct ignorance with education, but stupidity lasts forever."

Decide Who Counts

Columnist Ellen Goodman said that, over time, criticism doesn't feel so destructive. "When you're in your twenties, criticism is a hard thing to take," she said. "You write something and they write back and you cave a little. 'Oh, ouch.' But, when you are older, you just deal with it very differently. You have experience. You have more confidence."

And, if you are Ellen Goodman, you have a system. "One of the things that has been true my whole life is I only give a certain number of people chits to make me feel badly," she said. "I don't give every reader a chit to make me feel bad about myself." She gives the chits to her husband, family, a few friends she respects and her editor. "I live in a supportive environment," she said. "My husband is supportive, my daughter is wonderfully supportive, my sister and I have raised ourselves very similarly. I have a web of very close women friends. Those people are really my support system. I don't know how you find a system like that. You create it. There are some people you find that you connect with, then you build on those connections and maintain them. When other things collapse and you get into trouble, those are the people you go to. All of those things you create and nurture will, in turn, nurture you."

Being Liked

Too often, we assume that the secret message behind the criticism is that our critic doesn't like us. Why is it so important to be liked by everybody? Why do we fret so much when we realize somebody doesn't like us? We agonize over it, wondering, "What did I do wrong?" or, "What's the matter with me?" We desperately seek validation from others—all others—instead of from within. When we hear a little criticism, we latch on to it until it is monumental in our minds. This goes back to the chapter on self-esteem. People—men and women—with good self-esteem don't let criticism translate into worries that people don't like them. How many men do you see worrying endlessly about someone who doesn't like them?

Pat Schroeder laughed when I brought up our insatiable need to be liked. She had an answer. "Too many people feel they have to be liked by everybody," the former congresswoman said. "The good thing about politics is that you have to make 51 percent of the people happy. You don't have to make 100 percent happy."

Hmmm.

I think we need to keep telling ourselves that, especially since studies show women have the need to be liked more than men. "Wanting to be liked is something that is core to women's sense of who they are," said Yale psychology professor Marianne LaFrance. "We get the message from day one that our talent is in the social sphere, and the criteria for success is 'liking.'" The criteria for evaluating men has traditionally been in achievement and for women, in social success, LaFrance says. So, we think if we aren't extremely likable and socially popular, we must be doing something wrong.

Nobel Laureate Jody Williams says it's not worth the agony of trying to please everybody. "I was in my early teenage years when I figured out that no matter what I did, people were going to have their own version. Did I want to spend my life trying to be what everyone else wanted me to be? Or, did I want to spend it being what I wanted to be?"

The closer you are to the mainstream middle, the less likely it is that you will face criticism. Those who stand out often face a blistering dose of negativity. Phyllis Schlafly certainly did. The archconservative, antifeminist powerhouse rallied forces to kill the Equal Rights Amendment, which would have prohibited discrimination based on gender. Before she went to work on the issue, the measure had the support of Presidents Nixon, Ford and Carter. All but eight members of the Senate and twenty-four members of the House of Representatives were behind it. But, as the fight moved through the states in ratification battles, Schlafly found her power.

In attacking the amendment, Schlafly herself came under personal attack. She knows plenty about taking criticism. She was mocked, derided and constantly heckled. "I have a cheerful outlook on life," she said. "I always figure I irritate my opponents a lot more than they irritate me. If you hate somebody, you are the one who is hurt." As she campaigned against the ERA, she'd consistently encounter protesters who ridiculed her vision and attacked everything from her persona to her looks. Some mooned her. "I would just ignore it all. I laughed at them," she said. "They are the ones who had the problem. I don't hate anybody. There is just no way they can get me upset or riled to where I would say something that I would regret. I've been told that my unflappability is my most effective quality." That's it. If only we could get a good "unflappability" transplant. Then we could go about our business without worrying what other people think. What freedom we would have, if only we could let go of that need to be liked.

Of course, if you're on a mission, you don't have much time to worry about it. Jenny Shipley sure didn't after being elected prime minister of New Zealand in 1997. Her election brought her a barrage of criticism. After one term, her party lost control of Parliament and she now serves as opposition leader. Through it all, the condemnation was constant.

"I don't think it is easy to hear yourself criticized as viciously as you are when you are a key leader," she said. "There are fleeting moments when I ask myself, 'Is my commitment to this greater than my willingness to listen to this?' For me, they are only fleeting moments, although they are very raw and keenly felt. But it's the genuine feeling that men and women together must deliver the system of governance, and women have a right in that context, that keeps me focused and prepared to keep going. They aren't moments of doubt, necessarily, but moments of reality. And they are sharp."

Like the other women we've heard from, Shipley closely evaluates what was being said, even if it was hard to hear. "I ask myself if this is my problem or someone else's," she said. "If it's mine, of course it needs to be dealt with. But if it is someone else who is trying to undermine me or the fact that a woman leader exists, then I try to put it away. People will often say things to distract you. You need to differentiate between those that are genuine and need addressing, and those that are cheap and shallow attempts to say you aren't capable of dealing with your responsibility."

Shipley says it is only natural to want everyone to appreciate you and celebrate your efforts. It hurts when you hear something negative about all of your hard work—especially since you have given so much of your heart to it. She thinks that to be effective, you have to understand the difference between being an effective leader and being popular. She knows that if she's smart both may happen, but it doesn't *always* happen.

Your Turn To Criticize

When we are in positions to criticize others, we should remember how much we hate it ourselves if it's done unjustly. Some of us are supersensitive when it comes to being criticized, yet super-insensitive when it comes to handing it out. As a manager, it took me a long time to learn that anything negative that passed out of my lips was perceived a hundred times worse than I intended. Once, a reporter wrote a story for me that began with an especially boring lead paragraph. My note at the top was as blunt as anything your typical journalist might write, but it was horribly unfair. I wrote something like, *"I really loathe your lead. I detest it."* I thought I was insulting the paragraph. He thought I was insulting *him.* I'll never forget the crushed look on his face when he read my note. "You could just have told me to try something else," he said quietly. He was right, and I felt horrible.

Try to make your point without damaging relationships. Sometimes you can't help it, but being mindful of the fact that you are dealing with human beings may keep you focused on the issue—not the person. Hopefully, you are more concerned with solving the problem than placing blame. Deal with things as they come up because problems almost always get worse and seldom fix themselves. Even though it takes a great deal of assertiveness to confront someone's shortcomings, it is better to do it when the problem is simple, rather than when it's entrenched and complex. When the time comes, criticize in private, and don't make a big scene by yanking the person into your office so everyone knows he or she is going to get it. At the same time, be quick to praise publicly, with verbal compliments, kind notes or e-mails, and do this whether you are in management or in the ranks. Keep your mouth shut until you've thought out what needs to be said, and how you can best say it. Rehearse it in your mind. Imagine possible responses and how you can address them. If you are feeling angry, wait a day until you cool down. When you do start to criticize, make sure your intention is genuine and your words are constructive. If you are able to help others with good criticism, it won't be so hard to take when it is your turn.

Finally . . .

When I was twelve, my best friend, Lisa, told me my new purse was too big, just like every purse I'd ever had. At sixteen, a guy named David told me I was a "fat pig," right in front of the whole class. In graduate school, Professor Buddy Davis told me I was such a bad writer that no newspaper would ever want to hire me. I haven't kept a list of all of the criticism I have received, but it's funny how many specific examples I could list, compared with how few compliments I can even remember. And, that's weird, considering I've probably heard a hundred good things for every bad remark.

Why is it that we let criticism hurt us so deeply? Why can't we just evaluate it, then let it go? Instead, we collect all those negatives and file them away so we can maintain a general sense of insecurity. But, if we do what Gen. Kennedy and the other women suggest, we can turn criticism into a positive. We just need a little distance from it and the confidence to put it in its place. Look, Lisa was right about my purse, but, so what? David was a jerk and Buddy Davis was probably trying to put down the twenty-one-year-old "girl"—who already worked at a newspaper—sitting in his graduate school class. Whatever. It's time we all learn to discern what matters and what doesn't.

A MOMENT WITH . . .
LISA OLSON
Sports Columnist

"It is always an awkward situation. If it is your first time in a team's locker room, you have to look around to get your bearings. Sometimes, they are getting undressed, and that can be taken the wrong way. It's not a fun experience, ever—even if the players are nice. You are in there trying to get your story, trying to get out, and having to step over disgusting socks and jockstraps that have been thrown down onto the floor.

"I was writing a nice, positive story on a defensive back on the New England Patriots. Twice, I asked the public relations person to ask him to come outside to be interviewed because, if you can do that, it's less awkward. The player said no, he wanted me in there.

"I went in, sat on the bench and started asking about his game. Before long, I could sense something was going on. I didn't look around. A couple of players were coming up to me, and I'm sitting on this bench where my eye level was at the same level as their genitals. They were walking very close to me, standing in front of me trying to get me to look. I didn't. They yelled, 'Get her to look!' I didn't look up, so I was never able to identify them.

"Finally, I cut off the interview. I told my editor and he was livid. He wanted to write about it, but I didn't want to be the story. Instead, he called the general manager of the team. Three days later, the *Boston Globe* broke the story.

"Everything exploded. Victor Kiam, the team owner, went on the air and accused me of things like going into the locker room to get dates. The players said nothing happened, but the PR person had been in there and he was a decent guy. He said something really happened. When the team said it couldn't identify the players, the national media got involved and the NFL investigated.

"I didn't do anything wrong, but I constantly questioned myself. I'm not comparing myself to a rape victim, but a lot of women who are sexually assaulted question whether they did something wrong, as opposed to questioning the person who did it. That's what I did.

"I had to change my phone number five times. My apartment was broken into and someone spray painted 'LEAVE BOSTON OR DIE, BITCH' over the walls. There were rumors—people said I was sleeping with the whole team. Fans came up to me at Boston Celtics games and threw beer on my head.

"Some thanked me for standing up for what I did, but I didn't want that either. I just wanted to be a reporter.

"The NFL fined the team and the players individually. Some involved lost their jobs. That should have been the end of it, but it wasn't.

"One night, I went to my car to go to a Boston Bruins game and my tires had been slashed. A note on the windshield read, 'Next time it will be you.'

"That was it. I went back inside, called my editor and said, 'I can't do this anymore.' At the time, the *Boston Herald* was owned by Rupert Murdoch, and he called to tell me about an international program where he would send people out for four months at other papers to get a different perspective.

"I went to Sydney, Australia, and stayed for five years. I started my life over. That's what I did with my anger. I channeled it elsewhere. I didn't have time to be angry.

"It took a long time to get to the place that I knew I hadn't done anything wrong, that I was just doing my job. The whole thing was like an out-of-body experience. I look back on it and it doesn't feel like that was even me."

TEN

JEALOUSY, SABOTAGE AND THAT KNIFE IN YOUR BACK

I REMEMBER THE TONE OF four-time Iditarod champion Susan Butcher's voice when she had to correct me. I'd referred to her as the first woman to win the Iditarod.

She wasn't.

She was supposed to be, everyone assumed she'd be, but she wasn't. The year that everyone presumed she would finally win the prize she'd been closing in on for seven grueling years, nature turned on her. In the middle of the night, as she and her team of dogs ran first in the 1,049-mile dogsled race from Anchorage to Nome, a moose came after them. Two of her dogs were killed. Thirteen others were injured. Butcher had no choice but to quit. And from nowhere, Libby Riddles, who had previously placed eighteenth and twentieth and never even been considered a viable Iditarod contender, moved to finish first and won the ovation that Butcher had expected to hear.

Fourteen years after that happened, as I talked with Butcher, I heard her voice strain to explain what happened. "I was forced to scratch. I remember talking with my friends and saying, 'Boy, when somebody wins this race, it's going to be really hard on me. I should be in there.' The crowning blow was that it turned out to be a woman, someone who had never been competitive before. It was a very strange year. There were two freezes in the race, which are now illegal. But, they froze the race and allowed everybody that was at the back of the pack to catch up. Libby Riddles had been in fifty-fourth position in one of those freezes and was able to catch back up to being in first position."

I asked Susan about jealousy. She responded, "I absolutely had feelings of jealousy. I wouldn't have had them if I had an equal chance to beat her and been able to run in the race. I have always prized anyone who can beat me because, if they can, they've done a very good job. But, I was mourning the two dogs I'd lost. I was not being able to run the Iditarod, which I'd trained years for. It was a huge year of mourning. I was in a tough emotional state when somebody who was not even competitive before had won. And it was a woman. I just had it in my mind that I was going to be the first woman. I'd never allowed any sponsor to speak of me in those terms, 'Susan's the best woman,' but I was obviously doing it more inside myself than I had realized. I thought I was going to be the first woman and when I wasn't, that was hard for me to lose. I didn't want to feel like that."

Butcher admits to feeling jealousy, and the truth is most of us, if not all of us, have felt jealousy at some point in our lives. Yale psychology professor Marianne LaFrance says that Butcher's story is extremely important. "Here was a woman who made extreme sacrifices. She worked very hard. The American myth is the person who faces the challenges and odds will eventually be successful. We just have to keep at it. But, sometimes, somebody else gets there first. That's tough."

And, that brings out the green-eyed beast of jealousy.

The best definition for jealousy I've ever heard comes from Lenora Cole Alexander, a former chief of the U.S. Department of Labor's Women's Bureau. "What's jealousy? In short, it's 'Why you and not me?' That's the simplest way to put it," she explained. "It's not that easy for women to move up, so there is a lot of jealousy."

Activist Faye Wattleton, who heads the Center for Gender Equality, agrees. "Instead of saying, 'Why them, not me?' say, 'Why them? Let me go to work on me.' Don't attack them. When you get done being jealous at the end of the day, what does that give you? It doesn't give you their looks or their talent."

Of course you've been jealous of someone else at one time or another. And, of course someone else has been jealous of you. There's a theory that, in life, a third of the people you encounter will root for your success, a third won't care and the last third will root for you to fail. Too bad we have to encounter people from each of those categories on a daily basis. Some people assume that the more you win, the more they'll lose. They think success is finite, with only so much available. Jealousy is powerful, it's ugly and it's there even when we don't see or sense it. It seeps out when someone minimizes your success, attacks you personally or tries to thwart your progress. If anything, it should give you cause to appreciate those who do support you, and teach you to go to that network when trouble arises.

Think back to the last time you scored a big one, when congratulations were really due for your achievement. Some of your peers said nothing. Others limited their kind words to a quick e-mail sent out of obligation— even though their teeth were gritted. Some people sounded especially artificial as they choked out the words. How many people were truly sincere, happy that you'd accomplished something difficult?

Jealousy in Action

On her journey out of the cotton fields and up the ranks of organized labor, Linda Chavez-Thompson has suffered her share of backstabbing. Most strong women come up against someone who is determined to get in their way and it happened to her. Sometimes you have mentors, and sometimes you have *tor*mentors. She remembers when one boss was getting ready to leave his job and the press gathered for the announcement.

"Is Linda going to follow in your position?" one asked.

"That's up to the executive board," he answered.

"He could have said, 'I fully intend to recommend her, she's the only one who could do it,' " remembered Chavez-Thompson, now the executive vice president of the AFL-CIO. "He didn't say it."

A woman reporter approached her and said, "Linda, we know you are the one doing it all behind the scenes." "My eyes began to water," she remembered, years later. "I had to leave and go into the bathroom to cry . . . There were many times when that man would stop me, clip my wings. I was getting too far ahead of him. I felt so stifled." She vowed that she would never do anything like that to anyone who worked for her.

Where's the Applause?

Imagine what it is like to achieve something wonderful and hear that others aren't happy for you. Jody Williams knows all about that. After she won the Nobel Peace Prize jointly with the coalition she helped build, it got about as nasty as it could get. On the simplest level, it appears to be typical office politics on the largest scale: Boss hires subordinate. Subordinate excels. Subordinate gets recognition and attention. Boss gets jealous. Boss fires subordinate. Subordinate wonders what went wrong. The problem was, this dogfight was danced out in public, in the media.

Williams had been hired to lead the International Campaign to Ban Land Mines. Within five years, she and a coalition of 1,200 agencies, advocates and world leaders had won the passage of the historic 1997 treaty that banned use, production, stockpiling and transfer of antipersonnel land mines. The treaty was signed by foreign ministers from 135 countries and has subsequently been signed off on by eighty-one of their governments. They only needed forty to make the treaty international law.

The need for action was obvious. More than 400 million land mines had been deployed since World War II started, with more than 65 million being placed within the last fifteen years. Mines, costing between three dollars and thirty dollars, are a cheap way of waging war. But, the land mine legacy costs much more. About 24,000 people are killed or maimed by land mines each year, the Red Cross reports. With numbers like that, it would seem the issue would overshadow the politics of organizing.

As usual, it didn't.

Days before Williams won her prize, she was cut from the payroll of the Vietnam Veterans of America Foundation. Her former boss said her lone-wolf style wasn't working out. When she was awarded the Nobel, he criticized her in the press.

She responded, "Girls do all the work, boys want the recognition."

Here's how the *Boston Globe* described it: ". . . The same character traits that catapulted the now forty-seven-year-old Williams to Nobel glory—her brashness, bluntness, and lone-wolf style of leadership—have made her a lightning rod for controversy. She has been attacked in the press by former colleagues as an imperious self-promoter and as an out-of-control employee who hogged all of the credit and half of the prize money. She's been accused of betraying the ideals of the land-mine campaign and flouting the wishes of the campaign's steering committee by putting herself forward for the Peace Prize."

Forget the personalities, Williams was a top leader of a coalition that got the job done. Shortly after she and I talked, I met with a top official from the International Committee of the Red Cross while in Geneva, Switzerland. I asked about what happened to Williams. He said, "The thing that really killed them about Jody was that she was so good."

The public thrashing by her former comrades was one of the harsher experiences of her life, Williams says. "I got through it by continuing to do the work," she said. "It was seven or eight months of hell, sheer hell, but we knew why we were doing the work. We took the high ground. I didn't change because of the Peace Prize. *They* changed. It was their problem. The prize gave us a huge platform and I realized that. I used it to accomplish what I was trying to accomplish. I'm certainly not worse for it. You get through adversity. It does make you stronger, especially if you pay attention."

When the boss, the teacher, the parent or the media start giving big, wet kisses to someone else, it usually brings out the worst in the people who are waiting for the light to shine on them. "When somebody becomes noted and successful—whether it is a man or a woman—they become less a part of the group, by definition," said professor LaFrance, of Yale. "It's one of the costs of being successful. One becomes less 'one of the guys.' There is competition, envy, the feeling that the person has somehow changed, when in fact, what has changed is the perception that they are no longer 'one of us.' It's more common for women who don't have a long history of women before them who were entrepreneurs, Nobel laureates, winners of music competitions, and the like. It is more rare to find women out front, and it still makes us uncomfortable." LaFrance says that despite the illusion of equality, forces are still against women. "Some success is okay, but stunning success is not," she said.

Sylvia Earle remembers what it was like when, in 1970, she led the first group of women aquanauts in the Tektite II expedition to live for two weeks in a submersible, fifty feet below the surface of the ocean. She and the others became celebrities, being hailed in a ticker-tape parade and White House reception. That grated on their male counterparts in the program, some of whom actually suggested the women had worked harder than the men's teams in order to get more publicity. "That was absurd," she said. "We got our work done in *spite* of all the publicity. It is surprising what some people think—that the media attention is some kind of a great bonus. It is not. It makes it harder."

Like Williams, Earle realized the power of the attention she received and she used it to wake the rest of us up to the harm we are inflicting on our rivers and oceans. She'd tried to get an audience for those issues for years, as a scientist. It wasn't until she received attention for being an aquanaut that people listened.

Why Her, Not Me?

Astronaut Kathryn Sullivan offers one lesson that helps you put your jealousy in check: Instead of obsessing about what someone else accomplished, take joy from your own accomplishments. She learned plenty about rivalry and competition in her class at NASA. One of six women—the first to be trained as astronauts—she waited to be tapped for her first mission on a space shuttle. And she says that they were a competitive group and that they knew that one of the six women would be tapped to go.

But, the first woman was not Sullivan. It was Sally Ride—the first American woman in space. She says, "I would have loved to have been on that flight, but it just wasn't that flight." Eventually she went and she was the first American woman to take a space walk. And even though she didn't get the same glory Sally Ride got by being the first one out, Sullivan relished in what she accomplished.

Let's work on that for ourselves.

Too often, we get lost comparing ourselves to others and forget how much we've accomplished on our own. There will always be people who are smarter, more talented, savvier, more popular—whatever. Who really is "the best"? What does that even mean?

Instead of worrying about who did what, who got what, and who's going where, focus on your own path and decide whether you are doing what you want to be doing. Enjoy your accomplishments.

Be Aware

Every time someone was mean to my old friend Laura, her mother would tell her that they were probably jealous of her. We used to joke about it as we got older, invoking her mother's line whenever anybody did something to us that we didn't especially like. If a server in a restaurant was rude, she had to be jealous. If a boss criticized one of us, he or she must have been jealous. If we didn't get called for a second date, he certainly had to be jealous. We laughed about it.

But, when it came to identifying when people really were behaving out of jealousy, I had trouble seeing it. That changed when Gen. Claudia Kennedy, the U.S. Army's first female general, talked about the resentment some felt as she climbed so quickly through the ranks. She told me how she'd hear remarks here and there questioning why she was chosen for promotion. She knew it was jealousy.

As a reporter, I'd hear remarks questioning why I was given time for a project when others weren't, why something was played up on the front page, why I got a certain assignment, why I was nominated for an award, why the publisher took me to lunch—whatever. One coworker once said, "He treats you like a birth child and the rest of us like we're adopted."

I always internalized those comments, assuming there must have been something to warrant them: I probably didn't deserve my success, I thought to myself.

When Kennedy talked about the jealousy she encountered on her way up, I remember being struck by the force of what she said. Suddenly, there was an explanation for all of that catty backbiting.

"I put it down to envy," Kennedy said. "I think people who worry a lot about someone else who got something that they didn't are not attending to the right things. It's really none of their business. It's really just their business to be as good as they can be and stop worrying about the person on the left or right in terms of competing with them. What we really should be doing is competing with our own personal best—not competing with a peer."

Keeping Your Eyes Open

You've heard the saying: Know your enemies.

Who has something to lose if you succeed? Who seems bothered by your success?

Are these people subordinate, equal or superior to you in the hierarchy?

Which of these individuals is in a position to hurt you? Will they?

Is anyone actively undermining you behind your back? How serious is the threat? What will happen if you confront it? What if you ignore it? Is this person actively recruiting others to work against you?

Is there any way to diffuse the jealousy? Who genuinely cheers for you?

I've talked with most of the women in this book about the issue of jealousy and realize that it is out there in every work or competitive situation. The trick is to identify it. Instead of letting unkind words fire up our self-doubts, we need to look closely at what is being said and who is saying it. Why are they saying it? Is it true? When others are jealous of you try not to internalize it. Stay focused because jealous rivals will be happy if your progress is slowed and you lose sight of your goals. And don't escalate a bad situation by fighting fire with fire. That never extinguishes jealousy and in fact, makes it rage even more.

The Worst Color of Green

Too often, jealousy escalates into sabotage. After Judith Albino was tapped to be the University of Colorado's first woman president, there was an uprising that put her on the front page for months. Behind it all were some of the people who wanted her job. They leaked distorted information to reporters and met secretly with regents to try to undermine her.

She took the high road, assuming if she worked hard, everything would work out fine. But that's not what happened. "I should have seen a lot of things that happened early on as danger signs," she said. "There were attempts to deliberately twist my words and make me look bad. Things would come back to me alleging I'd said something that I had not said. Slowly, I began to see there was an active attempt to discredit me. I was often criticized for things I did not do, things I would never do, things that were totally against my principles. But, in leadership, you have to have a tough skin. I had the choice of taking it personally and dealing with it as a personal issue, or keeping my mind on the university and doing university business."

She kept her mind on university business until the Board of Regents finally had the votes to run her out after four and a half years. Even when her detractors declared victory, they did not give up trying to hurt her. They sent negative e-mails wherever she applied for jobs, publicly dooming her efforts to land a presidency at another major university. She remained on the CU faculty's psychiatry department until she was eventually recruited to be president of the five-campus Alliant University in California, where she now resides.

Looking back on everything that happened, Albino has gained an insight from which we all can benefit. "I felt strongly that if I gave all of my time and energy to the university and did what needed to be done there, the personal and internal political issues would take care of themselves. So, I never got involved in trying to combat the negatives and the criticisms, except when directly approached. In retrospect, that was a mistake. You have to acknowledge the problems internally and deal with them."

"Sabotage is a part of competition," said Yale psychology professor LaFrance. Some people can't stand it when others succeed and she notes that it is especially common when women move into male domains. To make sure she won't succeed, a saboteur may give her too much work to do or deny her the tools to do something. She may be left out, undercut, undermined and harassed.

When They Sink to the Lowest Low

Susan Butcher, the Iditarod wonder, has seen the worst kind of sabotage. While she was out on the course, someone changed the trail markings to throw her off the trail. She spent the entire night trying to find the right path and ended up falling eleven hours behind. She seldom talks about sabotage, but she knows it in its most raw form.

"There have been times when I have very specifically, positively been sabotaged out on the trail," she said. "I have been cheated against outright by a male competitor who had no excuse to turn against me other than I was a woman. I won't describe the specific situations because I have not shared them with anybody or made them public. But there were times when other mushers would say, 'We saw it happen to Susan, and it only happened to Susan and it only happened because she was a woman. This person should be disqualified.' But, they needed me to register the complaint, to say it had happened to me. I refused to do that."

She didn't do that because she believed it wasn't her job to go and change the mind of the individual who had cheated against her. She believes that it was her job to go out and beat him because she was better than him and do it well so that then, he would know she was where she should be. And that would get her the respect.

Butcher's solution to sabotage was to work harder and to not give up. She had to pull herself together and keep going.

Jealousy and sabotage are not easy obstacles to overcome and a few words on a page can't erase hurt feelings. But know that you can seek support and that all women have faced it in some form. Just remember to not let the green-eyed beast get the better of you when those pangs hit you or if you are the brunt of someone's jealousy.

A MOMENT WITH . . .
COKIE ROBERTS
Commentator for ABC News and NPR

"I can't imagine saying anything to someone cutting in line at the grocery store. It's not worth it. At this point in life, you pick your fights. It's not worth it to get hot under the collar about things that don't matter.

"I did have a little fight in the grocery store the other day because the person in the express line was totally incompetent and it took thirty minutes to get to the front. I was rushing, rushing, rushing after work and after I waited all that time they wanted my driver's license for the new computer bank. It was not my problem! I walked out. They had the information they needed on that check. But they sent a bouncer to come and get my groceries. I know it's easier to give them the information and spend that five minutes, but sometimes, you don't want to wait. And now if I do it, it's, 'Oh, that's Cokie Roberts! Look what she did!' But every so often, you snap at these things."

"I've got a husband I adore who loves me, a terrific job, and my kids are grown and off doing great things. They are lovely human beings and they are married to lovely human beings. I have a terrific mother who is still well and useful and productive. What more can I ask for?

"I have crummy hair.

"But, it's the first thing anybody notices and you can say anything you want, be stupid or brilliant, funny or irreverent, if your hair is looking bad, that's all anybody notices or comments on.

"I wish I could say that it's just all dumb. The truth is that the visual image is so strong. When you are trying desperately to get an idea across on television, which is very hard anyway, you can distract people from that idea because the visual image of you is somehow off. It could be some dumb thing. You could be wearing a scarf that some find distracting or you have dangling earrings that sway when your head moves."

"Of course it's different for women than men in broadcasting. The big question for us now is how old are we allowed to get? A bunch of the women who are my contemporaries are somewhere between fifty-three and sixty and it's going to be very interesting to see what happens. I noticed in New York they have this camera that makes everything look fuzzy. I hope they will bring it to Washington."

"I've failed at things. I'm a terrible athlete. I can't do anything artistic except sing. You'd just be flabbergasted if you saw my hand-eye coordination. My son once tried to play a game of Ping-Pong with me and thought he should never drive with me again. It took until I was grown up to be good at anything.

"I'm sure there are stories I could have done better. There were a couple of mornings when I did *Good Morning America* and I don't think they were thrilled with it. No one ever said it, but I wasn't invited back."

"I have never taken myself too seriously.

"My father was always in public office from before I was born, and then my mother was, so there was never a time when I wasn't in the public eye until I married. I grew up being in magazines and in the news and my mother was very clear that this was not hot stuff. It was that we were doing a certain duty because our father was in office and we were expected to be available to his bosses, the voters. But, we were no special someone.

"What people say to me now is, 'Oh, you're just like me.'

"They understand that my basic self is a suburban housewife that is doing a fun job. They don't think I'm some highfalutin somebody. And, that's wonderful."

ELEVEN

FIGHTING BACK

S OMETIMES, YOU HAVE TO FIGHT back. You have to tell that bully boss that he can't talk to you in that tone. Or that you want a male coworker to stop staring at your breasts. Sometimes, you have to ask why you continually get passed over for promotions by less qualified people. The decision to act is tough, life changing and scary. For years, I have argued that it is better to move beyond a bad situation than it is to stay behind and fight what may be a losing battle. After all, you deserve a good life. If a situation is making you miserable and you choose to stay and endure it, you are the one who pays.

But, I've changed my mind. The decision to stay and fight is an intensely personal decision that no generalities can address. I've had close friends sue and lose, and sue and win. I know an extremely accomplished woman who became so distressed by the experience of suing her employer (and winning) that she spiraled downward into a battle with alcoholism that she couldn't win. I've heard many women say they would never do it again, and I have seen women completely invigorated by the power they have taken back.

You have to decide what is right for you.

I present here several stories of remarkable women who fought back. Then, two of the nation's best civil rights attorneys will spell out how you can fight back as well. Whether the question is speaking up for injustice or taking that huge step and pursuing a problem legally, you need to know what it is you are after, and how you will be able to get it. You're about to hear from some women who have changed the world. Fighting back wasn't easy, and it wasn't always worth it on every level. But, they did what they had to do.

Meet Paula Coughlin, of Tailhook

Lieutenant Paula Coughlin was, is and always will be the female helicopter pilot who fought back after being sexually assaulted by her fellow aviators at the 1991 Tailhook Association's annual convention. Her courage forever redefined male/female relationships in the military, but the assault and its aftermath were personally devastating. "It was such a betrayal," she said. "I shared a kinship with these aviators, and I had been reduced to a party favor. My whole value system—not just my self-esteem and what I thought of myself, but what I had built my whole life around suddenly didn't add up to anything."

Some aviators had made a tradition of sexually molesting female aviators, aviators' wives and girlfriends at Tailhook conventions. Women would later say they were either too afraid to speak up, or felt they had somehow brought the attacks on themselves. But, Coughlin talked.

Her boss advised her to shut up about what happened and preserve her career. Instead, she pushed higher up in the chain of command, eventually gaining an audience with former President George H. Bush.

Empowered by Coughlin's courage and the national attention given the incident, other women assaulted at Tailhook started to talk too. When the final count was in, eighty-three women had been molested at the convention. The most the Navy would accuse its men of was indecent exposure, conduct unbecoming an officer, and making false statements to investigators. Still, the matter was serious enough to forever change the way the Navy treats women. Their revved up "zero-tolerance" policies now demand automatic dismissal for aggravated sexual harassment or repeat offenses. Navy Secretary H. Lawrence Garrett III was ousted. The Navy gave twenty-eight officers administrative penalties and thirty-three admirals were given non-punitive cautions.

"The biggest advice I give to women in this circumstance is, trust your instincts," Coughlin said. "You are not wrong. You have to know you are a good person. Don't rest until you either have brought them to the carpet for what they have done or until you find some other way to deal with it that works best for you."

The pressure and constant hostilities in her workplace forced her to quit the Navy. She won nearly $7 million in civil damages from the Hilton Corp. and the Tailhook Association, but she had to give up on the Navy that she had been raised since childhood to revere. "I have a terrible, icky feeling after I tell it," she says of her story, her voice breaking. "I don't tell it very often. Honestly, it left me just mentally disheveled talking to you. Once you put it away, revisiting the whole assault and everything of how the Navy handled it and what went on afterward was very difficult. I had bad Navy dreams over the weekend. That's really the essence of being victimized. I'm not the same person I was. That's a cliché. But, I hold memories I shouldn't have to hold, but can't lose." What a painful journey, yet hers has been one of many that set new boundaries for women and men in the workplace. It truly made history. Any woman who has to endure such hardship just to do what is right deserves our gratitude. Fighting back is so tough, and it is not for the weak.

Neurosurgeon Frances Conley knows that lesson well. It took her three hours to vent when she wrote about a resentment that had been festering for twenty-five years. "I have just resigned my position as a full, tenured professor of neurosurgery at Stanford University Medical School," wrote the brain surgeon to a California newspaper. "I did so because I was tired of being treated as less than an equal person. I was tired of being condescendingly called 'Hon' by my peers, of having my honest differences of opinion put down as a manifestation of premenstrual syndrome, of having my ideas treated less seriously than those of the men with whom I work. I wanted my dignity back." Those words would forever change her legacy in medicine, academics and society. It happened in 1991, almost five months before anyone ever heard of Anita Hill, and it sure made a splash in the news.

Building her career in neurosurgery, a specialty that had just five board certified women when she began, Conley figured she would have to put up with certain indiscretions. In fact, for some time, she had become "one of the boys" in order to be with the rest of the boys. She engaged in the banter and ignored many an insult. That stopped when the dean of the Stanford Medical School was about to promote a man, who Conley said had demeaned and outraged her by his sexist behavior, to be the next chairman of the department of neurosurgery.

She said the atmosphere in her department was one where male colleagues would sometimes run their hands up her legs in the operating room. "Even through that (lab) coat, I can still see the contour of your breast," she said she was told. That man's promotion would ensure an environment where such traditions continued. "Had I yelled and screamed about these things twenty-five years ago, I undoubtedly would not have been taken into training programs because I would have been labeled 'difficult,'" she said at the time. But, it was the nineties and she expected more.

Because the media wouldn't go away, the dean set up an investigative panel to explore the allegations she'd made in her editorial. To his surprise, dozens of other women came to meet with the panel and said they had witnessed and experienced the exact kind of behavior Conley described. Hopeful that something good might come out of the chaos, Conley rescinded her resignation until the investigation was over. "It was very lonely," she said. "I was by myself in there. I had tremendous support from people outside the medical school. One of the best things I did was gather around me about five advisors from all walks of life that I could call. These people were my kitchen cabinet." The man who she accused denied everything. He contended she was angry she wasn't made chair of the department and said it was all too convenient for her to get even by invoking her gender.

When it was over, he'd lost the department chair and Conley decided to stay at Stanford. "It was very validating," she said. "The nicest thing was to know that thirty women were willing to put very vulnerable careers on the line and say, 'Hey, Conley was right.'" Later on, the dean and the president of the university tendered their resignations. "The majority of the players I was dealing with were gone," she said. "All of them said, 'The sexual harassment scandal that has plagued Stanford has nothing to do with my departure.' Methinks they doth protest too much. Do I think it had anything to do with it? It had a hell of a lot to do with it. By that time, it had opened Pandora's box. The university and the medical school in particular had been inundated with other grievances."

Conley, who wrote about her experiences in her book, *Walking Out on the Boys*, is now chief of staff at the three-hospital Palo Alto Veterans Administration Medical Center. For other women debating whether or not to fight back, Conley suggests careful steps. "I think every woman has to do a risk/benefit analysis when she finds herself in a situation like this. Analyze your situation. Reactionary responses are not good here. Be thoughtful. You can't jump into it blindly. Too many women get ruined doing that."

How Tough It Gets

Sexual harassment and discrimination lawsuits are nightmarish experiences for most of the women who dare to file them. Winning can be sweet bliss, but getting to that point can be torturous. Paula Couglin won $7 million, but the process was painful. The trial was slow and hard. It impacted her family as everything in her life was investigated.

While Coughlin and Conley won their battles, Penny Harrington was not so lucky. After politics forced her out of her job as chief of police in Portland, Oregon, she sued. Unfortunately, she lost big. Now she says she would never advise anyone to file a lawsuit. "You are constantly going back, looking at every single thing that happened," she said. "If you have good lawyers, they are nitpicking everything you said and did, trying to pick up on what the other lawyers will try to do. You are in this tremendous victim mode, and that's not healthy. It was a tremendous strain on my health, on my finances and on my marriage. My marriage didn't make it." Harrington left Oregon for California so she could begin healing, but when her lawsuit went to court, she had to go back. "To go back into that city, into that courthouse, and look at that mayor again after all those years—it was terrible," she said. "It ripped the scabs off all the old wounds. And, I lost my lawsuit."

She wanted more than financial compensation. More than anything, Harrington wanted a neutral body to examine what had happened to her and say it was wrong. "That didn't happen. I'd lost, and there was no more hope that I'd be vindicated," she said.

Protect Yourself and Hold up a Mirror

So what can you do when facing a situation that may require legal action? I once sat in on a session where St. Petersburg, Florida, civil rights attorney Kate Kyres advised her client on how to protect herself from the men who were deliberately trying to impede her career. She told the woman to give it right back to them—but in a way that they couldn't retaliate against.

When I interviewed her, she said it is critical for women in the workplace to take control of the documentation of their performance. And, wow, does Kyres have the system. "Shine the mirror on the person who is violating your rights," she said. "This protects you." Reflect back what you are seeing, and do it in writing. Keep copies of everything. The bottom line should be, "Look,

I'm here to work. I love my job. I love performing my job day to day. But, I cannot do a job when someone is commenting daily about (fill in the blank)."

You shouldn't have to listen to sexual comments. You don't deserve to be degraded. You should be judged for your skill and not your anatomy. They shouldn't ask about your boyfriend, your dress or your dress size. If you are continually being denied a promotion, send a note that says you really love working there and want to know what you need to do so you can get the promotion the next time.

Kyres suggests always sending professional thank-you notes. *Thank-you notes*? She explains, "When you are constantly getting praise verbally, but there is something going on higher up that is discriminatory, send back professional thank-you notes. Something like, 'Thanks so much for complimenting me on the proposal. It means so much to me when my peers view me in such high regard.' That way when, six months later, they say that was a piece of crap, you have kept copies of all your thank-you notes. They are kind of self-serving, but they are a record."

She said she never advises people to send memos documenting situations. Instead, she tells them to send handwritten notes, which appears less threatening but are just as useful. Don't say, "This is to recap our conversation." Send a note that says, "I was taken aback by your comment that . . ." Or, "It saddens me that you'd say that . . ." If it's a proposition, put something on personal stationery that says, "No, I won't meet you at that hotel" or, "Please stop staring at my breasts every time you walk by me." Notes like that are invaluable because the person who receives it should protect the organization by passing it on to human resources. If the person doesn't, and you have copies, management will have to question why the concerns were never relayed.

Kyres once represented a pregnant woman whose supervisor was angry about the pregnancy and constantly made negative remarks about it. On a Post-it note, the woman wrote, "Dear So-and-so. I'm doing my job. You are not remarking about my job, but I am worried about my unborn child, and by not allowing me to eat crackers at my desk, I'm not only concerned that I won't get my day's work done appropriately, but that I'm harming my unborn child. Please help me by letting me eat a cracker at my desk." "Human resources sees that and says, 'Oh my God, that's a misunderstanding,'" said Kyres. "Sometimes, that's the only jolt they need. A good human resources department will get involved. They'll treat that woman with kid gloves for the rest of her pregnancy."

Kyres also added that it's hard for women to be so direct because we're sociologically trained to not offend people. So even when the worst behavior is happening to them, women think they have to make it better. They are afraid to take action. She also advises women to journal what is happening. "Journals are so important," she said. "It lets you know you aren't crazy, because every time you write it down, the demon is not put in the closet. It lets you know you are not nuts. There really is a demon, you're sizing it up and you are figuring out how to respond to it." Most of us tend to let bad things happen, then try to forget about them, she said. If you keep a list, it is easier to see patterns of discrimination. She adds that sometimes mere documentation is enough to fix the problem because most people want to avoid a lawsuit.

Making the Choice

Post–Anita Hill, the buzz was that *everybody* was filing EEOC complaints and sexual harassment and discrimination suits. Not so said Diane King, a Denver-based civil rights attorney who has won cases against some of the nation's largest corporations. "The vast majority of women find it far simpler to just quit and get another job," she said. Why not? I've long argued that the stress of a lawsuit isn't worth it. That it is so much easier to pack up your talent and go. For years, I argued with a woman police officer friend, telling her the only thing she'd win by fighting back against the sexists who ran her department was an ulcer. She'd won an award as the nation's number one community police officer, but she believed supervisors were intent on destroying her career. I constantly encouraged her to apply to other departments, but she stubbornly stayed right where she was, refusing to let the bad guys win.

Well, she fought back. The minute she and two other women filed their gender discrimination complaints, Officer Donna Saxer was no longer the victim, and suddenly she held her power like the strong woman she was. Regardless of how her lawsuit comes out, she knows she didn't let them mess with her. I was awed by her courage, and learned that some people win simply by putting up a fight.

"Fighting back is difficult emotionally and financially," said King, the lawyer. "But, if nobody fights back, the work environment is never going to change. That's a very strong motivator for women. They don't want this to happen to their daughters. The litigation process can be excruciating and scary, especially when the plaintiff seeks damages for emotional distress. Suddenly, your whole life is an open book. The courts allow the defense attorneys to ask you the most personal questions. The judge can order you to be examined by a psychiatrist who has been hired by the defense."

Attorney Kyres describes the ordeal. "Psychologically, it's like a woman is in the shower, thinking she has her privacy, but then looks up and sees her neighbor has been watching her," she said. "In the middle of this kind of suit, a woman feels like she has no privacy, even in the places she'd expect to have it. She feels utterly exposed, even to the people she had relationships or confidences with. They are in a system they don't understand. They are defensive and nervous. There is a real fear factor. It doesn't matter what the woman's intellectual capacity or socioeconomic status has been. They now feel like they are under the microscope." That's when the other side resorts to what is known as the "Nuts and Sluts Defense." They either paint the plaintiff as crazy, or asking for it. They dig through medical and psychiatric records. It often makes some women decide not to proceed.

Before King takes on a case, she warns her clients to think hard about what they want. She tells them that it's a very personal decision and that they must decide if it's worth it. She tells them she needs a commitment from them because she typically takes these cases on contingency and she has to work very hard with a lot of heart and soul. So the clients' commitment is essential.

Going into Battle

In a discrimination suit, the first step is filing a complaint with the Equal Employment Opportunity Commission. That takes at least six months to be investigated, but without that EEOC complaint, you aren't allowed to sue. King generally lets the EEOC complaints sit with the feds for 180 days, then yanks it and files suit because in 93 percent of the cases, the EEOC finds no probable cause that discrimination took place. "It was designed to be a place people could go without a lawyer to get some kind of remedy," she said. "The problem is that people think that's the case. They don't realize they aren't going to get much satisfaction there." It's a long haul. Lawsuits often take two or more years to resolve. Most cases settle out of court.

The first hump is always psychological. You have to realize that you are being treated unfairly, and have the power to do something about it. "The only thing that is common in these cases is that, as women, we tend to think, 'It must be me. I'll just work a little harder. I'll just dress like a nun,' " said King, "We think we can control things and fix them, so we keep trying. It takes a long time for women to realize they can never fix it. No matter how hard they work, how well they work, how pleasant they are, they aren't men. They are never going to be a part of the club because of it. There is nothing that personality and charisma can do to fix that."

With so many companies putting emphasis on training employees about harassment and discrimination, there are fewer cases of harassment arising out of ignorance. Men and women tend to know there are boundaries when it comes to raunchy remarks and jokes. King said the big rule is, "If it is welcome behavior, you can say or do what you want. If you have an atmosphere where there is a lot of sexual joking, that's not illegal unless one person doesn't like it. The standard is whether there is unwelcome contact. If a woman participates in the dirty jokes and is not offended by them, that is not a hostile work environment."

Where it gets sticky is that the rules can change. Any employee can wake up one night and decide that the behavior is offensive. While you need to go through channels to file a complaint, King warns women not to trust the sincerity of a human resources person who sounds concerned. "They are there to help the corporation," she said. "They are there to make sure the company is covered legally. You should go to them because, legally, you are required to try to work through things internally and give them the chance to do the right thing. But, don't count on that."

That's the sad part, because most people would rather have a good job than a good lawsuit. Kyres, the Florida civil rights attorney, said many women have good cases but don't want to go through the trauma of a lawsuit. It takes plenty of internal fortitude. By the time a woman questions whether she has a case, her self-esteem has already been challenged and compromised. "To go forward, it requires self-esteem and confidence that is almost super-human," Kyres said. "They are not only going against individuals, but against corporations or public entities to which they have had a lot of loyalty. Now, they are asked to speak of things that, in their minds, make them disloyal." And it becomes even harder when they feel they are fighting a corporation and the individual who discriminated against them.

But as each woman challenges that structure, she changes. Kyres says, "She becomes a person she never believed she would be." These women are not only affecting their own lives, their families' lives, the women after them and coworkers. They are changing corporate mentality. They feel they are part of a better world. That's why I think my clients are among the courageous few that will try to enforce the laws as they were intended."

When the Environment Turns Hostile

From day one on the job, as hard as it is to set boundaries, don't accept situations that make you uncomfortable. At first, try gentle reminders. Then try some of the advice suggested by the attorneys in this chapter. If you are in a sticky situation, try to make sure others witness it. If you aren't able to get witnesses, document when things happen, make sure you tell others about it right afterward, and keep a good journal. Don't forget to write your "mirror notes" to put in writing kind words or difficulties without the formality of a memo.

When things get tough, get a little perspective by asking a coworker you trust whether the problem is your gender or your ability. If you are told you don't measure up, find out what you need to do to boost your skills and move forward. If the problem isn't you, come up with a strategy that protects yourself emotionally and professionally. If you are passed up for a promotion, don't make the assumption that it happened because you are a woman. That may be the reason. But, look around. How many men were passed over? The number of opportunities dwindle the higher you go up the ladder. Are you as qualified as the person who got the promotion? If so, you've got decisions to make. And, if you are going to travel the route of the EEOC and the courts, find a lawyer who is passionate about your case and will take it on a contingency. Often, you will need to pay up front for the EEOC portion of the case. Look for someone who specializes in employment law and is a member of the National Employment Lawyers Association (www.nela.org).

I am so mindful of the fact that, if not for those daring women who fought back, we'd still be working in a climate where male superiors could demand sexual favors in exchange for jobs or promotions. We'd still be powerless to challenge a paycheck that is less than our male counterpart's. We'd have no recourse if we were passed by for promotion because our boss didn't like working with women.

We owe everything to those women who fought back, and we especially owe thanks to those who fought back—and lost. The system is hard and often isn't fair. Whether or not they win their cases, they have been bold enough to say, "Stop it now." Even if they don't get the validation they seek from the courts, they should get it from us.

A MOMENT WITH . . .

MARILYN VAN DERBUR ATLER

Debutante. Miss America 1958. Incest survivor.

Until age fifty-three, Marilyn Van Derbur Atler maintained the paralyzing secret of incest. Once the former Miss America came forward and told the world what her millionaire philanthropist father had done to her from the time she was five until she left for college at eighteen, she became the world's most visible survivor. Now, ten years after making the truth known, and joined publicly by one of her three sisters, she continues her crusade to help others deal with the agony of abuse.

"My biggest nightmare was that people would find out that I was an incest survivor. Then my life would be over.

"The shame is what imprisoned me for fifty-three years. It's not what perpetrators do to our bodies, but what they do to our minds. My father tattooed my mind with shame. With incest, you are completely alone.

"More than 95 percent of the letters I've received are from women between thirty-five and fifty, the age most of us begin to come to terms with what happened.

"The research is consistent. One in three to four women, and one in seven to ten men will be sexually violated by the age of eighteen. I assumed that fondling would be less violative than penetration. It's not true. As I have traveled and spoken and listened to hundreds and hundreds of people, I have learned that it isn't what is done. It isn't whether there has been penetration or fondling, or whether it has been once or for years. What matters is the betrayal and shame that it brings. People have asked why I didn't tell my mother. I did, when I was forty-eight years old, after my father died. She said, 'I don't believe you. It's in your fantasy.'

"My mother never came around. She had to acknowledge it because there was too much evidence. One sister came forward publicly.

"If I had come forward as a child, it would have been, 'Look what you have done to the family. You have ruined this family. Not your father, *you*. Most mothers will stay with the fathers and sacrifice the children. Not all, but most.

"That was very clear in my mother's case. She protected my father to his death, but I realized when she passed away three years ago, she was protecting herself, her image. She used to say, 'I had fifty-two years of a perfect marriage.'

"For me, recovery was six years of complete dysfunction. Recovery means flashbacks. You aren't remembering the abuse, you're living it. I wasn't remembering my father coming through the door. It was, 'My father is coming through the door. Tonight.' My life completely shut down. I had voices in my head. I cried all the time. I had night terrors every night. I was what middle America would call 'crazy.' I didn't know if it would ever end.

"The most important gift I can give is the hope that it will end. When I talk with survivors, they know. They can feel the peace I have finally found. It will end, if you do the healing. That means you have to walk right into the terror.

"All of us have to be aware that childhood sexual abuse is pervasive. One in nine women will get breast cancer, and we all get our mammograms. If mothers truly grasped that one in three to four children is sexually violated, then they would be proactive in protecting them. The abuse is rampant. There is inappropriate touching between brothers and sisters that usually starts between six and eight. Sit down with all of your children together—and it's critically important that they be together, because what you say to everybody empowers. Say, 'As you are growing into your sexuality, we need to talk about what is appropriate between brothers and sisters.'

"Most children don't tell. Most adults don't tell. But, ask. Ask if anyone has ever touched them in an uncomfortable way.

"Then, they just might."

TWELVE

FALLING DOWN

IF ONE OF WORST THINGS about failing is the embarrassment, imagine what it was like to be Shannon Faulkner, the first woman cadet at the Citadel, who bailed out after just six days. *"How could she?"* everyone asked. Her exit was fodder for groans, jokes, anger and disappointment, with most people being quick to blame Faulkner.

For two years, she had fought the famed South Carolina military school in court and in spirit to allow her—a female—to be allowed in. Finally, when the U.S. Supreme Court refused to bow to the Citadel's insistence that she be kept out of the academy, she was admitted. Faulkner had already made history by being the first woman to attend the Citadel as a day student—reporting for class for one year, thanks to a court order—but she hadn't gone through the rigorous physical demands of cadet training.

By the time she gained full admission, her weight had climbed from 150 to 190 pounds and people questioned whether she was up to cadet training held in one hundred-degree South Carolina heat. She didn't last long. After one day as a cadet, she entered the school's infirmary and did not leave until she checked out of the Citadel for good. "On Friday morning, when I ate my breakfast, I decided then and there that I couldn't put myself through it anymore. I physically was not going to be able to walk off campus if I didn't put an end to it, and I didn't want to be carried off campus" she said, recounting the extraordinary physical and emotional stress she'd suffered over those historic six days.

She called her mother and asked for a ride home. Her dad, brother and one of her lawyers made the four-hour drive to pick her up. "My lead attorney from New York was on the phone yelling at me not to give up, saying there had to be something we could do medically," Faulkner remembers. "I set the phone on the bed and walked away." Her brother held her when he saw her, telling her that if she could just go back to her room in the barracks one more night, she'd be able to make it. "He said, 'If you can't stay for you, Shannon, stay for me,' " she recalled. "I told him, 'Don't make me hate you.' When I told the Citadel I was leaving, they wanted me to creep out the back door so the press couldn't see me. They said, 'We can get you off campus and nobody will know you are gone.' I said, 'No, I came in by the front door and I will leave by the front door.' " It rained hard as she left. She remembers that the moment they hit the highway out of Charleston, the rain stopped and it turned into a glorious day. "Everyone was quiet the whole way home," she said. "There was nothing to be said. There was a lot of anger and disappointment in that car. At me, in some ways, but at that point, my family didn't know anything. My lawyer didn't know anything. There was disappointment that everything we'd fought for was so suddenly over."

She said she had told no one about a frightening encounter at the grocery store, just before she moved on campus. Faulkner said she was grabbed by a man who told her that if she showed up at the Citadel, he knew just the place where he could see her parents burn to death. She saw his alumni ring when he grabbed her face. That was the first time she'd been touched, physically, in the ordeal. All of the other attacks had come through her lawyers or parents, in the form of letters or phone calls. And she told no one what had happened for ten months.

So, the day Faulkner left the Citadel, everyone assumed she was bailing for one reason: She wasn't up to the challenge. She felt like a failure then, but time has given her a new perspective. "I'm not a failure," says Faulkner, now a high school English teacher in Greenville, South Carolina. "I walked away from it and I'm still alive. I succeeded. I walked into the Citadel. I was a cadet. I reached my goal, my first goal, which was to get there. I went a year and a half. It took much more for me to leave than it did for me to stay. I took more ridicule. Even those who supported me turned against me when I left. They said I didn't have what it took to stay, that I'd hurt women."

Some people speculated that she was in it for the money and the publicity. "I didn't receive anything for going," she said. "There was a movie deal in the works, but the day I left, that fell through. The book deals fell through. In the eyes of the public, I was a failure. It made me feel terrible, horrible. Very, very bad. I did a day of interviews, and then shut down."

She blamed it on the stress she'd gone through for the previous two years, on all of the hatred that was focused on her and on the isolation of being the only woman on campus. She admits that all of that played a part in her decision to leave but says that the grocery store incident was the straw that broke the camel's back. It took her two years to get to the point where she could just be Shannon Faulkner, not "Shannon Richey Faulkner, plaintiff."

"I can't say there was any one thing that brought me back," she said. "I think it was just a lot of time. I can talk about it now and not start crying or not want to throw up or not get a migraine headache. You know, I look back at everything I've done and, wholeheartedly, I would do it again. I don't regret filing my lawsuit and I don't regret leaving the Citadel. I don't regret any of it." Luckily, for Faulkner, time heals, even in the worst circumstances.

Thank goodness you probably won't have to see your failures displayed on the front page, but it still hurts when it happens. Failure is inevitable at some point, especially if you are going to stretch and test yourself. Too many people won't risk stretching for fear of failure. But, as long as you are taking risks and testing how far you can go, you are going to experience some loss. Expect it, deal with it, but don't harp on it. And, so what if you do fail? You have every opportunity to succeed again. As long as you focus on your dreams and persevere, you will find more success than failure. We hate failure because it makes us feel like we don't measure up. When we stumble, we feel stupid because, in part, we worry about what other people will think. Some people may actually gloat at our difficulties, and that's painful. The word "failure" is so loaded that we cringe when we hear it.

I'm always amazed when people move on to other cities or jobs and always, always send reports back of wild triumph and success. Nobody ever seems to want to admit they left and actually had a harder time. Well, anybody who has made a significant life change knows that there is good and bad in every new experience. Decent people will *respect* you for daring to try. There are many, many decent people who offer emotional support when it gets rough. They'd rather hear you being honest than faking it. By being truthful, you gain so much in terms of human connection. It is much easier to be friends with a real person, rather than a person who feels the need to be "on" every minute. And remember, everybody has moments of triumph and moments of struggle.

Hail to the Chief

Those of us who have tried and failed have learned a hard, but valuable lesson: Failure is hardly the horror we expect. It's awful at the time, but once you climb out of it, you generally find you are better off than you were before. It's a matter of learning not to define yourself by your failure, but your ability to rise above it. Think about Penny Harrington, the first woman to lead a metropolitan police department.

First, she became the darling of the world media when she got the top law enforcement job in Portland, Oregon, but then came the day when the mayor told her that it was either going to be her or him and that she needed to resign. So, she did. Suddenly, she couldn't even find work as the manager of an RV park. It was the same year that Harrington had been named "Woman of the Year" by *Ms.* magazine. Her story shows how much it hurts to fall, but how good it feels to win again because she ended up finding a job that brings her much satisfaction.

Just about every crisis that could happen to a police chief happened to Harrington: Budget cuts. Staff cuts. Allegations of corruption in city government. She remembers, "That department has never seen a period of time like that in its life. There was a crisis every day, and these were huge, huge things that had the community on the verge of riots. In some ways, that was very exciting. But, it never gave me a chance to take a breath and start implementing what I wanted to do."

She reorganized the drug unit, and then the union put out the word that she was soft on drugs. The department was making more arrests and seizing more drugs, but the take was she was soft on the issue. Morale was awful. The union became so angry, it warned the mayor that if he didn't get rid of Harrington, members would launch a recall movement against him. She says, "He knew that when we'd taken on those ethical and performance issues, it would upset the union. He said he didn't care. Everything was going the way it should go, but morale was bad. And then he fired me." She was asked to stay on as deputy chief, but she walked. "Why would I stay in an organization that doesn't believe in what I'm doing?" she asked. "I was so angry. The only thing I blamed myself for was being so naïve," she said. "I wondered how I didn't see it coming. I was angry at the unfairness of it, and I immediately started looking for a lawyer. I thought, they can't do this. It's illegal."

She spent two years looking for work. At first, she tried to find work as a police chief in another city. "I'd been the chief of police in one of the biggest cities in the United States and I was naïve enough to think I could go out and get another chief's job somewhere else," she said. "I'd always be a finalist, I'd always get the interview and I'd never get the job. I was working with a headhunter, and they stopped calling me. Finally they said, 'You're never going to get a job in policing. Stop wasting your time.' That was horrible. I knew it was true, but to hear it spoken just about did me in. So, I quit applying."

Harrington had been in charge of a $57 million budget and knew she had many of the same talents and expertise that a CEO of a company should have. But the business world was quick to reject her, telling her that she wasn't qualified because she was "in policing." Harrington eventually found work as a recruiter in the electrical industry. Six months later, she was hired by the state bar association of California as the assistant director of investigations.

Then, she found her voice. Harrington now leads the National Center for Women and Policing—a project of the Feminist Majority. That organization gives voice and support to women facing the same kinds of difficulties Harrington did as an officer and a leader. It works to get more women into policing, and help the ones who are there to ascend to higher levels. She says that, at first, she really missed the excitement of policing but that today, she wouldn't go back for anything. Not because she's bitter, but because she's fulfilled in what she's doing now. She also believes that her best decision was moving out of Oregon and heading to California. Before she left, she'd hear her name in the news daily—usually in a negative light. Now, she's introspective about the experience. It's not an all-consuming black cloud from her past, but rather, the experience that led her to a positive new challenge. "You do learn from things," she said. "Then you have to go on and do something else. I feel most sorry for the women who get trapped and can't get beyond the victim stage. If you stay there, you're victimizing yourself. You're going to be there forever. What's the point of that?"

Sometimes the gods decide we need a growth experience more than another success story. Haven't we grown enough already? Unfortunately these lessons keep coming along to remind us that we are works in progress. The thing to remember is that failure is not defeat. It's just a reminder that we are humans, not super-humans, that we can't appreciate our successes without suffering a few failures.

Sometimes we fail because we don't try hard enough. That *is* a failure, but it can also be a lesson for future endeavors. Sometimes we fail because we don't have what it takes to pull off a particular challenge. But don't we get points for trying? Of course we do. And don't we get points for learning something about ourselves in the process? Absolutely.

Give yourself a zillion points for at least having the guts to go for it. Look at all the people who live their lives fearing failure—or success. They don't dare try anything different. They might spare themselves the pain of individual failure, but looking at the big picture, if they are too afraid to try, they aren't living to their full potential. Meanwhile, every time you scare yourself by trying something untested and unknown, you are stretching to your full height.

When you feel like you've failed at something, the last thing you want is some sort of Pollyanna perspective telling you how you are a winner for just trying. Falling down **hurts.** You aren't going to feel a lot of comfort by my telling you that this is just another stop on your journey, a moment of self-definition, blah, blah, blah, blah, blah.

I've had a few of those moments of "self-definition." The biggest lesson I ever had came from a boss who didn't support my initiative to improve our newspaper's coverage of women. Like many local papers, women and women's issues were mostly relegated to the features section and lacked a significant presence in editorials, columns, or in business and news stories. Our publisher—the big boss—supported the effort to improve women's coverage and asked me to start a task force. I invited seventy of the most powerful leaders in the state to serve on this task force, and they eagerly accepted. Among them were the state attorney general, major business leaders, the governor's chief of staff, members of the legislature, state supreme court and the city council. Despite support from the publisher, that huddling of powerful community leaders so infuriated a top editor that when the task force finished its six-month assignment and issued its report, my career suddenly hit the skids. I was told, flat-out, that I would no longer be covering women's issues and that I would never have the chance to pursue my career goals there. So, I left. At the time, I felt defeated and somewhat depressed that my genuine efforts to do what was right had backfired. How could I have been so naïve?

But, guess what? That close-minded and sexist editor turned out to be the greatest teacher I have ever had. If not for him, I would never have known firsthand the resistance that so many women face in the workplace on a daily basis. I would not have understood personally that intelligent women can—and do—threaten insecure men who will retaliate. I would not have shared my experience with other women, only to find out that so many women have suffered the same treatment. Most important, I would never have known that this book was even needed. I was half-tempted to dedicate it to him, but I see my mother as a much better role model.

Everybody has known moments of defeat. Think of all those people who achieved great success—and great failure. Michael Jordan missed half of his shots on the basketball court and Ted Williams missed six out of ten times at bat. Thomas Edison once said, "I speak without exaggeration when I say that I have constructed three thousand different theories in connection with the electric light . . . yet in only two cases did my experiments prove the truth of my theory." Well, that was enough.

What if he never found the method that worked? Would he have been a failure? That man was pursuing his passion. He did the work he loved and he felt good about it. Regardless of whether his lightbulb worked or not, he was living his dream. That's what we need to focus on. We might lose money or time, influence or patience. But we still win when we lose, as long as we have done what matters to us.

"Some people think that if they fail, something is the matter with them," said Ellen Langer, a professor of psychology at Harvard University and author of *Mindfulness*. They let a setback define who they are, when it is only a moment in time that may not have worked as well as they'd wished. "With some people, any failure in life is taken as an indication of their basic worth," Langer said. "Other people search for situational explanations of *why* something went wrong, rather than questioning their basic worth. Doing that allows you to stay in the process of what you are doing, not constantly evaluating how good or bad you are."

Langer suggests using the techniques of mindfulness to give you greater perspective when things turn tough. Mindfulness is an awareness that cultivates the ability to see things as they are from moment to moment. It stems from a Buddhist philosophy. "When I play tennis, I play each point as if my life depends on it," she said. "I don't care whether I win or lose it, but playing it is important. I am actively involved in the process." That's the trick. Engage in the process, not the outcome. Make sure you aren't using setbacks to define who you are as a person, she said. Just learn to enjoy what you are doing, while you are doing it.

Stop Worrying About Yesterday

For Joycelyn Elders, failing was a matter of continuing on as the strong force she always was. When she was sworn in in 1993 as surgeon general, it didn't take long to realize that she was more like the people than the politicians and her way of playing politics wasn't to pull punches, but to throw them. She lasted eighteen months.

Surviving attacks for her stands on abortion and birth control, poverty and health care, Elders suffered especially harsh criticism when her son's drug problems surfaced in 1994. She was finally undone when her remarks about masturbation were reported. Instead of playing victim, Elders played warrior and continued on her crusade, returning to academics and making hundreds of speeches every year about the issues that have grabbed her passion.

"Our political leaders in Washington knew I was right. Nobody ever called Joycelyn Elders a liar because I was talking about the facts of the matter. But, they called me a 'Condom Queen,' an atheist and a lot of other things," she said. "They felt I was an atheist because I wanted to teach children about sex and tell them about condom use. They said that meant I was against God and had to be an atheist. I probably had been to more churches than any of them. That was OK. I don't wear my religion on my sleeve. That's between me and my God."

When she spoke at the United Nations on World AIDS Day in 1994, she was asked if she felt masturbation would reduce the spread of AIDS, and if young people should be taught about masturbation. "My response was that I thought masturbation was a normal part of human sexuality, but we don't even teach children about other aspects of sexuality. We should stop lying to them about masturbation, telling them hair is going to grow on their hands, that they are going to go blind or they are going to go crazy. That was primarily it," she said.

It took a week for the story to break when a reporter used it as an example of why Elders was a liability to President Clinton. "It got interpreted by certain press that I wanted to teach children how to masturbate," she said. "First of all, nobody needs to teach anybody how to masturbate." When she was asked to explain the remark, she couldn't even remember what she'd said. Elders was told to resign, but she refused to step down until she talked to Clinton about it. Chief of Staff Leon Panetta told her that the president— her old ally from Arkansas—was too busy.

But, she insisted. "All along, the president had defended me," she recalled. "Everytime I'd see him, he'd put his thumbs up and say, 'Keep it up,' even though I was being ripped into day after day." This time, it was different. "The president called, he said he was sorry and I asked him, 'Mr. President, do you know what I said?' He said, 'Yes, they've told me.' I said, 'Have you heard it?' He said, 'It will be best if your resignation is on Mr. Panetta's desk by two o'clock.' "

Too much was happening for Clinton to stand by her. "I put the phone down, went into my office and just sat there. I called my secretary in and told her what happened. I told her not to say anything because I had to get myself together. She didn't, but as soon as Elders got back out to her desk, it had already been released to the press. She hadn't even written the resignation letter yet."

She says that speaking her mind was not a failure. That was success. "I don't know how to say anything but the truth," she said. "When you are born in the country and you are poor, you don't learn to be devious. You don't learn to sugarcoat anything. You don't have time. My mother always told me to 'Always speak the truth. And the day you see the truth and cease to speak is the day you begin to die.' That is what I believe."

But Elders did sense some failure in what she had dreamed of accomplishing in terms of HIV and teen pregnancy prevention. "I thought I had plenty of time," she said. "I didn't think I needed to be in a hurry." Still, she feels good about what she did. "Things worked out. I went right back to my work at the university. I really feel good about who I am. I feel very good about the job I did as surgeon general and I feel very good about what I am doing now. Something my mamma told me was, 'Never throw away your tomorrows worrying about yesterday.' I had to decide I couldn't sit around and worry about not being surgeon general. I had to decide what I was going to do next, and move forward."

What To Do when Things Start Looking Bad

How many times have you read of extraordinary success coming to those who seemed perpetually mired in defeat? Coco Chanel was a flop as a singer, but went on to become a legendary designer and manufacturer of the world's most famous perfume. Anita Roddick's Body Shop stores were born after years of struggle with a hotel and restaurant operation. Beethoven's music teacher said he was "hopeless" as a composer. Michael Jordan didn't make the cut on his high school basketball team. I especially like the famous failures of publishing: Dr. Seuss was turned away by twenty-seven publishers, Jack Canfield suffered 123 rejections for *Chicken Soup for the Soul* and twenty-five publishers passed on *Gone With the Wind*!

All of that success came to people who were bombarded with negative messages telling them they were doomed to failure, yet they didn't let initial negativity hinder them. They kept fighting. Sometimes you have no choice. You lose something that matters to you: a job, a mate, a project, an opportunity. Life can take back what it gives and you can't control what happens to you. What you can control is how you deal with it. Don't let another person or external force push you down or destroy your spirit. Don't wallow in self-pity or embarrassment. Take that moment as what it is: One of the low points on your journey, which will teach and inspire you to even greater personal success.

It can be hard to know when to give up when it appears that you are going to fail at something you are pursuing. Make certain you are truly going to fail before you quit. Don't give up just because things start looking bad, because a situation that looks bleak today may actually turn around tomorrow. If you truly care about a challenge, take it to the wall. Do *everything* you can to make a success of it.

If it doesn't start to work out, take an intermediate step before quitting: Give it to the wind. Step back and breathe a little, get some distance from your effort and let yourself feel "whole" with or without a success in that endeavor. That is the way to feel success in your heart. And, during your cooling-off period, you may see the situation begin to change.

Don't give up too soon! Too often, people give up when success is one or two hurdles away. They bail in the middle of the race, rather than pushing a little harder toward the finish. Be deliberate. Don't fail because you let your dream slip away. Know that you've done everything you can before you give up, because you can feel a degree of success and satisfaction by knowing you've done everything possible. It just didn't work out.

Use your moments of setback to help you define who you are, and what you want. Learn from these times. Know exactly what went wrong—and right. Nothing is a complete failure because, even though you might not have accomplished what you'd hoped, you did accomplish something—and that should be celebrated.

At least you tried.

The Hardest Fall . . .

Remember comedian Margaret Cho who read nasty graffiti about herself in the bathroom of the club where she was performing? Well, at the young age of twenty-four, she faced some pretty horrendous experiences. She'd skyrocketed to stardom with all the hype surrounding her television series, *All American Girl*, then crashed in a matter of months. From the start, she didn't feel comfortable with the show's writing and felt the pressure of producers telling her she needed to do something about the "fullness" of her face. She was ordered to lose weight, and she followed along as they hired her a trainer and a nutritionist and put girdles in her dressing room. She took diet pills. The result was a diet that was so harmful, she began urinating blood and damaged her kidneys. She didn't shake the addiction to the pills, which made her stress even worse. The show floundered from its debut and by midseason, the network ordered its cancellation.

Critics heaped the blame on her. The tabloids castigated her with cracks about her weight. Cho figured her star fell because she wasn't good enough, and coped by feeding drug and alcohol addictions. "It became this Judy Garlandesque phase of my life and it was a cycle I didn't get off for a long time," she said. "I fell into such a depression that it was really incredible how insane I got," she said. "I just felt so much like I had failed. I didn't have any career anymore and I didn't have any talent. I felt like another Hollywood casualty, which, in essence, I was."

But there came a point when Cho realized that she'd have to get it together, or die. She's feeling good these days, having shaken her addictions and has turned into one of the most successful women comedians in the world. "I still feel I haven't achieved what I wanted to," she said. "I held myself back by being a drug addict and an alcoholic, by being insecure and not thinking I had a place to be in the industry."

But Margaret picked herself up after her defeats and continued. The women in this book have all endured some type of failure, some more public than others. They share their stories after enduring the torture of falling down but the important message is that all of them have rebounded and rebuilt their lives, a testimony to the possibility that awaits us after we encounter hard times.

If at First You Don't Succeed

1) *Don't quit too soon.* Take it to the wall and give it everything you can. Be creative and determine whether there are some other avenues you haven't considered.

2) *Take a break before you give up completely.* Get a little space between yourself and the situation.

3) *Realize that everyone experiences some degree of failure* at the whim of someone else, whether it is a boss, corporation or life mate. Don't assume that because this happened to you that you are the one with the problem.

4) *Drop the word "failure" out of your vocabulary.* That's enough to make you miserable.

5) *Realize setbacks are inevitable in life,* and what matters is what you learn and how you rise again. Make a list of things you learned—positive and negative—in your experience.

6) *Forgive yourself.* Move on.

7) *Start making plans for your next challenge.* As you review your plan, see if there is something learned in your setback that can help you succeed in this next round.

8) *Realize what matters most.* It's people, family and heart. Don't get hung up on things that don't define you.

A MOMENT WITH . . .
GENEVIEVE SANGUDI

On the night of May 27, 1990, the world unraveled for Genevieve Sangudi, then fourteen, and her family. Civil war had broken out in Liberia. Few of us heard of the atrocities of that war, but Sangudi has dedicated herself to making sure we all learn something about it.

"Terror and fright used to be something that I knew from a movie. Something that comes at you from the dark. But, this terror is a fear of humans. You can't turn the light on and make it go away. You can't call the police. It is a fear of the capacity of human evil. You are afraid of what lies in other peoples' eyes. Their ability to commit indescribable atrocities. That makes you afraid of humanity—your own humanity.

"It makes you think. What if you have enough food for yourself, but your neighbors are starving. Will you share it? If you were supposed to turn your son in for having been a soldier, and that would save your family, would you do it? But, that's your son! Or, what about the fathers who had to watch their daughters being raped? Do you watch that and save the lives of your family members or do you try to stand up to protect your daughter, putting the lives of your family at risk? How does a father deal with that? All of a sudden, these are the questions that are most important. They are matters of life and death.

"We stayed in the house for about three months without ever leaving. Those three months were absolutely terrifying. I don't remember sleeping, not once. There was heavy, heavy fighting one night, with bullets flying through our windows. Lots of bullets. We all had to stay on the floor of the hallway because it was the only room without windows. I thought I was going to die.

"I don't remember crying, not even once. I can't remember anyone in my home crying. I had no desire to cry. I'm the biggest crybaby in the world. I cry when I watch TV. But there? What are you crying for? There are human skulls on the side of the road. What is there left to cry for?

"My parents were looking for any way out. One of the rebels took a liking to us and would visit us every night. My mom told him that we were trying to leave the country. He took her to his superiors, they took her to their superiors, and finally, she met up with someone who could actually do something about it.

"They wanted to be paid.

"I was very ill with malaria, which I had gotten from mosquitoes. There were no hospitals, of course, no doctors. Nothing works when there is war. Everyone is in their house trying to save their own lives.

"We were driven to a rebel house to get our pass. One of them said, 'You can go, but I want your daughter to stay with me to be my wife.' This was a very delicate moment. You can't really say no. He has a gun. But, my mom is a real diplomat. She acted like she was honored. She said, 'She's a very good cook. You don't want her right now because she is so sick. Come and get her after she gets better.' And he was okay with it.

"After five days, we crossed the border into the Ivory Coast. There is no real border. Just a little footbridge, and we were in another country. Two steps and you are safe. It took weeks to adjust to the fact that we could walk again, in the day or at night. We were free. But then, you still feel like, 'These people don't know what's really happening. They don't know where I was five days ago.' That's where the real isolation is.

"We all came to America after nine months. You get here and no one knows what happened to you. How do you laugh and go to the movies and go dancing when a few months back you were in the midst of such madness? I tried to forget and live the picture-perfect life, but it comes back. For me it came back during college, when Rwanda happened. Genocide was happening again, and I relived it. I went through a very deep depression and I felt guilty for being so unhappy. I thought, 'Look at me. I made it. I'm doing well. My family is all alive.' I didn't think I had the right to be sad. The true problem was that I hadn't dealt with everything.

"I worked on it a lot. Now, I feel like I've been lucky. Blessed. It's my absolute responsibility to speak about what happened and do everything I can to prevent it. I now am one of the organizers of Global Youth Connect. This is what I needed to find my place in America among a group of young people who are dedicated to preventing genocide and ending human rights abuses. So many people see something wrong and just say it's wrong. Not enough people think they can do something. But, I have this fear that if I don't do something about it, it will happen again.

"That's what drives me."

BALANCE

THIRTEEN

SURVIVING PEAKS
AND VALLEYS

JUST WHEN YOU THINK YOU'VE made it, you start to slip. You're up, you're down, you're up, you're down. The problem with getting to the top in this competitive world is that it's so hard staying there. Sarah Weddington got me to think about the notion of peaks and valleys in life because I'd assumed that people like her reached the top and stayed there. Maybe she wondered what to do for an encore after she took *Roe v. Wade* before the U.S. Supreme Court and won, but who else would have even expected her to need one? "There isn't anybody who isn't going to have ups and downs," she said. "I call them 'course corrections.' All of us have had mountaintop experiences, but you don't ever stay on the mountaintop. At some point, you are going to end up back in the valley, either voluntarily or involuntarily."

I've often said that my professional and personal lives have rarely been in sync at the same time. I used to think that if I could just make the two halves of my life come together in some great confluence of good fortune, I could truly be happy. What I didn't realize was that the natural cycles of good and bad times actually offer a certain kind of life security. I can take joy in what is going right without registering too much defeat from what isn't working. But, without creating a good life balance in your mind, the valleys in life can seem oh-so-deep and oh-too-devastating. "Every worthwhile thing in life, be it your career, be it your relationships—every worthwhile thing in life has peaks and valleys and requires sustained effort over long periods of time," said Carol Dweck, a professor of psychology at Columbia University who specializes in achievement motivation. If you focus only on the setbacks, you lose that perspective, she said. "Then, if your work isn't going well, you think you are a failure," she said. "If your relationships aren't going well, it means you are a failure. It does not give you the perspective to escalate your effort. Instead, it makes you give up and withdraw your effort, just when it is needed most." Think about that. If you get discouraged and give up, you've lost the big-picture vision that reminds you that it is the time to try even harder.

That "big picture" outlook is important in the growth process says Harvard psychology professor Ellen Langer. If you are trying to do something you haven't done before, or are trying to do it in a different way, you may encounter a setback or great difficulty. Is that a valley moment?

The biggest challenge in all of these up-and-down moments is keeping your attitude straight so you don't spiral downward. You know how that works: A little setback can become monumental if you allow your mind to distort it enough. Step back for a little perspective, and try to determine how each individual obstacle affects the whole of your life. Chances are, you won't even remember two-thirds of your worries five years from now. Don't let the crisis of the day mess with your mind. You're truly dealing with the same madness the rest of us are facing.

The Balanced Approach

Few people rise to the top without encountering adversity, conflict or obstacles. Listen to Ret. Gen. Claudia Kennedy, the first woman three-star general in the U.S. Army, who has a very balanced approach to tough professional times: "I think I've had periods of achievement and other periods that weren't particularly great," said Kennedy. "For a while there, I was thinking I was setting up a pattern of making some huge mistake I'd need to recover from every two years." She's felt that. Sometimes, she's struggled with her own performance. Sometimes, other people have gotten in the way. Her rise to the top seemed meteoric to those watching from the outside, but like anyone else, she has endured her own trials. "Sometimes I have to say, 'Look, stop struggling so hard. Just do some minimums for a while. Get through this bad period,'" Kennedy said.

And still, she was the most successful woman in Army history. Just goes to show you, trouble visits everyone. As frustrating and difficult as it got in the low periods, she remained focused and driven. Those moments of self-evaluation are great moments of personal definition. Sometimes, it is important to step back from a difficult situation and understand what you are after, why you are after it and how the immediate difficulties are just a short-term hassle.

When it gets tough, she focuses on the image of a duck putting oil on its feathers so the water will roll off. "Sometimes you have to add a little more oil so it rolls off easier. I always think of that image," she said. She also tries to lighten up. "Don't take it quite so seriously. What you really need to do is laugh at much of the conflict you have at work, particularly if it gets real intense. Detach a little, and look at it. Say, 'What a bunch of yahoos!' You have to wonder, 'What is this crazy system I'm dealing with? Have we all lost our minds?' "

If it gets tough, remember, *you are not defined by your work alone.* You are an intelligent woman and can pack up your brainpower and abilities and go elsewhere if necessary. Do *not* let a tough situation pull you down or make you doubt who you are. And, realize that there is so much more to life than any one piece of our world, like work.

"Sometimes, you get a wake-up call," Kennedy said. "For example, you might be notified that a friend of yours is dying of cancer and you think, 'Come on. What am I dealing with? Is this all that important?' I think of that often. On my very worst day, it is still better than what 98 percent of the people in this world are dealing with. Some of this business we get so wrought up over is absolutely a fly speck, compared with what other people live with."

What a humbling notion. The world does not revolve around our individual crises. There are still women in this world who aren't even allowed to work! There are women who live in violent homes where they have to worry whether they or their children will be killed. There are women who go in for a routine pap smear and find out they are going to die. And there are women who have no place to live. It goes on, and on, and on. Just think for a moment. As bad as it sometimes feels when we start to fall, we've still got it pretty good.

Learn whatever lesson there is to learn from this experience, own your piece of it, but don't let it destroy you. We live in a world where we can't be appreciated or loved by everybody every minute. As tough as the bad times are, we can use them to know ourselves better, and find out how strong we really are.

Have you ever gone through one of those spells when you have had to finish three weeks of work in three days—and pulled it off? Or, contrast that with one of those torturous dry spells when you couldn't manage to crank out any more than the minimum? Everybody has. When things are really humming, it's hard to notice the time flying by. Slumps, on the other hand, can be excruciating.

They used to make me crazy. One minute I was cranking out copy like a madwoman, working late hours and basking in accolades from my editors. The next minute, I didn't want to write anything and would slip out for a two-hour lunch. I'd get so paranoid over my lack of inspiration that I felt certain that all those big-shot bosses were spending all of their time watching me and wondering whether I was ever going to spring back to life. Of course, they weren't. But, it took a few years for me to realize that, in a creative field like journalism, slumps are practically necessities in order to be ready and charged up when serious news breaks without notice. After I figured that out, I learned to deal with—and enjoy—my inevitable downtime, and I stopped worrying about it so much. Every single slump was followed by a work frenzy. It all equaled out in the end.

Those experiences helped me as an editor because I knew my reporters needed some downtime in order to be up when they had to be up. If the slump stretched on for too many weeks, I'd make a little remark and things would get moving again. I'd also pass on the advice that reporter Randy Loftis gave me a million years ago when we were still at the *Miami Herald*. He devised the best end-the-slump technique I have ever known. His technique:

1. Define your project

2. Write down every single step you will have to take to complete the project, from coming up with the idea to sending it on to the next level.

3. Check off the steps one at a time until you are done.

Poof! No more slump. It sounds elementary, but it works! The hard part is motivating yourself out of the slump to the point where you are willing to take that first step.

The Valley Within

Sometimes, you experience a personal low at the same moment you are enjoying the highest professional high. Gayle Greer did. She had the office, the assistants, the title, the respect, the money and the perks of being right at the top, but, inside she'd hit bottom. Her story is a reminder that it's up to you to decide whether you are winning or losing, and to define for yourself what success is.

When she started, Greer was the only black woman in the administrative ranks of the cable industry. Her titles kept getting better on her way to being senior vice president of Time Warner Cable, but she felt isolated and she resented the fact that she was surrounded by peers who were all white males. Despite the perks and accolades of her position, she couldn't stand the fact that her fight to diversify the workplace had left her labeled for what she wanted.

"If you are the type who wants no conflict and wants to live a nice, quiet life in peace, then to go along is to get along. That's what it's about," she said. "When I learned that, when I finally got to the place where I didn't care anymore, that's when I knew I had to move on. Other people used to say, 'Cool out, take a vacation, that's just the way it is.' I resented that they didn't care. And then I got to that, too. I would just sit there as they would drone on and I'd be thinking about something I'd do in the next hour or the next day or over the weekend. I wasn't saying anything either. Banging your head against the wall drives you crazy, so you turn off. That's not me either. I knew I had to walk away."

Imagine turning away from such success. Greer said she worried that she would spend the rest of her career wandering aimlessly around her house, wringing her hands and "becoming a drunk." She didn't know what she would do with herself. She had always lived by the calendar and she was constantly checking voice and e-mail. And she worried that no one would want her, even with her remarkable work history.

But, she did what she had to do. She'd already "made it," but only according to other peoples' definitions. Being true to herself was another matter. "As I got healthier, I started seeing my own value," she said. "I recognized I had something to offer, even if it's not within the confines of a job. I was going to be OK. Life was going to go on. I was going to get better. The longer I've been away from Time Warner, the more foreign it seems to me. I have lunch with my old colleagues and they tell me what's going on. It was all going on when I was there, but I hear it now and it's like, 'That is *really* weird.' "

Greer partnered with a tech-wizard and started mining Internet potential, much like she did during the cable revolution. Her business has soared, and she's as busy as ever. She now has a new, stronger sense of success that came out of reassessing what her soul needed when she was in that valley at Time Warner. "I am loving what I am doing now," she said. "I find something very intoxicating about being able to determine your own destiny, and have that feeling of being able to sit at the table and make decisions about things. And whether they are right or wrong, I have that freedom to do that."

The change inside her has been dramatic she says and she realized that there is life after making a decision to move on. A life that is better suited to who she is.

The Course Correction

Once I was done talking with Sarah Weddington, I realized that *everybody* goes through ups and downs requiring difficult professional and personal adjustments. Weddington shared a comedown that came when she worked as an advisor to President Carter. She envisioned a cabinet position for herself during his second term, but Carter didn't get reelected. "Until that point, I'd had an office above the Oval Office and spent weekends at Camp David," she remembered. "And then one day I was in the White House looking at an article someone had put on the bulletin board entitled, 'Fifty things you can make for Christmas for less than five dollars.' Everybody I knew, including me, had just lost their job."

Weddington tapped into her professional network and connected with a woman who was a college president. The woman offered her a chance to teach, and taking the time to put a class together gave her a chance to reflect on everything she'd been through. It was a temporary job, but it gave her a chance to gather her strength to move forward. She later went to work for the Democratic governor of Texas, and then *he* did not get reelected. "As they say, I had another 'opportunity to seek new challenges,' " she said.

Enduring the ups and downs was a matter of tapping into her professional and personal networks. A professional network helps you to find those new challenges and your personal network helps you to get through the tumult. "First, you rely on your personal support network," she said. "They are the ones who gather around you. Second, you start calling your professional support network." Her personal support group included her closest friends, some of who stood by her from the beginning. "They'd been there, helping me from 1969 on," she said. "We'd worked together so long that, if I'd have lost that case, they would have known that I'd have done everything I could to win it, and they still would have been behind it. And, if I'd won it, they would celebrate with me. It's important to have friends who liked you before you had an important title, who will be your friend long after you have that title."

Alas, balance. It's not as elusive as it seems if you just open your eyes to what you have. Let's go back to Weddington's suggestion about the personal and professional support networks that she keeps. As much pain as she felt when she floundered after losing her job, didn't she get a certain amount of joy tapping into the lifelong friendships that gave her such unconditional love and support? Even though circumstances may have pushed her into crisis, didn't she get some satisfaction in knowing she was not alone, that people she cared about would be there to help her through the difficult time, and that she'd survive it no matter what? Of course.

It's hard to keep your mind clear when you find yourself in a struggle, but what better time to relish in what you have? If your personal life is bottoming out, can you find a degree of joy and satisfaction from your professional life? Granted, there are times when both the personal and professional arenas look pretty bleak, but fortunately, those times don't last forever. Something always budges and you can get back to appreciating what you have while discovering a deeper part of yourself that will enable you to deal with what is still wrong.

Reassessing Yourself

The beauty of course corrections is that they give us an opportunity to reflect on our journey and decide if we are on the right path. If you've started to slip after a period of great professional success, ask yourself whether it's so great at the top if it means you have to struggle so frantically to keep your place there. If you suddenly find yourself on the outs with a boss or perhaps even lose your job, don't use the moment of crisis lamenting what went wrong and who did what to whom. Instead, focus on what you want to do next, and use the lesson of what happened in the past to find an environment and challenge that is a better fit for you. If your seemingly wonderful relationship suddenly implodes, build yourself up so you are strong enough to be alone, or strong enough to let someone else touch your life in a way that is less destructive.

Maybe you are in a lull or a down season. Don't waste time wallowing over what's going wrong, just use the time to check in with yourself and see if you are on the path that is most meaningful to you. Instead of harping on yourself because you might not be succeeding by somebody else's measure, focus on your own definition of success, and look hard at the priorities you have set for your life. Tough times can be a catalyst for rebirth, either for a greater commitment to what you are already doing, or for a whole new series of challenges and endeavors.

Sometimes, it may seem as though you are being tested—and you are. Nothing worth having comes easily. If you want it, earn it. That means committing to your dream, regardless of how tough it gets. It also means recommitting again and again.

Take Care of Yourself

All of these ups, downs, course corrections and slumps can be crazy-making. So can your intense devotion to a job, mission or relationship that takes more than it gives back. Don't let yourself burn out. Psychologist Barbara Distler of the University of Illinois says, "The biggest thing to pass along is that burnout can be prevented if people just respond to their own stress."

Okay. Here's what she suggests. Instead of ignoring your stress signals, pay attention. If you find yourself wanting to cry at work a lot, and that's not the way you normally are, something is going on. Or, if you are suffering headaches or feeling more irritable, ask what is going on. "People tend to downplay these signals or ignore them and just keep pushing forward, rather than doing things that will help," said Distler, who specializes in work-burnout issues. "People often wait until they are at a crisis point to take a vacation or rest on the weekend. Don't wait until you need to spend two days doing nothing but recharging your body." Taking care of yourself is an ongoing process, she said. Set good limits in terms of how much you work. Take vacations, spend time with family and friends, and make sure that fun is a regular part of your week—not just a luxury that happens once or twice a year.

Do what she calls "self care." Take an afternoon to do what you enjoy. If it's cooking, sailing, golfing, escaping, indulge yourself. Always, always do this, even when you are not stressed. Then, at the first sight of a stress symptom, intervene. "Say, 'Wow, I'm starting to overdo it. I'm not going to take on that extra project this week,' or, 'I'm going home early.' Don't wait for it to become more extreme."

Sometimes that's hard to pull off, since society puts more of an emphasis on working longer hours, taking your work home with you and always being accessible to others via e-mail, cell phones and beepers. Distler agrees that it is getting harder to set limits on demanding careers, but says it is important to retain control. "Take a step back and evaluate what is going on," she said. "Think about what your real goals are. What are the consequences you'll face if you set better limits on your work. If you used to leave work by five-thirty, but now you never get out until seven, pull back and evaluate. Is that how you want to be living? It's nice to be doing a great job at work, but is that the only thing you want in your life?"

But What About the Peaks?

I've been talking about the valleys for far too long here, especially since we generally enjoy so much more success in life than hardship. We just don't seem to notice. Every time you meet a goal, every time you score a victory, celebrate it! Relish in it! Live it, breathe it, enjoy the moment for all it can bring.

Just don't shrug it off and move on to the next challenge, and don't limit your celebration to an occasional congratulatory dinner out when you get a raise or achieve something huge. Wake up every morning being mindful of all your talent and success. Think about how far you have come in the past one year, five years and decade. Remember what you envisioned success would be when you were in your early twenties, and look at how much you have done.

If you aren't good at doing that in your head, do it on paper. Make a list of your ten greatest accomplishments, and don't overlook the most important things, like the friendships you have established and the family relationships you have in your life. Then, write down what you had expected to achieve in your life. If you didn't meet all of the goals you'd set, did you replace them with other more emotionally fulfilling experiences? The point of this kind of introspection is to give you the power of knowing your value as a human being has many dimensions—not just career and not just home.

Every time you catch yourself struggling or worrying, give yourself a time-out and look over what you have accomplished. Think of everything, from what you did in school to what you achieved in every job you worked. Even if you left a job feeling like something went wrong, look back on it and remember all of the things that went right.

We don't celebrate our success very well says workplace consultant Stephanie Allen, author of *Having It All Isn't Everything*. "First, we were taught not to brag about ourselves," she said. We feel uncomfortable basking in our own glory. Allen said it is important that we not only celebrate our success, but the success of others. Celebrate their promotions. Hail their achievements. Make them a part of your team of celebrants, she urges.

Keep a cluster of friends and confidants who are as happy for your success as you are for theirs. Enjoy the good moments because you have worked so hard to achieve them, and remember there are always good moments in life, even when your days seem painfully difficult. Doing that is the most vital part of finding balance in your life because knowing and appreciating what you have makes it so much easier to deal with what is missing. When things seem to go negative, force yourself to focus on the positive. Remember how much good fortune you have.

We aren't doomed by the inevitable difficulties that pop up, but rather, we are challenged by them. It's all part of the process, and tough as it may seem, it's the ultimate test of who we really are.

Surviving Peaks and Valleys

- **Know your talent.** Know how marketable you are. ALWAYS have your resume ready so you can leave.

- **Take risks.**

- **When you start to get fed up, analyze what's going on.** Is the problem with your company or the situation? Will your replacement suffer from the same hassles? Did you make matters worse by ignoring it or fueling it, or does the blame belong with other people?

- **Constantly remind yourself of how much you have accomplished.** Don't wallow in what has gone wrong, but rather, bask in what you have done right.

- **Don't automatically assume that it is your fault** when something goes wrong. The workplace is rarely fair.

- **Make a "secret file" about yourself.** Keep a log of every word of praise, every discussion of your accomplishments. Keep all notes, memos and paperwork supporting your success. If you need to self-promote, the paperwork is there. If things turn sour, you've got documentation to show your worth. You've also got the goods to help you get a better job.

- **Enjoy your success!** Since obstacles won't go away once you've "made it," relish in the good times. You've worked hard to make it happen, so enjoy it!

A MOMENT WITH . . .
MARY-ELLIS BUNIM

The executive-producer of MTV's *The Real World* encounters what is real.

"You shouldn't defer life. You can't count on it being there, you can't count on it staying the same. You have to seize the opportunity for today.

"I had to get breast cancer to know that lesson.

"I've had it twice. The first time was ten years ago, and I had it again last year. It made me reassess everything about what is important and how I wanted to live. Life is now a matter of recognizing the opportunities to be happy.

"The first time around, I found a little lump doing a breast exam. My breasts were notoriously lumpy, so I would have them checked all the time and I would check them as well. The lump I found was very small. It didn't show up in a mammogram. I had no history of breast cancer in my family, no reason to suspect anything, but they said it was clearly cancer. I had a lumpectomy and radiation.

"Afterward, I did a lot of volunteer work so I could stay close to all the research. Twelve months later my best friend got it and had to go through nine months of chemo. Since then, it has happened to countless people I know.

"About a year ago, I found another lump. I went to a surgeon who had been checking me periodically and he said, 'Oh, this is nothing. This is fibroids.'

"I took a long trip to Vietnam, came back and went to him again. I said, 'You know, this is bothering me. It feels different than it did a month ago.' He took a biopsy and said, 'See, it's clean. Just forget it.'

"Another month went by and I knew. There was no question in my mind. I said, 'I don't care if this is just fibrocystic disease, I want it out.'

"He said, 'Okay, if this will give you peace of mind, you should have it out.'

"I went into surgery and I didn't have anesthesia—just a local. I put this wonderful music on my headset and relaxed, because he was so convinced it was nothing. A half hour later, my doctor patted me on the shoulder and said it was over.

"He told me he wasn't sure, but it didn't look right. The next day, he confirmed that it was cancer.

"I had found that lump when it was less than one centimeter, and by the time he got it out, it had grown to more than two centimeters. It was aggressive. I had a mastectomy and reconstruction, which was a major thing. It's huge surgery.

"The recovery has taken about a year. There have been three or four surgeries, and I consider myself cured—but alert. And I do believe if you listen to your body and stay on top of what it is telling you, that you have a fighting chance.

"The morale to this story is, take responsibility for your own health.

"Listen to your own body. Don't be intimidated by other people telling you that you are wrong. In more cases than I can count, doctors have said, 'Oh, it's nothing,' and it ends up being cancer. Get other opinions. Most people know what their body normally feels like.

"Today, I woke up at the beach and it was overcast and foggy—really eastern kind of weather, and I took a walk and it was just wonderful. It is important to seize wonderful moments as they happen. Recognize when people are nice to you or recognize that something is particularly pretty or know when something makes you smile. If that can happen once or twice a day, you have it made."

FOURTEEN

GETTING A LIFE

I WAS A TWENTY-FOUR-YEAR-OLD REPORTER, completely obsessed with my work, and I needed my time card back. My boss told me to adjust it so it reflected at least some of the eighty-plus hours I'd put in to crank out a series at the last minute. So I went to the editor's office and told his assistant, Joyce Duarte, that I needed to make the change. "Gee, Fawn. Is it really worth it?" she said, looking at the hours logged on my revised time card. And then it hit me. It wasn't worth it at all.

Live to work? Or, work to live? It's your choice. After the "Is it really worth it?" question in Joyce's office, my relationship with work changed forever. Work remained an important part of my life, but it stopped being all that I had. I became a spirited adventurer who lived for the big picture, enjoying travel, sports, the outdoors and the youth that I'd almost sacrificed to workaholism. I no longer surrounded myself with people who would only talk about work when they were off duty. I found friends, like Joyce, who had this same balanced appreciation for living large, and living now. In the process, I've lived and I've laughed.

So few people allow themselves to live large. They restrict themselves by the roles they have chosen as career woman, wife, mother, etc., and allow those parts of their lives to hold them back when they see opportunities to really enjoy living. I'm not sure if they are bound by guilt or fear, but they will never know their full range as human beings if they don't take a few chances and challenge their boundaries.

Some people do that, without losing their ability to be a good career woman, mother or wife. They challenge their limits and insist upon time for themselves so they can experience life in new ways. Those people know how to live, and they are the ones I want as friends.

I was lucky to have someone shake me out of the workaholism mode when I was twenty-four, and if you haven't had your awakening yet, let me ask you something: *Is it really worth it?*

It's Business. Business isn't Everything.

Among the many women I have worked for, three didn't date, didn't socialize, didn't exercise, didn't travel, didn't take vacations and didn't live well at all. One spent more than a decade taking crap from a verbally abusive boss who would publicly humiliate her with great frequency. Another had only one emotional connection outside the office: her dog. The third was a bitter beast of a woman who muttered nasty remarks under her breath when one of us would leave for vacation, receive flowers, become engaged or have a baby.

They lived their lives in black and white, and as they tried so hard to gain fulfillment from their work, they missed every opportunity to find fulfillment from within. They never explored any of the many dimensions of growing as an individual, choosing instead to work and work and work. The tortured expressions they wore on their faces said everything to me: It really wasn't worth it.

Some people derive a lot of joy from their work. My dad sure does. He's seventy-four and still working almost full-time as a pharmacist. He *loves* what he does, and is one of those worker bees who chose to "live to work." But, he has a family, he loves to exercise, he takes classes, enjoys traveling and has a lot of other interests. So, there are people who can make work the center of their lives, without losing a sense of balance.

Carly Fiorina likes what she does as CEO of Hewlett-Packard, but realizes that's only part of who she is. She doesn't live in one dimension, but many, knowing that who she is as a person counts a lot more than how she scores as a business leader. "I like the high-wire act. I like the rush of having to stay concentrated in order to be successful. If things get easy, I get bored," she said. "But, while I love what I do and am challenged by it, work does not define me as a whole person. I still have a soul, which is defined by things outside of how I make a living."

Fiorina likes to spend time with her family and friends. She has outside interests, like gardening, listening to music, and she loves to dance. And she has fun with her work. "Life is so unpredictable and most things are out of our control. To me, that means making the most of the present," she said. "I know that sounds corny, but I do believe that." She knows that those who lose themselves to their ambitions pay a hefty price. "I have seen many very talented people really do damage to their careers because they were so focused on the next thing that they didn't spend the time or attention they needed on the current thing," she said.

Hmmm. Live in the moment. We've heard that before. Someone once told Fiorina, "What you are is God's gift to you. What you make of yourself is your gift to God." She doesn't remember where she heard it, but the thought has stayed with her. "You have a choice," she said. "Recognizing that the choice is always yours is important. Having self-possession and self-awareness is important. And, having the self-confidence to try enough different things that you really learn who you are and what you are capable of is important. That requires risk. It can't be done without risk or mistakes." That's just life. Accomplish what you can, but focus your heart on your soul. She believes that in the end you've got to be happy with who you are and proud of who you are. No amount of money or power or success can make up for the unhappiness that you may feel.

Striking a Balance

How many times have you seen articles talking about the magic of balancing your life? Obviously, it's a hot topic, but it wouldn't be so hot if most of us weren't having a hard time doing it. The first step is to stop worrying so much. Let go of the past and stop losing yourself to the future. All you've got is now, and there are no guarantees about anything else.

I often think of how my mother, at age 66, suffered a massive stroke that disabled her and took her independence from her. This is not what Mom expected out of her golden years, but I have never seen a person so able to draw joy out of every single moment of life. "It's not what happens to you," she has told me again and again. "It's how you deal with it."

The key to dealing with it is living in the moment. One of the ways to learn how to live in the moment is through mindfulness meditation. As mentioned in Chapter 12: Falling Down, mindfulness is a Buddhist philosophy that what you are doing in the moment is most important. "If you are eating, you should be about eating. If you are walking, you should be about the walking, not the arriving," said psychotherapist Kim Vaz of the University of South Florida. "Honor whatever you are doing in the moment as the most important thing." No easy task, especially in today's world where we are tethered to the rest of the world by our pagers and cell phones and pocket computers.

Harvard psychology professor Ellen Langer, who has researched the concept of living in the moment—or mindfulness—as her life's work says, "The way to be in the moment is to first accept the inherent uncertainty in the world in which we live. The more you count on things to happen as expected, the more you travel a path of mind*less*ness. It is the healthy respect of uncertainty that can help lead you to the present."

A friend once told me her therapist had found the heart of her problem. She was never, ever in the present moment. She was told to start practicing by consciously spending ten minutes a day in the present. My friend was unnerved by the thought, as she was always, always thinking of something else. Spending ten minutes a day in the present was a *huge* challenge. If that kind of exercise would be a challenge for you, start practicing. Free yourself from all of that worry anxiety and start living in the moment, enjoying the richness of your everyday life. When you feed your dogs, take pleasure in how much they appreciate you. When you eat your dinner, relish in the taste of the food and the people around you. As you drive to work, look at the beauty of the trees and notice what is happening in the world around you.

Are You Going To Live Half of Your Life, or All of It?

I will never forget the story of Gurnelle Jones, a woman who rode on the same six-hundred-killer-mile bicycle trip I took in Arizona a few years back. Jones, who was seventy-five at the time, told us that she'd lived her life in "quarters," sacrificing everything of herself to others until she had to take her own turn at living. This woman is my hero. I found her again after running her name on the Internet. It popped up in the results of a 10K race. When I contacted her, she again told the story of her life in quarters—only now, at eighty-one, she is in a new quarter.

"For the first twenty-five years of my life, I was under the command of my mother and father, and spent three years with the Navy in the WAVES (the Women's Auxiliary Reserve). Somebody was always telling me what to do. Then the next twenty-five years, I was married, so I had a husband and four children and I was mostly under his control. I got a divorce when I was fifty-one, and for the next twenty-five years, I was going to be my own boss. I was going to do what I wanted to do when I wanted to do it, living where I wanted to live without anyone else's opinion. That's what I did, I have had the most wonderful life."

The third "quarter" was filled with abundance, adventure and challenge. After her divorce, she trained for a new career, then retired to work part-time in a bicycle shop for the fun of it. After that, she worked summers busing tables in a Grand Canyon restaurant because she loved mingling with foreign tourists. She's done long-distance bicycle touring all over the world, and wrote a book on cycling when she was seventy-one.

I love her story because it shows how we are always on the verge of a new beginning. If she's not mad about being eighty-one, why should we lament turning forty? If she's found opportunity and challenge throughout her life, how can we use the excuse that we can't go for something because "it's too late"? Our time is right now. We can either choose to live half of our lives, or all of it. And like Gurnelle Jones, I want to live all of it. "Retirement? There shouldn't be such a term," she said. "Life is just progressing along to the next thing you want to do. Do it! DO IT! See what's out there!"

I asked her about the fourth quarter of her life, now that she's eighty-one. "This last quarter? That's the icing on the cake," she said.

Caring for Yourself First

Imagine the nerve of a woman who dares to put herself first! Weren't we socialized to take care of everyone *but* us? Don't we all hear some inner voice that tells us we are being selfish when we put our own needs ahead of others? Well, that's got to stop. There is no way we can deal with the pressure of everyday living if we aren't putting ourselves first, taking care of our minds and bodies so that we can go out and deal with the rest of the world.

You laugh. You don't even have time to take care of yourself. Well, the women mentors in this chapter are going to show you how to make significant life changes by following five steps:

1. *Break down all of your demands.* By breaking up all of the pressures in your life into smaller pieces, you can deal with them one at a time.

2. *Make time for yourself.* Even when you think you don't have a spare minute, you do.

3. *Create your own space.* Have a place that belongs to you, alone, where you can read, relax and meditate.

4. *Break the cycle that is pulling you down.* Just go out and start living.

5. *Be creative about how you really want to live.* Explore your values about living, and make sure you honor them.

You can't make major changes until you start caring for yourself and learning that you are worthy of the best in life. Judith Albino learned that after an especially rough experience. After she was forced out as president of the University of Colorado by the Colorado Board of Regents, she had to confront her identity and how she was living. When she took the time to take care of herself, she realized why things were so hard when she was in the midst of battle. "The day that I woke up and was not president any longer, I wondered what I was going to do," she said. "The transition out of a very demanding position is difficult. One day, your time and attention is needed by everyone. Your opinions about everything are important. You have more work than you could possibly do. Suddenly, you are just one voice among many, and no one needs anything from you. That was certainly an adjustment. But, it didn't take too long."

She immersed herself in her work as a faculty member at the university. Just when she was getting used to a secondary role, she was recruited for the presidency of the five-campus Alliant University in California. At first, she said no. But after she was convinced to take the job, she learned a lesson in balance. "It's clear to me now that I do my best work when I do take some time for myself," she said. "And, I think I'm a better judge of the people around me. There are two things I would tell people now. One is to be sure your job is a good fit for you. And second, take time for yourself. There were times when I was president at Colorado that I was so exhausted. I'm sure, in part, that was from some of the personal attacks that went on, but it was also the long hours I worked. I was not at my best."

Now, she takes vacations. She lives.

Changing Gears

There is so much more to life than ambition and challenge.

There is also a lot of living to be done. When I first talked with Iditarod legend Susan Butcher, she'd completely changed her life with the birth of her daughter, Tekla. She's since had another child.

"Before my daughter was born, I had a single focus," she said. "Now I have at least a double focus and this winter, in addition to my dog mushing and Tekla, my husband and I are building a house. I have to be very clear about what my number one priority is. That is Tekla. Period. If she needs me, I'm there for her and she does get the majority of my time."

That's a huge change because before motherhood, the dogs and training were 100 percent of her life. She still has to do the balancing act between family and career, and says she feels like she fails at it sometimes. "That's why I'm not doing the Iditarod right now," she said. "I would fail at the balancing act. I hope to go back to running the Iditarod at a certain point in my children's life. If that doesn't happen, it doesn't happen. I can manage that."

So, she does smaller races now—three hundred to five hundred miles, or ten to twenty-five miles. The training is less intense and she doesn't have to devote so many days to the race itself. She's completely changed her attitude about living and lives in the moment.

I'm sure some of this "take time for yourself" approach may sound good on paper but seems completely impractical in the chaotic life you now lead. But it is possible to find the calm within yourself, regardless of how impossible the concept seems. Reverend Suzan Johnson Cook has and she's living in the same demanding world we are. Everybody wants a little piece of her: her congregation, the women she reaches in her motivational speaking, politicians all the way up to the highest reaches of government, and her husband and kids. Still, Cook can find solace.

> "I was once in Florida with my mother, when I got a call from my daughter Elizabeth. She ended her one very long sentence by saying 'There is a fire in the Oakland hills and we have to evacuate in twenty minutes, what should I take?' You start to rank things in importance. It's, 'Get out of there as fast as you can. If you can, take the animals, and maybe the photographs.' My many books, that would be a great loss. My plants, they are irreplaceable. But the main thing is life.
>
> "The winds favored us in that fire. Others lost, but we survived. It sharpened our focus. What matters is life."
>
> —Oceanographer Sylvia Earle

This Baptist minister, who operates from a storefront church in the Bronx and yet influences thousands of American women through her motivational speeches and writings says that there are ways to find solace, despite whatever mayhem we've found for ourselves. She is the author of two books: *Too Blessed to be Stressed: Words of Wisdom for Women on the Move*, and *Sister Strength*.

Of finding calm in the frenetic world, she says, "I think many women are tired. Many of us are trailblazing into industries that are traditionally male. The culture is still male and when you go to a day's work, you then come home and have to have time for family. You look around for time for yourself and you've given out all of your 'oomph.' Your strength is gone. It is very difficult to prioritize and focus when you are burned out. When you feel tired you make wrong decisions, bad decisions, decisions that aren't right for you. You are too tired to think clearly." Have faith, she suggests. Be hopeful. Look around and decide what you can handle, one thing at a time. Decide what is pressing on you that you can't stand, then work on that. "You need to identify what is upsetting you," she said. "Identify it, confront it, move to the healing process."

> "We know the meaning of life. It is not a $50 million contract for seven years. That's not the meaning of life. The hardest thing to teach is that peace of mind is so much more important than the biggest bank account. You have to be the best you can possibly be on this earth, and you have to grow as a person."
>
> —Women's basketball legend Teresa Edwards

One of the most important necessities is finding time for yourself. Alone time. "If that means, instead of taking a lunch break you go to a park and take a 'me break,' do it," she said. "Find whatever amount of time you have that no one else can capture." She manages that by starting her day at 4:30 A.M. "If I am going to have any time to myself, I have to get up before my children do at 6:30," she said. "I get up early and capture that hour. Sometimes people come up to me and try to be social. But that's my prayer hour. You have to set your boundaries. If that is your time, it's your time."

Find Your Space

I am convinced that every woman has to have her own space where she can spend time alone and just "be." Finding that space is another matter. My friend Pam has been putting together her own room for the past week, impatiently moving the furniture, installing a water fountain and hanging pictures so it will be instantly perfect. The other day, she had me come over to see what she'd done. We walked in the room and were astonished by what we saw. Sitting next to her new desk and under one of those beautiful pictures was her husband's briefcase and his laptop computer. As though they belonged there. As though it were his home office, his room, his space. We stood there, slack-jawed and speechless.

Another friend, Teresa, told me there is no room in her home for her to have her own room, so she thought she'd claim a corner of her formal living room for her favorite chair. After all, nobody uses a formal living room, so she might as well make it hers. She made the space warm and spiritual, with candles and other treasures. As soon as it was ready, her teenagers decided they loved that chair more than any chair in the world, and staked it out for themselves. When they weren't in it, the cat was. The only person who didn't have access to that special place was Teresa.

Just about every woman I know who has claimed a space as her own has had to fight a turf war to maintain it. Even if the only space you get to call your own is a chair in the corner, it is worth the fight. Use your space to meditate, journal, read, create, rest and relax. Go there for five minutes or five hours, whatever you can spare. Fill it with your own energy. Decorate it so you own the space. And don't forget to sit the family down and talk about why it is so important that you have a place of your own.

I once visited a friend in California and stretched out on her cushy couch for a glorious afternoon nap. Her living room was so sweetly lit by the sunlight and it was a perfect moment. When she came home from work, I told her how wonderful it was on that couch, in that room. "I've never done that," she said. "Not once, in all these years." Take your time. Take your space. You aren't living for the rest of the world, you are living for *you*.

Breaking Out of a Bad Cycle

One of the biggest challenges to improving your life is just making the decision to break out of a destructive cycle. Kathrine Switzer, the pioneering marathon runner, says that a lot of women she deals with are grossly overweight and have many other health problems. She says many of them are miserable at home, miserable with their kids and are basically paralyzed by some kind of fear to break the cycle. Switzer's advice is that you just have to start. To take an action. Just doing something positive begins the process of change. "The reason I push women to get out to walk or run is that they then take ten or twenty or thirty minutes a day and have a window of time to get things clear and focused," she said. "You also get an endorphin rush from exercise. Most women have never had that before. That allows them to feel positive about something. If you feel positive, you have a sense of hope. If you have hope, you can have courage."

Take a break. Just go outside and walk. Or run. Do something to get out of your rut and take care of yourself. Switzer says that an amazing feeling of empowerment will translate into all areas of your life.

Now come the hardest questions of all. You've grown up. Do you like what you see? Spiritual teacher Brooke Medicine Eagle challenges us to find out what really matters, and then free ourselves to explore a life filled with higher personal rewards. "Often, we have patterns set up that say 'Compete. You'll never get anything in life unless you push somebody else down and get on top of them.' Someone else has to lose in order for you to have what you need," she said. "This is the opposite of the truth that we are all in this together, and that helping each other is how we all can create an abundant, sustaining and happy life. It's certainly not by damaging people or by hurting or competing with one another."

Whoa.

Medicine Eagle said many of us are starting to wake up to that concept. People in business are looking at the bottom line and seeing that it isn't working if they focus only on money. "It is caring and relationships with people that makes business work in the long run," she said. "Thankfully, those values are coming into the workplace. It's worthwhile in both the long and short run to emphasize them. Yet, in order to bring them into the workplace, you must work on yourself in other ways."

She'll show us how. Medicine Eagle begins by working on self-esteem through meditation and reaching into her own "higher self," she said. "Through touching into the great 'Source of Life,' I am stepping out of my intellect and into my heart where things are connected," she said. "As I connect deeply to life, I start to realize that I am an absolutely unique being that has incredible gifts to give. That I and everyone have a powerful kind of uniqueness, which means the gifts I have are rare and no one else is going to bring what I have to give forward."

Slow down!

"Life now is so rush, rush, rush," she said. "It's not workable to rush, rush, rush—hoping life will suddenly be peaceful and nice. Instead, we need to look at the choices we are making by asking these questions: What do I value? My health? My sanity? Being with my family and having my kids feel nurtured and loved? What? Is another car and big wages more important?"

Certainly you've seen people who have chucked it all and left corporate life to do something less financially rewarding but more spiritually fulfilling. I've watched coworkers quit to live on sailboats, teach English in Paris, become massage therapists, major in theology—to name just a few. Many of them took huge pay cuts, learning they could live twice as well on half as much money.

Look at the choices you've made and decide whether they have made things easier, made your family happier and created more goodness for your life. Do you have a real connection with your family, community and friends? Do you get to relax and enjoy your life? Look at your basic values. Look at the connection.

Don't continually tell yourself, "Well, *someday*, I'm going to have enough money to be in a place that I can retire and have everything I want and go where I want and do what I want." What if it never happens? "Most people find out that is not how it works," she said. "Some do retire and find they are beat up or worn out. Or that these retirement communities are awful." Or, that they don't have their health. Or the financial security they expected.

Medicine Eagle suggests meditation as a place to begin. Sit up in bed for fifteen minutes every morning, and do some exercises with your heart. Focus on something you appreciate, perhaps a sunset over the Grand Canyon or the moment your child was put in your arms. Maybe you want to think of a person you appreciate. "Gratitude and appreciation strengthen the heart," she said. "Feeling your own personal heart and your own personal heartbeat, being grateful and appreciative while being still for fifteen minutes centers you and strengthens your heart and the center of your self." She also suggests a five-minute break at your desk where you relax or meditate. Or, mini-naps where you can regroup.

Becoming present in this moment can be a matter of doing something as simple as having a massage that brings attention back to your body, rather than what you need to do at your job. Or, listen to music and feel the soothing energy. Choose something that you absolutely love. Focus on what is important.

It's not enough to make a decision to treasure the moment and live in it. Go deeper, and decide whether you are getting the quality out of your life that you deserve. Do what you value and what means something to you. Decide whether it contributes to life and your children and your community.

If the most significant relationship you have in your life is with your job, then you have made a dangerous choice. The workplace can be unpredictable and harsh. Counting on it for your self-definition and value leaves you in the position of having outside influences measure whether you can feel good about yourself. If times are prosperous and you have a boss who appreciates you, then you may feel wonderful. If you have a bad boss, you won't. Or, if the company has cutbacks or layoffs, you won't. If someone gets promoted ahead of you, you may worry too much that it is a reflection of you as a person, rather than just another day in a crazy work world. If your coworkers are in bad moods or are mean-spirited, you may internalize all of that negativity.

The world around you is so much larger than the room in which you work. It is so important to take time to leave your realm and realize that. I once worked at a newspaper where several newsmen had their ashes encased in the marble walls of the lobby. If anything taught me about balance, it was that oddity. I would never want to be so defined by my job that I'd want my final resting place to be right there in the walls. I want my final resting place to be in the wind.

Getting a Life

- It's just a job, it's just a job, it's just a job.

- Don't wait any longer. If you put other things ahead of yourself, you'll spend your life dying instead of living.

- Make sure you exercise three times a week for thirty minutes at a pop. Movement makes you feel better. If you start with this kind of minimal commitment, you'll be able to maintain it.

- Give yourself time to relax. Your family or your boss can survive without you for ten or twenty minutes a day. That's a start. Walk, read, listen to music, take a bath, light candles. Do something that makes you feel good and alive.

- Drink plenty of water. It's healthy and it makes you feel healthy.

- Respect yourself enough to allow for a good night's sleep.

- Take care of yourself. Protect your body, protect your soul. You don't have to put everyone else's needs ahead of yours.

A MOMENT WITH . . .
ARACELI SEGARRA

She climbed Mount Everest in the IMAX movie *Everest*.

"I don't know whether I was the fifth woman to climb Everest or the twenty-fifth or fiftieth. It's not important.

"On my first attempt on Everest in 1995, I wasn't feeling good. I was cold, I was going to get frostbitten and I wasn't strong enough. So, I decided to go down. The team had spent two years looking for money and preparing for the expedition, and I turned around 2,400 feet below the summit. I didn't care about that summit, especially if getting there would mean I would lose a finger and wouldn't be able to climb again.

"I learned a lot from that. You can lose a lot. But, if you have clear ideas where your limits are, then you can keep trying and trying for the rest of your life. And you can keep enjoying everything.

"People think I am strong and can run a marathon, but I can't. I just go slowly.

"I know my own reasons for climbing. Some people don't climb for the right reason, which is climbing for *you*. There are some people who do it just to be on the list or to be proud in front of other people. You don't have to feel proud in front of anybody if you are doing it for yourself.

"The summit I reached was not the real summit for me. By the time I got there, I'd been climbing nonstop. I'd had no sleep at all—just a little rest. I'd left the tent at midnight and climbed the whole night, and had been climbing the whole day before. So when I got to the summit, I was cold, tired and hadn't eaten at all.

"I wasn't sitting there, looking at the landscape with a nice, warm day and having a picnic. It is thirty degrees below zero. It's like, 'All right, nice view. Let's go down.' Also, you can run out of oxygen if you stay too long and you don't want to do that. And, there is one other thing. The later it gets in the day, the clouds come in and you could get stuck in a storm. Going down, you could get lost.

"We were more excited to reach base camp than we were to get to the summit. It's hard to tell you what I felt when I got down there. That was my team waiting, and I just wanted to hug everybody.

"If I had to choose between the two months of the expedition and the one day of the summit, I would choose the two months. It's about relationships.

"Life is easier than we make it out to be. You are up there on Everest for two months with a drum of your stuff, and you are happy. You come back home and you have light you can turn on and off, a tub with water, a bathroom, a machine to clean your clothes. And, you worry about your car because it has a scratch. You think about that all day and, oh, you forgot the laundry and you forgot the bread. Some people have a bad day just for that.

"Why worry? Look at all the things we have and be happy. I can be happy just sitting on a mountain."

FIFTEEN

FAMILY MATTERS

I USED TO HATE IT when editors would have me ask women of power the question, "How do you do all of this *and* raise a family?" I thought the question was insulting, especially since I was never told to ask it of men. But, after talking with so many women who are trying to do it all, that remains *the* question. How do women do such extraordinary things without letting their home lives fall apart?

All of the women I talked to about this had their own system, touching on everything from carefully selecting a supportive mate to expanding the family circle so no one is neglected. What hit me was how each of the women warmed as they talked about their children and families. It was so heartening to know that the greatest achievements are human, that family counts more than ego or work success. Some admitted sacrificing too much at home—and coming to terms with what they had to do to right the wrong.

I once had a dream that I'd found some quality time to spend with my daughter, but I couldn't even remember where I'd left her. Alas, I decided not to have children. That's why I am floored by stories like the one Dr. Nancy Dickey tells of her adventures in parenting. How did she do it?

Dickey's first pregnancy was during medical school. The second one came during her residency and the third when she went into practice. "It was flying in the face of authority," said Dickey, who made history as the first woman president of the American Medical Association. "This was a new medical school and they hadn't had many students. None of the women had the audacity to get pregnant."

She didn't tell anybody she was pregnant until it showed. She wore a girdle as she interviewed for residency programs all over the country. "It was against the law for them to ask me if I was married, but these guys would say, 'Do you intend to have a family?' I'd say, 'Yes, someday.' Under my breath I'd say, 'Soon.' I figured I wouldn't get good consideration if they knew I was going to have an eight-week-old infant once I started my internship."

Once she'd won her internship, she called to let the program director know. He was good about it, scheduling a lighter rotation right after the baby was born, and the tougher ones after that. Her husband was very supportive and when she was on call he would bring the baby in and wait while she would breast-feed between patients. However, she doesn't recommend that path to other women. Her friends took much better care of themselves as they started their families, but Dickey was so focused on doing what she needed to do professionally that she made sacrifices of herself and her family. In the 1970s, as she set up her practice in Texas, medicine was different. Doctors lived and breathed their work, putting in long, long hours, and Dickey was no different. But, despite the harried life of medicine, she would plan an outing every week where she'd take the children to the beach, the museum or some other special place. When she traveled, she always took one of her children with her. She even coached soccer. But the reality was that if she was going to succeed as a doctor, she had to play the way the men did, putting medicine before everything else. Since the men didn't ask for special considerations because they were parents, she felt that she couldn't ask, either. "I felt that if you had beaten on the door and said, 'I want to come in and play,' you needed to say 'I'll play the same way the rest of you play.' But, as there have been more women come in, they have been able to say, 'Hey, listen. I think there is some foolishness in the way you play.'"

Now, women physicians have time to deal with family issues, as do men. The profession is not as all-consuming as it once was, and that's been good for families and doctors. Physicians have become more aware that they need to preserve their sanity and humanity. "Nowadays, we spend more time with our families," Dickey said. "In some ways, that's not been good for patients because we have created a more impersonal style of care because we aren't there twenty-four hours a day, seven days a week."

Dickey said the question women most commonly ask her is how she juggles multiple roles. "They want to know how they can mix all these roles of wife and mother and community leader and politician and physician and whatever else they have," she said. "No matter how much progress we have made toward equitably sharing roles, at least for my lifetime, it looks like women still carry more than their share in the vast majority of cases." Usually, Dickey laughs and tells them that if they can go without sleeping and eating, they'll save a lot of time. "Seriously. I don't sleep eight hours a night," she said. "I sleep more like five or six hours so I have two to four extra hours to do things."

She also says that choosing the right spouse is essential. If you don't have a partner who is willing to help out, everything will collapse. "I couldn't have possibly done what I've done without a supportive spouse," Dickey said. "If I had to battle a spouse saying, 'Why are you doing that, do you realize you are cutting into my time?' I think that would have been the straw to break the camel's back." She also suggests prioritizing and learning how to delegate those things that can be delegated, like housecleaning. I asked her if she lived that way. "No, I haven't lived that philosophy," Dickey said, "But maybe middle age is telling me you can't do everything all at one time."

Live and learn

By comparison to earlier decades, we now live in an age of enlightenment. At least most of the work world has figured out that career women do get pregnant and can manage to be both a mother and a professional. Yet, enlightenment doesn't do much to help the women—millions of women who find themselves harried and hurried over all of the demands they are trying to satisfy. Who has time to take care of herself, her kids, her job, her mate, her home, her dreams? "Something's got to give," said psychology professor Carol Dweck, of Columbia University. "You can't be perfect at everything, and a woman who can accept that and go on from there is going to have a much easier time than a woman who constantly feels guilty and inadequate for not doing everything a full-time career person can do. They have to face, realistically, what is possible. Admit what help they need and go on from there."

Dr. Maryanne LaFrance agrees. "The idea that anybody can do it all is preposterous. Yet, despite all the beliefs that a lot of modern marriages are egalitarian and have the assumption of shared child care and domestic efforts, women still do the majority—if not the totality of the domestic side of work. Even if they are working fifty, sixty, seventy hours a week at a job, women still seem to bear the brunt of the burden. They are also supposed to be great moms, great hostesses, have the perfect house, perfect meals, perfect children, perfect hairdo and perfect whatever," said the Yale psychology professor. "I don't think that has changed."

LaFrance knows some lawyers who realized they couldn't have their work obligations, child obligations *and* home obligations all at once. So, they decided to just let go of the housework. "The house was a mess," she said. "They deliberately decided to let it go. But, in most houses, they aren't able to do that." Instead, they figure out other alternatives.

The Woman in the House

When Pat Schroeder went to Congress in 1972, reporters asked her what she feared most. "Losing my housekeeper," she said. "Editorials slammed me for being so petty," she recalls. "They wanted me to say something very profound, like what I feared most was not being able to move a major bill in my first term. Hell, that's easy. That was a piece of cake. They didn't understand. I would say, 'There is no member of Congress who is in the jeopardy I'm in if my housekeeper leaves. If my housekeeper leaves, my life stops.'"

Schroeder's main key was putting family first. "If it wasn't, the whole thing would unravel like gangbusters," she said. "I put down all sorts of rules. I'll do breakfast, I'll do lunch, but I don't do dinner. Half the time we'd be in session, so I'd have my family come in and use the House dining room. A lot of people would say, 'I can't believe they're eating in the House dining room.' Well, where else are you going to eat with them? My children would even do homework in the office. You have to work it out." She felt extra pressure to make it work, knowing that people were watching to see if she failed her family. Men may have failed their families in order to pursue their politics, but Schroeder knew she couldn't. She literally operated on two or three hours of sleep and felt fortunate to get through it.

Looking back on it, there are whole years she can't reconstruct. "I know we had Christmas, but I don't know where it was," she said. "It was just a very busy time. My husband was supportive—pretty amazing for that generation. It doesn't mean he ran around and did everything. He wasn't Mr. Mom. But, he was very supportive. Most men his age were just horrified."

The Real Home Computer

ABC News star Cokie Roberts thinks what talk-show host and columnist Chris Matthews told her was especially insightful. He said that every household has a computer that keeps track of the immunizations, meals, stocking of the refrigerator, washing the clothes, getting the birthdays straight and picking up the dry cleaning—and that computer is the wife's brain.

"That's true," she said. "We don't even think about it, that's what we do. We try to get some help and whether that comes in the form of child care or a husband or whatever, but I look back on the years when the kids were home and I was working unbelievably hard and I don't know quite how I did do it. We didn't have very much money. I didn't have some fabulous nanny who ran my life. We had sitters and an au pair who would take care of the kids, but there was nobody going to the grocery store, getting kids to lessons and all of that. I just sort of did it. Put one foot in front of the other." When her children were young, she remembers how her friends' mothers set about instilling guilt in them for working and not doing enough for their children. Her mother, the spirited former Congresswoman Lindy Boggs, stepped in and told Roberts, "Cokie, your kids are fine. Give it a rest." "I think she is right," Roberts said. "That angst can give kids a sense that they aren't competent people and need to be angsted over all the time."

She took her lead in child rearing from what she learned from her own parents. Her father, the late Congressman (and Democratic Majority Leader) Hale Boggs of New Orleans, took his children seriously. She learned to do that with her own kids. "Children are intelligent beings whose views should be taken seriously," she said. "Political views, views on books— include them in the conversation. We always had family dinner—at 9 o'clock. My kids revealed years later that they'd already eaten at six at their friends' and then they'd come eat again at our house. Sunday dinner was my absolute favorite. Nobody was allowed out. That was a period of conversation. It was sometimes unpleasant when the children were at each other, but we'd share views and everyone's views were taken seriously."

The need to prioritize is obvious when a woman has so many demands on her. Sometimes, something happens to make them realize their priorities are way out of whack. Think of it as a wake-up call. As a senior executive with Time Warner Cable, Gayle Greer was on the road about 80 percent of the time, usually leaving her son behind. "I will never forget the day when he was a senior in high school and he asked me if I would be traveling on a certain day because a couple of coaches wanted to talk to me about a college scholarship," she said. "It blew me away. College? I hadn't even thought about it. I wasn't living in the present. I was so intensely holding on to whatever it was, keeping all the balls up in the air. Then it dawned on me, this kid is leaving. I became a much better parent."

She had always tried to prioritize what was important in terms of managing her career and being a good mother. Timing was the biggest challenge, she said. "It's the PTA meeting versus the board meeting," Greer said. "Do you take this business trip? Do you take him with you? Or, do you try to send somebody else? It's always juggling time." The other challenge is one of companionship. Greer missed having a second parent to help, since she was a single parent from the time her son was twelve to nineteen. "It's a huge job to raise a child. It's the biggest job I have seen. It's even harder when it is one person trying to do it. I think there is something about two parents raising a child that is very important. It is difficult when you don't have that companion, and it's difficult when you don't have that second point of view. The kid has to deal with one person."

That meeting with the coach deeply affected Greer. She said she questioned whether she'd been a good parent. Greer never missed one of her son's football games after that. The two have built an extremely close relationship. The last time we chatted, Greer told me she couldn't focus on anything other than the wonders of being a grandmother. Her daughter-in-law went into labor unexpectedly, and who was the only person there to coach her in delivery? Greer, the former workaholic.

Labor union pioneer, Linda Chavez-Thompson, had her own wake-up call as well. She'd been working long hours and traveling a great deal for her position with the international labor union. She eventually gave that position up because it interfered with raising her daughter. "I'd taken her away from my mother when we moved to San Antonio and I was only home every other weekend. I was working around Texas and she'd say, 'Mom, I want you home right now.'" Her daughter was only seven at the time, and she'd cry when she'd talk with Chavez-Thompson.

So, she quit the international job and took a pay cut. But she was able to be at home with her daughter. She worked at the local union from 1973 to

1995 as assistant business manager, then business manager, then executive director of the office in San Antonio. As her daughter grew, so did Chavez-Thompson's influence, culminating with her post as executive vice president of the AFL-CIO. How does she feel? She says, "I am very fortunate. I have done what is good for what I believe in, what's good for my children, my local union, my international. It's what I hold in my heart. It takes stamina, and it's worth it."

The Solo Path

If it's hard in two-parent households, imagine the challenges faced by women raising their children alone. Right now, Census data show there are 20 million children under eighteen being raised in single-parent households—that's about 28 percent of all children. And, 84 percent of those children are living with their moms.

Fifteen years ago, Claudia Laird was building her career in a male-dominated industry (her company manufactures polyethylene tubing) when she divorced. She tried to figure out how to manage her 2- and 5-year-old sons while keeping her career on course. "One misstep financially or healthwise, and I'd be in a really tough place," remembers Laird. "My mission was to be sure I had a flexible schedule. I had to have a lot of flexibility. And, I was in a situation where what counted was that I got my work done. It didn't matter what time I did it, or where I was. Sometimes, that meant getting up at 3 A.M. so I could leave at 2 or 3 P.M. You talk about juggling. You just do what you have to do."

She knows she missed some of their ball games, but she did the best she could to be everywhere at once. Like most single parents, the toughest moments came when somebody got sick. "Then, the whole thing can fall down," she said. "There's such a domino effect." She managed raising her children while advancing her career. She heads LIDCO, the tubing company, is president of CATALYSTIC, an Internet company, and even is producing films. All of that comes second to her boys she says. "My

> "You can do anything, but you can't do everything. You cannot be everything to everyone at one time.... You have to set realistic expectations for yourself, and let the human dynamic come ahead of whether or not you have changed the linens every Monday, faithfully and religiously. You can't be saturated with responsibility twenty-four hours a day, seven days a week. You can't do it all. It's time to accept that."
>
> —*Marilyn Ware, chairwoman of the board of American Water Works*

view on parenting is that you need to respect the fact that you brought them into this world," Laird said. "They didn't ask you to bring them here."

One bit of wisdom that the mentors offered repeatedly was this: Know when you need to ask for help. Then, ask. Whether you are parenting on your own or with a partner, don't try to do it all alone, advised Aida Alvarez, who led the Small Business Administration and served on the Cabinet through the Clinton years. You don't have to be in it alone.

"I'm often asked how I do so much at once. The way you do it is you recognize that having children is a partnership with more than one person," said Alvarez, who had an eight-year-old daughter and a stepdaughter in college at the time of our interview. Alvarez copes with the demands of parenthood by expanding her family of caretakers to include others. "We all have families in one form or another, by blood or closeness," she said. "If we only looked at ourselves as part of a bigger unit, it wouldn't be so intimidating to have children. Children benefit from having different caretakers, different parents. It's not just a relationship between a father and mother."

She considers herself lucky because her mother stayed with her family for the first six years of her daughter's life. There are good baby-sitters, there are aunts and uncles and so many other people who want the opportunity to share in parenting, she added. And, there is always day care. Just make sure you investigate who is taking care of your children by checking the day-care center's records with the state's licensing agency. If you are hiring a nanny, go to the police department and pay for a criminal background check or try a search online.

"Instead of thinking it is all the responsibility of one person—usually the mother—realize it's a responsibility and a joy to be shared by all," she said. "I am actually encouraged as I meet a lot of women juggling families and careers who are taking turns with others. There are many more stories about househusbands, men who work at home or stay home with the children. There is more openness about discussing the possibilities. People are less tied to the old, rigid roles."

The Toughest Role

Acting in some of the most challenging roles in Hollywood is the easy part for Academy Award winner Frances McDormand, who is probably best known for her role in *Fargo*. Parenting is so much tougher. "Controlled chaos is easier than spontaneous chaos for me," McDormand said.

When You Have Too Much To Do and No Time To Do It

Prioritize and organize. Have a "to do" list for every day, and try to get through it. Make tomorrow's list at the end of your workday. Don't over-schedule your life.

Focus. Know what your major goals are for the week and don't get distracted.

Know when you are at your best. If you are most productive between 3 P.M. and 5 P.M., that's when you should be doing the hardest work. Never fritter away your peak hours on phone calls or other distractions.

Clean up your mess. Clutter makes it harder to do your job.

Quit procrastinating. Just do the hard or unpleasant tasks you have to do first and don't lose time worrying about them.

Set deadlines. Know how long each assignment should take, and try to complete it on schedule.

Don't get stuck in the mud. If things aren't clicking with what you are doing, either take a break or switch to another assignment and come back to it when your mind is refreshed.

Use your commute to your advantage. Do work or read when you are on mass transit. If you are in the car, listen to tapes. Have work with you when you are waiting for meetings in other offices.

Schedule alone time. Clear your mind and focus on what you need to do and how you intend to do it. Or do nothing. Let your mind and body rest.

Have smart meetings. Have an agenda, and send it around before the meeting. If you have a choice, use it to decide which meetings you will attend. Handle what you can in e-mails and conference calls, but when you meet, don't let things drag on endlessly.

Delegate. Don't be proud or stupid about doing what other people are able to do. You don't have to do it all, you just have to see that it gets done right. That goes for career work and housework.

Return phone calls during lunch. Leave a voice message, that way you spend one minute instead of ten connecting.

Know what counts. Few people will ever remember which meetings you missed, but your children and spouse will never forget.

Consider your timing. Maybe you would rather jump off the fast track while your children are young.

She mused on a play she'd done seven times a week that included a one and a half-hour monologue, a bunch of rolling on the floor and throwing herself around the stage. "That was a breeze," she said, "whereas Sunday I had a bowling party for my son's fifth birthday. I needed Valium. I was begging someone for it. I had a glass of wine at four in the afternoon. This was extraordinary. There is something about the structured, organized chaos of my professional life that does not tend to prepare me in any way for my personal life, my private life." She wondered whether that would come with practice. She'd been acting for twenty-five years, and doing "the motherhood thing" for just five. When she's out on acting jobs, she can check in and out of her work. She's never done a theater production for more than three months, and she's not interested in doing a television series that lasts seven years. According to her, the thrill of the job is that it keeps changing. But with parenting she says, "After three months of knowing my son, I thought, 'Okay, now that's done.' Then I thought, 'No, it isn't. It's going to change constantly. You'll never stop, because this is for the rest of your life.'"

> *Delegate.* Don't be proud or stupid about doing what other people are able to do. You don't have to do it all, you just have to see that it gets done right. That goes for career work and housework.
>
> *Return phone calls during lunch.* Leave a voice message, that way you spend one minute instead of ten connecting.
>
> *Know what counts.* Few people will ever remember which meetings you missed, but your children and spouse will never forget.
>
> *Consider your timing.* Maybe you would rather jump off the fast track while your children are young.

McDormand and her husband, director Joel Coen, adopted their son, Pedro, when he was six months old. "I have always had a knowledge that I wanted to be a parent," she said. "I always wanted to have a kid. We tried biologically, and it didn't work." She and her husband waged the same infertility struggle that affects more than 4.5 million American couples each year. "During the whole reproductive investigation that often happens with older people trying to get pregnant, it was up to me to make the decisions because, after all, it was my body," she said. "Frankly, I was lucky I was with a partner who knew that. I still had to make the decision about what medical steps I was going to try. But, once we started the process of adoption, it became so much more equalized. The idea of adopting was always an easy thought for me because I am adopted, as well." When she'd feel shaky about it, Joel felt strong. When he was getting nervous, she felt more positive. Then they met Pedro, the South American baby who became their son. "After that, you don't have time to worry about things," she said. "You just go with it."

All Things Being Equal

Leading New Zealand as its first woman prime minister, Jenny Shipley had to count on the partnership with her husband, Burton, when it came to parenthood. He was the one who convinced her that she could raise her children and go into politics, and he helped make it happen. "Burton would bundle them up and take them with him as he worked around the farm," she remembered. "If one wanted to stay home, he'd say 'Mothers do things too. Ben, you're coming with me.' There is a very supportive and shared responsibility. I am fortunate in that respect."

Not that it's been a breeze. Her family is like any other with the usual conflicts and challenges. To make it work, they carved out family time, and have been fiercely protective of it. "When my children were smaller, we had a family diary and if they wanted to do something, they wrote it in the diary. Each Sunday, the family would sit down and we would talk about what I had to do and what they needed to do. Everyone was respectful of each other's needs. It wasn't always Mum who would do it. It might be Burton, it might be Granny, but it still saw that the needs of the children were met and recognized."

Burton was at the forefront of men acting as a full-time caregiver. Even though he was self-employed on their farm, he was the one who went on school trips and the like. "He broke a lot of those molds for children to see and he broke down attitudes in the quite conservative community in which we live," Shipley said. "It's worked." She was taught to believe in herself and that's what she wants for her own children. She says her daughter has grown up to be self-assured and at twenty-two "is her own person." And, her son? His unusual upbringing has translated into an open-minded approach to gender roles. "He melts my heart at one look, and he's a very able young man as well," she said. "He is an extraordinary commentary on a child who has grown up with fathers and mothers doing substitute roles. Ben thinks men need to cook dinners and clean and do family housework. We had to do that, chip in, in their earlier years if we wanted to go skiing and do what families like to do. The roles got merged and muddled. Ben has to be the most wonderful catch for any female because he has no hang-ups about men and women doing particular things. He is likely to say, 'I'll cook tea tonight' and do it with flair and panache."

So, there's the reward. Whether you are running a country or making it at your day job, you make the sacrifice and you wind up with one of those incredible human beings that you helped create. All of that difficulty, and look what happens in the end.

For Dr. Bernadine Healy, the former executive director of the American Red Cross, the reward of motherhood was far greater than anything she experienced professionally, as she opened the doors to research in women's health. But to her, parenting alone was by far, the more frightful challenge. "My daughter was an infant when I became a single mother," said Healy. "I became the breadwinner, working as an associate professor and running a cardiac care unit. I had no choice but to work. I had to support my baby. I was scared." It was a difficult time, she said, but it was also a beautiful time. "When my daughter tells me about the strength I gave her, I think it was woven into our relationship when she was born," she said. "I respect her and admire her. Sometimes you encounter these cruel, prejudicial concepts, like single mothers are bad or working mothers are bad. Society's ills are blamed on these 'social deviants.' Learn to understand people, one by one, face-to-face, and don't make these general comments. Likewise, you can't receive those signals, either. Don't let people beat you down or build you up for what you are."

Healy's daughter, now in her twenties, wrote her mother a letter before Healy underwent surgery. "Everytime I look at it, I am overwhelmed," she said. "She said the greatest gift I gave her was her strength. If I can give my daughter a sense of values, a good work ethic and a sense of strength to know she can handle life's ups and downs, then I have succeeded."

Lessons from Mom and Dad

"My father and mother fostered the belief that we should be the best we could be. They didn't put on any expectations or limitations. They encouraged us to take responsibility and set career goals and get on with it. I was brought up to expect to be treated as equal and to act as equal, as well. We were encouraged to form our own opinions. That is very much what led me to be the person who I am today. Quietly confident to believe I am as able as anyone else to lead a country."
—Jenny Shipley, former prime minister of New Zealand

"My parents were my role models. They taught me about justice. There's nothing more important than education, that the sky was the limit, or maybe not the limit, that we could do anything we wanted to do. But, we had to be good people. Fair, decent, law-abiding. And we had to love this country."
—Helen Thomas, legend of journalism

"I can't recall ever being made mindful by my parents of girls do, boys don't, or boys do and girls don't. It was about my talents as an individual. I was never confronted by that conflict in signals. When we were kids, we would set off on a Saturday morning on our skateboards or bicycles or skates or just our feet, and we had nothing we were going to do in particular, except to go off exploring. There was nothing nefarious or mischievous. We just wanted to see what all was out there."
—Astronaut Kathryn Sullivan

"When I was born, I was always told I was the best baby born in the world. I was nurtured by my parents, grandparents, aunts, uncles and all their associates. So there were three, four or five people at nursery school graduations. All of our siblings got that. Our community was very important. When we went to my mother's church, they wouldn't ask if I was going to college, it was, 'Where are you going to college?' Then they'd put five dollars in my hand and say, 'You go there and do well. You need to be class valedictorian.' I thought, 'Dang, I need to do well.' I went to college with the confidence that they knew I would succeed."
—Rev. Suzan Johnson Cook, author and pastor

"I grew up in a family where both my father and mother inspired me and my brother and sister to believe we could do anything we wanted to do. There was never any conversation or inference in my upbringing that women could do this and men could do that. That women are this way and men are that way."
—Carly Fiorina, CEO, Hewlett-Packard

"Nobody in my family ever told us that there were things we couldn't do because we were female, or things we couldn't do because we were poor or things we couldn't do because we were Native American. When I hear such admonitions from other parents, it makes me grateful for how I was raised. We didn't feel there were limits on what we could do. Growing up, we learned about interdependence by watching people barter. People had milk or bread or fruit, and they would trade. We had a sense that

everyone was dependent on everyone else for survival. But, the single most important lesson I learned by watching people in my community is that it is important to have a good attitude and keep your mind free of negative thoughts. That's what I observed. I saw people facing the most daunting sense of personal or financial problems, yet they always found something positive in their situation. That had a profound impact on the way I looked at the world. And, it impacted the way I look at other people. They looked at the positive, rather than the negative. That's important. When you meet people, you can focus on the positive attributes rather than the negative ones. It's your choice."
—Wilma Mankiller, first woman to lead the Cherokee Nation as principal chief

"I remember what my dad said when I called to tell him I'd made one star. He let out a yell, then he said, 'OK, celebrate tonight. Tomorrow morning get working on that second star.' Pushy, pushy, pushy. There were no women two-stars."
—Ret. Gen. Claudia Kennedy, U.S. Army

"The four visions my mom left me are, 'Always do your best, that's good enough;' 'Never throw away your tomorrows worrying about yesterday;' 'The day you see the truth and cease to speak is the day you die;' and 'If you want to get out of the cotton patch, you have to get something in your head.' "
—Dr. Joycelyn Elders, former U.S. surgeon general

A MOMENT WITH . . .

WILMA MANKILLER

First Woman Chief of the Cherokee Nation

"I didn't set out with any grand goal to be actively engaged in the world around me. I wanted to love life and do what I could in my own way to help people around me and be of service in some way. Whether I have accomplished that is for others to judge. But, I have lived a full and active life with incredible opportunities.

"Growing up in the Cherokee community, I saw people facing the most daunting sense of personal or financial problems, yet they always found something positive in their situation. That had a profound impact on the way I looked at the world. And, it impacted the way I look at other people.

"When I was growing up, we went to California on a Bureau of Indian Affairs relocation program and took a step backward. We were left in rough housing projects where there were no female role models, no support of the extended Cherokee family or the Cherokee community. There were no female professionals in my community. No one I knew in my immediate circle of friends was even going to college.

"But living in the Bay Area had an impact on me. I was coming of age during the beginnings of the women's movement, the anti-war movement, the Red Power movement, the civil rights movement. There were changes in the music, changes in how we thought and how we lived. It was a tremendous time of change in the country and it touched me in a very real way.

"I saw women—not just men—but women speaking up on important issues. They weren't just standing in support of men, but they were stepping up and taking leadership positions for themselves. That had a big impact on the way I looked at women and the possibilities for women.

"When I ran for election in 1983, I took every dime of savings I had and used it on the campaign. That was risk. I have never regretted that.

"We live in a relatively conservative area in eastern Oklahoma and I expected my politics to be the issue. I'd been involved in many things that would be considered liberal or even radical. I thought those would be the issue. They weren't.

"The issue was my being a woman, and I wouldn't have it.

"I simply told myself that it was a foolish issue, and I wouldn't argue with a fool. I ignored it and focused on the real issues. When it would come up and someone would say, 'You're a woman, how will that affect your leadership,' I said 'Thanks for asking, now lets talk about health care.'

"I did have my tires slashed. And one time when I was marching in a parade, a fellow folded his hand into the shape of a gun and did a pretend shooting of me as I walked on the parade route. That somehow bothered me more than anything. There were other things, like people burning down my signs on the billboards, but it was that man that I remember most.

I could have dwelled on the hateful things people were saying to me, but I'd have lost the election.

"We are all interconnected, not only on one another for survival, but on the natural world for the survival of the earth itself. It is very, very important for people to remember that. There is an increasing sense of isolation. Individuals isolate themselves from one another. There appears to be less involvement in the outside world. But it is important to stay involved and realize how dependent we are on one another for survival."

SIXTEEN

IT'S OUR TURN

ON ROBBEN ISLAND, WHERE NELSON Mandela was incarcerated, the prisoners had a motto, "Each one, reach one." The imprisoned doctors, lawyers and other learned men all took responsibility for educating each other. "From that grew the mighty anti-Apartheid movement," said Nobel Peace laureate Betty Williams. "We women need to do that for each other. I know that one person can make a difference."

Too many of us are lost in our own daily hassles to worry about taking care of the rest of the world. After all, we have it pretty good. We have good jobs, make fairly good money, and experience greater opportunity every day. So many of our frustrations are momentary. There doesn't seem to be much cause to start a woman's revolution now because the revolution happened already and we are receiving great benefits from it. But, why is it that most of us look with admiration to women like Williams who try to make the world better, but we don't take the initiative to personally get involved and help?

After Williams won the Nobel Prize, she was invited to travel throughout the world and see some of the conditions children endure. Her horror led her to establish the World Centers of Compassion for Children and lead a new crusade driven again by her sense of injustice.

There are mornings when she gets up and doesn't want to do what she knows she must. "I'm a human being. We all get tired of it," she said. "The trip I leave on tomorrow is going to be strenuous and grueling—ten days, three time zones. I thought this morning, 'I don't want to do this Russian trip.' But within 10 minutes, I'm saying to myself, 'Stop being selfish.' Then I go and I see the children in the orphanages and I'm angry one more time."

One person can make a difference. Find your calling. Don't let anyone pick your issues or tell you how you should think about them. But, don't be silent and don't choose ignorance. Be active in this world. And, if you are ready to help other women, that's great, because we need your help. We have a generation clash that is alive and well in the women's movement today. Some of the women who devoted their lives for the advances we enjoy today see too few of us standing up and pushing for more. We have come so far, but we have so much further to go. The women who brought us to this point want to know why we're standing around, idling.

The big problem is, the injustice isn't as visible as it used to be when women were fighting for basic equality and reproductive rights. Young women today don't experience what it was like to be prohibited from applying for certain jobs, playing in sports, working while pregnant, etc. The discrimination against women used to be blatant. Sarah Weddington, the attorney who won *Roe v. Wade* against the U.S. Supreme Court, remembers, "They always said 'Women don't, women can't, women shouldn't.' I got so tired of hearing it." When she finished law school, she was told she could not apply for a credit card without her husband's signature. It didn't matter that *she* was the one putting *him* through law school. She waited until she ran for the legislature and passed the equal credit bill. Then she got her own credit card.

Faye Wattleton who heads the Center for Gender Equity says she has heard others complain that younger women are not as active as they were. But she says, "I'm not sure that is true. We often think that others have to have our precise experiences to understand what we are talking about. I give younger women more credit than that."

Why the clash between women? Perhaps those who fought so hard expect younger women to be carbon copies of the women who came before them, she suggests. "The younger ones haven't seen women die from illegal abortions," she said. "The conditions are different. Through our behavior, they can see how we deal with injustices out of our own experience. We came to the positions that we did out of our experiences. They will, likewise." What does matter is that women stick together and support one another.

She's right. We *are* a majority, but we act like a minority. We don't have to be monoliths, but we should get it together on issues of importance. "Women certainly haven't achieved the power of the vote and if you look at the representation of women in elective office, it's a sorry state of affairs. We still have a long way to go. Social movements don't often happen with great flair and drama. They often have breakthroughs, like women having the right to vote. But transforming that right and its powerful potential into reality is the long work of history," Wattleton adds. And the impact of our support is not only for the individual woman, but for all women.

Changing things is scary but extremely important. "Do other women see you standing out against injustice?" she asked. "Do they see you standing out in support of other women? Do they see you out there trying to reconcile community strife? Younger women need the benefit of conversation about social responsibility and what it means to be obliged to give something back, for the privilege of their privilege. Keep fighting," Wattleton urges.

Sarah Weddington remembers the jubilation after *Roe v. Wade* was won. "We had the sense that the words of *Roe v. Wade* had been written in granite in indelible ink." How wrong they were. The forces opposed to abortion came back, and they are still mighty. She says it is much easier to rally forces to change things than it is to get them to stand up and say, "Let's keep things as they are." Keeping abortion safe and available has proven to be the toughest test, she said, because few people under forty-five can remember what it was like before *Roe v. Wade*. They've grown up knowing that if they want an abortion, most can get one that is safe and legal.

"There is such a tendency for people to assume that the problems have been solved and that discrimination does not exist," Weddington said. "When they do run into discrimination, they tend to say 'What have *I* done that was wrong?' " But, when something bad happens, you need to take a careful look at the situation. Maybe you are not to blame. Maybe you've just butted up against some of that old, sexist behavior."

Several years ago, I worked on a year-long series on domestic violence that provoked quite a reaction from the editor of my paper. While working on the project, I met some of the strongest women I'd ever encountered. These activists kept talking about people who "get it" and people who don't. At first, I kept wondering, get *what*? And I remember that once I got it I wished I hadn't figured it out. Life was so much easier when I didn't know.

I'd always felt that as a female investigative reporter, I had received the same pay, support and attention as any of my male counterparts. It wasn't until I started writing about women's issues that I learned how threatening this was to the old order, and how fiercely they would guard their positions.

The moment when I "got it" was when a top editor of the paper came back from vacation and became enraged when he saw his Sunday paper, which led with the first installment of the domestic violence series. I had reported on the week I'd spent at the Denver SafeHouse, and the photograph of a woman with two black eyes took up most of the front page. *"Everyone knows women get beaten,"* he huffed at me later. *"No one wants to read about it."* A couple of months later, another editor criticized a column I had written about some of the sexist remarks lobbed at me while I was covering the legislature. *"It's not as though they took their dicks out and exposed themselves to you,"* he snarled.

Oh. I GET IT.

But, too many women don't get it because they take their freedom for granted, especially if they haven't been directly affected by discrimination. "They wonder, 'What *is* the problem?'" said former Congresswoman Pat Schroeder. "One of the most shocking days I ever had was going to the first class of graduating women at the Air Force Academy. They just lit into me. They didn't know what the hell I was talking about, because they'd never been discriminated against." But, think. If any of those women grads had been born even a year earlier, they wouldn't have even been allowed to attend the Academy.

If we don't push for change, change won't happen she reminds us. And look at the amount of stress women deal with because issues like day care aren't addressed. "We wouldn't have the vote if it hadn't been for a lot of women going and chaining themselves to the White House in their lovely white dresses," Schroeder said. "Women were the first to picket the White House. If we knew our history, I think we'd all have to say we are acting like wimps today. Our foremothers would say, 'We did all of this and you won't risk speaking up about day care?'"

But Wait! What About the Third Wave?

The Suffragists were the first wave. The feminists of the 1960s and 1970s were the second wave as they fought for economic rights, reproductive freedom and educational opportunity. And the third wave is the group of feminists born sometime around the late 1960s or early 1970s.

"We are the first generation of women who knew about feminism from the time we were born," says Kim Allen, one of the leaders of

3rdwwwave.com, a web home for voices of new feminists. "We've always known there was a women's movement. It is expected that women should have equal rights. We're the first generation to experience that our whole lives. Because of the work of the past feminists, we can finally afford to disagree. We can pick and choose our own political agenda rather than adhering to just one. This is democracy. We all have our own voice, just like men."

One of her colleagues, Janis Cortese, said she knows the women leaders who preceded her are wondering where the feminists are. "It's a problem of perspective," she said. "The second wave was like the beachhead assault team. After the beachhead was secured, we came in like the feminist corps of engineers. We're back there building the bridges and the Quonset huts. The front-line troops don't think we are doing anything because they are standing on the beach asking where we are. We're breaking our backs setting up the tents and bridges. Feminism now extends much further than that first beachhead."

What tents? What bridges?

Cortese says it's a daily challenge. She works as director of marketing for a male-dominated telecommunications company. "What I'm doing as a woman performing my job in a competent fashion and gaining their trust by simply doing my job is more effective than any slogans or sign waving could ever be. The day-to-day things ink into their minds every day." She believes that young women are making their contribution, she said, even if they aren't conscious of it.

What's Left

If we look at the larger picture, there is so much to celebrate. We break barriers every day and enjoy a degree of opportunity and promise that women couldn't have imagined even thirty years ago. Still, we have so much more work to do. We've lost our momentum, and we have to find it again.

You are busy. Many of these issues are not on the front burner anymore. It's harder to mobilize when the masses aren't feeling the sting of injustice, but the injustice is there. If you and every other woman in America would just take two minutes every month to send one letter or e-mail to lawmakers or corporate decision makers, almost two billion opinions would be expressed! If every one of us gave one dollar a month toward our issues, that would be $2 billion! What if everyone gave two dollars a year to breast cancer research? That's $280 million worth of research. Imagine what would happen if all 140 million of us stopped buying products from a given company. Or if we really did get it together on an issue like gun control. Thanks to technology, it takes very little effort to make our opinions known. It also makes it easier to offer financial support to our causes. The women in this country are 140 million strong! Let's use our strength.

Back in the 1970s, when Betty Williams mobilized the women of Northern Ireland together in protest against the violence, she knocked on doors and talked to newspapers. Today, she could reach millions with a good list of e-mail addresses.

I much prefer thinking the world is wonderful rather than focusing on what's wrong, and I generally avoid people who go on spewing negativity. It makes me uncomfortable. But, somewhere along the way, friends started confiding in me. I have lost count of the number of friends who were sexually abused by fathers and uncles. Some were battered by their families or spouses. Others were raped. Then there were the ones who were completely devastated financially in divorces. And I've had so many friends express such frustration over being discriminated against at work. One, who was a top-ranking police official, endured screaming tantrums by her chief, and one time, he actually *threw furniture* at her. I've had friends who were so undermined by their male coworkers that their computers were hacked into and paperwork stolen. And I've had too many friends who have been stricken with breast or ovarian cancer.

One of my best friends, lawyer Jeanne Elliott, was gunned down in the courtroom and paralyzed by a client's enraged husband in a divorce case. He was a cop. All she did was fight for fairness for his wife, who had been battered during the relationship. He served less than 15 years, but Jeanne will never walk again. We don't all have to commit our lives to crusades to right the wrongs of the world, but we owe it to women like Jeanne to carry on and be strong. Every one of us needs to become involved because if we don't, our collective strength will be wasted.

> "Because the word 'feminist' is not easy to wear, I feel obliged to say, 'Yes, I am a feminist.' As a trade unionist, I had to fight with the same energy for equal pay. I feel for the women who were attacked because they said they were feminists. There are so many reasons to push for equal opportunity. You cannot just spoil half of the labor force."
> —*Ruth Dreifuss, first woman president of Switzerland*

Joycelyn Elders says to make your voice heard and learn how to make your point so you can maximize your effectiveness. Elders makes sure she is ready for anything, no matter how much resistance she encounters. "Don't back down," she said. "Once you do that, you've been had. Decide the points you are going to make. Organize them and try to get everyone to come to the same place where you are. I always end it by asking, 'What is *your* role in changing this? What can *you* do to make a difference?'"

For a woman who was fired for her frankness as U.S. surgeon general, Elders has a wonderful sense of calm and purpose. "I have absolutely nothing to lose by speaking my mind. I have long since accomplished more than I ever thought I would," she said. "I'd done that long before I even went to Washington, so when I got there, I had nothing to lose. I had nothing to lose then, I have nothing to lose now. That's true freedom."

She knows the power of one.

What One Person Can Do

Jane Goodall. Now that is one amazing woman.

The famed primate researcher and anthropologist has set up programs in twenty-seven villages near her research center in Gombe, trying to help impoverished women gain education, skills and self-esteem. The average family there has seven children. Goodall's people work to educate the girls in hopes that the birth rate will drop. "The excitement of it is being able to have an impact," she said.

We affect the world by our choices she says. We don't have to buy cosmetics tested on animals. We don't have to buy genetically engineered food or products made in far-off countries with child slave labor. We shouldn't support environmentally unfriendly companies, either. She reminds us that we can use our power by choosing what or what not to buy. And this kind of thinking will help the future for our grandchildren.

Too many people feel that society owes them something, rather than the reverse. "What's happened to us? Does it make sense that you can sue a company when you are stupid enough to burn yourself with hot coffee? They've done a huge disservice because it's hard to find a cup of hot coffee anymore. We take so much for granted today and it is so easy for people to grouse about what they don't get. Something costs too much. They had to wait in a line. You just say, 'Imagine being a Kosovo refugee.' Imagine being a woman in Afghanistan who can't even go to a doctor because men aren't allowed to look at women and women aren't allowed to be doctors. There are ethnic cleansings going on around the world. But, people get angry that someone is driving too slow and there's all of this road rage. Or they get angry when they get held up on an airplane because there's a technical fault and they have to get off. They get angry and shout at the personnel who had nothing to do with it. Would they rather be in the air and have a crash? Is that what they want?"

Goodall suggests contributing to the greater good of society, to do your share. "Maybe it's boring in your workplace, but work isn't the only part of your life," she said. "You have evenings, weekends, holidays. We can influence other people by what we say and what our attitudes are. Even in the most boring job, you can make a difference with your fellow workers, just with your attitude."

Most of Goodall's time is spent traveling the world with her message. That message? DO SOMETHING. "Every individual matters, has a role to play and makes a difference," she said. "We have this huge collective power—if only we'd use it. But, we have this great 'me-ism.' You know, 'I'm one person. I live in an expanding world of people. What can I do to make any difference?' It's apathy. What we do makes a difference for the future."

Without Women, Everything Stops

Perhaps one of the most powerful stories I heard in researching this book was shared by Ruth Dreifuss, the first woman to serve as president of Switzerland. Dreifuss, a strong feminist whose desk sits in front of a poster of women protesting for labor rights in the 1950s, tells of the historic women's strike in her country in 1991:

"Twenty years after having reached civil rights and ten years after having reached new laws on marriage and five years after having reached a law on equal opportunity and looking around and counting the number of women in Parliament as heads of corporations, the women said, 'If we do not show where we are and what we are doing, we will not progress,'" she said.

They showed their power in one day. The women of her country of seven million people decided that on that day, June 14, they would all wear the same color—pink.

"It was a general call for women to stop work or to go out at least for a few hours and join women on the streets," Dreifuss said. Not just women in the workplace, but women at home too. "We had more than a half a million women in pink," she recalled. "It was impossible not to see that women were everywhere.

"The slogan was, 'Without women, everything stops.'"

Can you imagine what we could accomplish in this country if we all banded together for one another and stood still for ten minutes?

Dreifuss wears a pin of the sun as her trademark symbol. "We were too long in the shadow," she said. "Let us come out of the shadow."

Coming Out from the Shadow

So, if you think you are one of those women who are too busy to do anything, below is a list of ten things you can do in less than ten minutes. If you have ten minutes, you *do* have the time and you *can* make a difference. Don't be silent about your opinions and don't ignore the issues of the day.

Ten Things You Can Do in Less Than Ten Minutes

1. E-mail a public official. Letters or faxes are even better.

2. E-mail the "letters to the editor" section of the newspaper.

3. Send a quick e-mail to all your friends in your e-mail group sharing your concerns and telling them where they can send their own e-mails. Then, get them to spread the word to their friends.

4. Write a check to your cause and mail it.

5. Call in to radio shows to express your opinion.

6. Vote.

7. Call and complain when you see an injustice. Better yet, write.

8. Only do business with companies that share your agenda, and let those that don't know why you are going elsewhere.

9. Encourage and support other women.

10. Confront those who make sexist, racist or other offensive remarks.

11. Wear a political T-shirt, put a bumper sticker on your car, make your opinion known.

Where to Start

Finally, here are a few helpful Web sites that can get you connected with the activist within.

www.congress.org

Enter your zip code and up pops the list of your representatives in Washington. Click again, and you have their e-mail addresses. Click again and you are voicing your opinion to all of your representatives at one time. You can also e-mail the heads of many federal agencies, as well.

www.house.gov

Home base for the U.S. House of Representatives.

www.senate.gov

Home base for the Senate.

www.cspan.org

"Public affairs on the Web." It's nonpartisan and it's good. Look for issues, see how your representatives voted and find who to contact.

www.now.org

The site for the National Organization for Women. Come here to learn the facts about virtually all issues concerning women here and globally.

www.feminist.org

Home to the Feminist Majority Foundation. This is a great site for getting updates on issues *and* suggestions on how to get involved.

www.hardwonwisdom.com

Meet with other women who share your concerns. It's a place for support *and* activism. It's my Web site. This is where we'll band together and make things happen.

http://www.ncadv.org

National Coalition Against Domestic Violence. Describes the issue, public policy and legislative concerns and resources.

A MOMENT WITH . . .
SARAH WEDDINGTON

The attorney who won *Roe v. Wade* in the U.S. Supreme Court

"One day, a group of us were having a garage sale. I was talking with two women who had been involved with giving out information on how to prevent pregnancy, but sometimes they were asked about options when there was already a pregnancy. These women wanted to know if they could say it was legal to get abortions in California or New York, or if they could tell women good places to get illegal abortions.

"I told them I'd look it up in the library.

"When I filed our lawsuit challenging the constitutionality of the Texas statute, I did not think I was filing a U.S. Supreme Court case. I thought I was helping some *other* case to get to the U.S. Supreme Court. We knew we needed a pregnant plaintiff, and we chose Norma McCorvey. She'd gone to a male attorney in Dallas and said, 'I need an abortion.' He said, 'I can't help you with an abortion. I can help you with an adoption.' Her life story was, in part, that she'd run away from home when she was about eleven, she'd had drug and alcohol problems, and she'd had a child that her mother had taken to raise.

"We started working on *Roe* in 1969 when I was twenty-four. We argued it in the fall of 1971 and went back and argued it again in the late fall of 1972. The decision was issued on January 22, 1973.

"One thing that helped propel the issue and the case were all the horror stories that were out there. Almost everyone knew a horror story of someone who had had an illegal abortion or tried self-abortion.

"When a male lawyer called to offer his help with the case, Linda Coffee, my co-counsel, and I were delighted. We were willing to have anybody help us who would. But, the issue became who was going to argue the case in the Supreme Court. Without telling us, that same gentleman filed a paper that said he would argue the case. A lot of the women attorneys involved felt strongly that it was a woman's issue and a woman should argue it.

"At first, we asked to have two attorneys present the argument—that gentleman and me. The court said no, just one. I talked to the clients. They said, 'Sarah, you filed it. You've been with it the whole way and we want you to argue it.'

"My concern was that I had such limited—no, practically nonexistent—trial experience. I had done uncontested divorces, wills for people with no money and one adoption for my uncle.

"I spent endless hours in what we call 'Moot Court' with other people playing the court justices, asking me questions and getting me to sharpen my arguments, be more assertive and make sure all the arguments that needed to be made were included, regardless of the questions I got. I spent a lot of time preparing.

"What made me the most tense was the importance of the issue. Once the Supreme Court decides a case on an issue, it's unlikely they will decide a similar case for many years. We didn't know how far the ruling was going to go, but we knew if we won, abortion would be more available than it was before the case. If we lost, it would mean we'd have to keep working in the legislatures and on public opinion to change the laws.

"Of course, I didn't sleep much the night before oral argument. I had spent three years getting ready for that moment.

"I had a lot of people in the courtroom who were very encouraging, so when I went in I saw faces of people who wanted me to lose, but also faces of people who were silently cheering me on.

"It was one of those moments when I said to myself, 'I have done everything I know to do.'

"Then, Chief Justice Burger said, 'Mrs. Weddington, if you are ready, you may proceed.' I rose to represent the women of America who wanted to make their own reproductive decisions."

CONCLUSION

BREAKING NEW GROUND

The Pain is Mandatory
The Agony is Optional

E VERYTIME WE HAVE A GOOD day at work, collect a decent paycheck, and see ourselves advancing beyond the expectations we had when we first started our careers, we need to thank the women who came first. They are the ones who suffered. Because they broke trail for us, our challenge has broadened from seeking a chance to participate to earning our chance to lead.

In many ways, this is our duty, considering what these women went through. The basic opportunities that we take for granted were an everyday battle for the women pioneers.

Remember Penny Harrington who became the first woman chief of a metropolitan police department? She went into policing in 1964 when police were men and women officers handled "women's work": juvenile and sex offenses. Period. No work on the street, no rising through the ranks. "I got tired of it," she said. "I didn't understand why I couldn't do anything else. The only reason I was given was, because I was a woman. I decided I wasn't going to take that anymore."

To get a fair chance, she had to file forty-two complaints of sex discrimination in the Portland, Oregon, police department. The department had eight hundred officers at the time. Harrington was one of eighteen women. She organized the women. Half wanted to fight for equal opportunity, half didn't want to fight at all, but agreed to remain silent, so the women officers would not be fighting amongst themselves. One at a time, the discriminatory rules were tossed out, but not without encountering resistance at all levels. "I used to tell myself, 'Don't let the dirty bastards get you down.' It got so bad. When you are identified as the out-front person, they'll come at you from all angles. Part of the problem is, you don't know what to take on and what not to take on. I was afraid if I gave in on anything, I would lose on everything. If someone said 'Hi Honey,' I filed a complaint."

At first, male officers resented her. Some told her she was taking a man's job. But, as she fought her battles, she won change for everybody. Promotions and transfers were no longer based on connections. And, men who'd been hindered by the old system of favoritism liked the changes. She eventually won their respect and support.

However, others set her up to fail. After she made sergeant, she was placed in charge of a multimillion dollar computer system when she, nor anybody else, knew anything about computers. "I had never seen a computer, yet they put me in charge of designing one for forty-three departments," she said. She made it a success, working a full shift, nights, holidays and weekends. "I knew if I failed, they would fire me," she said. "I kept saying, 'Just keep going. Keep going. Keep going.'"

Moments like that, when you are all alone in an arena where the masses want you to fail, are the toughest moments of all. For Harrington, the pressure eventually got to be too much, and she suffered a stress breakdown that forced her to miss six months of work. That experience taught her not to take everything on and how to choose her battles. She says it was tough to learn but that you have to be realistic about how much you can do.

Ahh. Exactly. There are times to engage in battle and times to hold off. Knowing what to do comes down to knowing your environment and knowing yourself. Pick your battles by evaluating the timing, possible outcomes and potential repercussions of your involvement. Finally, consider how you are feeling. You must make yourself a priority, and only do those things you are up to doing. Be mindful of your needs, and don't take on a new crusade if your reserves are so depleted that more tension will push you over the edge. Take care of yourself! Your first duty is to yourself, and that means keeping yourself strong by scheduling ways to help yourself physically and emotionally. If exercise helps you with stress, then work out. If you'd rather enjoy a bubble bath or a massage, then go that route. But, always, always take care of yourself, because it is tough breaking new ground.

Being First

You'd think the first person in line would get the best seat in the house. But, not when it comes to trailblazing. When you're among the first, there is no road map. You'll encounter criticism, roadblocks and self-doubt. You may wonder why you're bothering. Hopefully, your work will result in all the appreciation and accomplishment in the world. It might, but remember, it might not. Sometimes you might feel the door slamming in your face, and you may not sense that your efforts are pushing it open for others. As you push to go where few women have gone before, you might get labeled an "instigator," a "troublemaker," or, (gads!) a "FEMINIST!" The status quo likes to discredit those women who pose a threat, in hopes of shutting them down. Don't let it happen to you.

I had a particularly ugly experience a few years back when my boss completely lost it after I wrote an article questioning whether a woman in the news would have been so vilified by the press and her colleagues if she had been a man. Quoted were fifty of the most powerful men and women in the state, including business leaders, lawmakers, state supreme court judges, academics and the like. I made sure that the group was diverse, so I included liberals and conservatives. One, Gale Norton, sits on the Bush cabinet now as Secretary of the Interior. Some said her gender played a role, some didn't.

That editor, who had supported every controversial story I wrote as an investigative reporter, became infuriated when I showed him the printout of what those important people had said. He screamed, "THOSE ARE NOTHING BUT A BUNCH OF LIBERALS AND FEMINISTS!" I tried to calm him down, reminding him that a feminist is simply someone who believes in equal treatment of men and women, but he screamed, "THAT'S NOT WHAT IT MEANS!" His face was so red I thought he was going to have a stroke. He threw the printout at me and waved me out of his office. For years after that incident, I felt like a pariah.

It wasn't until I interviewed activist Faye Wattleton for this book that I realized I hadn't done anything wrong. That little incident was my introduction to the kinds of fights others wage at work every day. "It feels bad when that happens," Wattleton told me. "It feels bad because you are human. But you might want to take some comfort in the fact that, one hundred years ago, a woman wasn't sitting where you were sitting and wouldn't have dared said that to her boss."

She says that sometimes we lose perspective and can lose the sense of where we are in the evolution of history. "Would you have even had that conversation forty years ago?" she asked me. "Thirty years ago? Not only are you in that job, in that chair, but you have said something. You talked back. You didn't go back into the 'I'm so dumb mode.' And, I would bet you changed him a bit even though he reacted badly. I've seen people transformed, even though they resented it at the time. They'll come back and say, 'I think you are right,' or the next time they hear it, it won't be so foreign and repugnant to them. The fact that you were able to feel your own intellectual empowerment should not be minimized or dismissed. This little illustration is the lesson women sometimes forget. Yes, it feels bad, but years ago, it wouldn't be on this level." The reward, she explained, is that I was even in that job, in that position, in that office to have that confrontation.

I have such a black-and-white approach to matters of right and wrong, expecting that injustice should be fixed the moment it is identified. Unfortunately, it doesn't work like that, and no matter how passionately I believe something may be right or wrong, others may disagree just as fervently. Progress is a slow-moving, back-and-forth experience.

Judith Albino, the college president, remembers getting her first academic job in 1972. At that time, the department at a large university on the east coast was under pressure to make an affirmative action hire. "They assumed I would fail in a year so they could hire the man they really wanted," she said. "But, I did not fail. I did what most women do. I used my social skills. Women are socialized to put other people first and try to ingratiate themselves. I think the burden is always on women to help men feel comfortable with them. I've talked to a lot of women about this. We resent it." She worked in that academic department for twelve years and assumed men had changed and become more accepting of women. But when she moved into a job in the administration and was the only woman in the executive ranks, she realized things hadn't changed much. "Men hadn't changed. I had helped a particular set of men to adapt to me and now I was going to have to do that all over again."

She faced the same situation again and again and again. By the time she got to lead the University of Colorado, she had to go through the same "education" process again. But irregularities with her promotion ubsequently sparked an uprising against her and made this experience a killer. Her reward for that struggle was a public crucifixion and eventual firing. At the time, I thought the spectacle would ensure men would run the university for another two decades. The regents replaced her with a man, but after he left mired in controversy, the regents cleaned up their search process, made sure they did not set someone up to fail and brought in another woman, who has since soared. Things really did change, although Albino wasn't there to enjoy it. Still, if she hadn't fought her fight, it never would have happened.

Surround yourself with support. Women trailblazers carry a huge burden because they are under intense scrutiny and don't have a broad network of support, says psychologist Jackie James, director of the Murray Research Center at Radcliffe College at Harvard. The center focuses on the study of women's lives. "There is no path, there are no models and they are inventing all the time," she said. "We owe them a great debt. They are paving the way for others, but I think that adds to the burden as well."

When a trailblazer has trouble, it can be big news inside an organization or even in the external media as some critics relish in a failure and consider it a black mark against all of womankind. When trailblazers encounter difficulties, the naysayers puff up and use the incident to generalize about how women have gone too far. That's why many of these pioneer women feared that, if they failed, they'd fail us.

Build a support network on the outside with people who share your mission and views. My friends have helped me through my toughest moments. Individually, they were fighting their own battles and suffering the same kind of criticism I faced. We'd get together for dinner or a night at a spa in the mountains and buy ourselves giant, PMS-sized bags of peanut M&Ms to help us cope. Instead of experiencing the isolation of being the "lone wolf," I had unlimited validation from people I loved and respected. Those were tough times, but they weren't the "Bad Old Days." They were good, because through it all we had each other and made sure we took care of ourselves physically and emotionally.

If you don't have a good support network, build one. Join women's groups like the National Organization for Women or the American Association of University Women. Find other strong women by aligning yourself with the domestic violence, reproductive rights, rape crisis and other women's movements. Find other trailblazers who know exactly what you are feeling, whether or not they understand the particular dynamics of your work environment.

Don't forget to log on. Thanks to the Internet, it is even easier to connect with other bold women in chat rooms and on message boards. Because the dot.coms come and go so rapidly, do a search for "women's message boards" or "feminist message boards" and you will find thousands of women who will listen to you, encourage you and give you advice.

When you need support, ASK FOR IT. Let your friends know when you are feeling down or shaky. Come right out and say, "Hey, I'm having trouble here. Let's go out and talk," or, "I need some encouragement," or, "Help me. I feel like giving up." Use your support network whether you are fighting for political and social change or are just trying to do a good job under tough circumstances. You don't have to be a crusader to need others to help you be strong.

Discrimination in the Pulpit

You can also draw strength from the past because I certainly do. Everytime I catch myself worrying about some particularly rough situation, I think about how much harder it was for women before me. I live an hour away from the Rev. Margaret Towner, who made history when she became the first woman ordained as a Presbyterian minister. She shares a home with two roommates, and they all call themselves the "Golden Girls of Sarasota." The sad part of it is, Towner doesn't have much choice about how she lives her golden years. After suffering wage discrimination throughout most of her career, she didn't have the kind of salary that earned the kind of pension that most of the male ministers got.

If office politics are harsh on women, just imagine what it was like in the church. "I got a lot of letters after I was ordained," she said. "Most of them were very positive and encouraging, but there were a number from women and men who were angry. They were citing the letters Paul wrote that said women are to keep silent in church, women are not to ask questions in church, and if women want to know something, they should ask their husbands when they get home. I got letters from people who said they were praying I would change my mind and renege on my vows. Some men wrote proposing marriage to save me from my predicament. Others wrote that I was a sinner for being ordained. I was overwhelmed. Numb."

After her ordination in 1956, she was still in her old job as minister of education at a church in Pennsylvania. The church allowed her to bring communion to shut-ins, but she was never invited to preach in that pulpit. When it came time for the communion celebration on Sundays, Towner was always relegated to the fellowship hall for overflow, where she would mime—

not speak—but *mime* the actions as they were coming over the loudspeaker. "Being the first and breaking in, I was trying to help the male population and clergy be able to accept women and not be offended by overzealousness or overaggressiveness. Later on, the women in the clergy may have gotten angry or belligerent, but I figured I needed to build a support community first, which I was gradually doing."

She did talk back when she discovered the other assistant minister was getting a better salary. He still hadn't even finished his seminary training and she'd been there a year longer than him. "I was getting a very low salary," she said. "So, I went to the board of trustees and said I would like to have a commensurate salary. The trustees were very rude. They said, 'You don't have any right to be asking for a raise. You don't need to have a better salary. After all, you are going to be getting married and you'll be taken care of. Besides, you're a woman.' I said, 'Well, I'm sorry, but I feel I deserve to have as much as the other assistant.' They said, 'No, he has a family and needs to take care of them.' To argue with them in that mood would have been fruitless."

Rev. Towner soon had a chance to move to a church in Kalamazoo, Michigan, as assistant pastor. She was invited to preach in the pulpit there, but the senior pastor would get phone calls from men and women who said they did not want a woman up front.

Her solution was to find alternative ways to be accepted. She tried to break down their attitudes gradually by getting to know people and participating in clergy events. At first, she loaded her sermons with Gospel and insight, trying to show her intelligence. "If I had to hear those first sermons again, I'd cringe," she said. "You can't put the whole Gospel in one service. They were much too academic. Not free enough. Too stiff. I felt I had to show my educational savvy."

For a long time, she said, many of the women in the clergy wanted to be "one of the boys." "Starting out, we women felt we had to excel," she said. "We had to be much better than the men in order to be received and accepted. We should have just been ourselves and done the best job we could and let the criticism roll off our backs." Then they discovered they had unique gifts to bring to ministry. Gifts like caring, patience and understanding. By focusing on those strengths and being a source of comfort for parishioners, the women claimed their own power in the pulpit.

Solitary Confinement

When a woman challenges the system and takes a lead, she becomes isolated. The status quo generally wants to protect itself, and doesn't let go of its power easily. Its greatest power comes by cutting off the rebels, labeling them as crazy and on the fringe.

I've mentioned the task force I coordinated several years ago, which brought in the most powerful people in the state to focus on my newspaper's coverage of women. I tried to enlist other women in the newsroom to help, and their behavior shocked me. Our paper had no local women columnists. It ran few national women columnists, save for Hollywood gossip, Dear Abby, Miss Manners, etc. More than two-thirds of the letters to the editor were written by men. And, women business leaders were angrily complaining that the little coverage they got was derogatory. When I tried to get other women in the newsroom to help push for improvements, I found a couple of loyal supporters—and plenty of criticism. One female reporter immediately went into the managing editor's office to alert him to the "insurrection" I was trying to cause. A midlevel editor told me, as we left for lunch, that it was "politically expensive" for her to be seen with me. Another woman reporter sent an e-mail to me that said, "I don't know why you're stirring everything up. There isn't anything wrong." The absolute worst part of that experience was that some of the people who criticized what I was doing were people I'd considered my friends.

> "It's very scary being first. So many people are depending on you to make changes. People say, 'Now things are going to happen because Linda's there.' People of color say, 'It's about time.' The women, too.
> They expect so much of you. And, they should. It is scary because it's up to me. Either I make it happen or I don't. But it is so wonderful to be in a position to offer advice, ideas and change the direction of the labor movement."
>
> —*Linda Chavez-Thompson, executive vice president, AFL-CIO*

If you ever feel you are being cast aside from your own peers because you are standing up to a wrong, I salute you and stand beside you. I know how it hurts. There is nothing more crazy-making than other people telling you how wrong you are when you know in your heart you are right. It's what I call the "Marilyn Munster" syndrome.

Hopefully, you've caught this 1960s television sitcom in reruns because it's the best. Cousin Marilyn is the only "normal" member of this family of kindly monsters. She's a sweet, extremely attractive blonde who doesn't look at all like Frankenstein or Dracula or any other monster in the house. Yet, living amongst Herman, Lilly and Grandpa Munster, Marilyn thinks *she's* the weirdo.

The F-word

The more you stand out, the more likely it is that somebody is going to call you that nasty f-word, "FEMINIST." I wouldn't call myself a feminist until I was thirty-three years old and Pat Blumenthal, then a leader with the National Abortion and Reproductive Rights Action League, read me the definition of feminism out of the dictionary.

I include one here so you can see how "scary" the word really is.

fem • i • nism

Pronunciation: (fem'u-niz"um),—*n.* **1.** the doctrine advocating social, political, and all other rights of women equal to those of men. **2.** (*sometimes cap.*) an organized movement for the attainment of such rights for women.
3. feminine character. Source: (Dictionary.com)

What's the big deal? It's the formal definition of that bumper sticker that says, "Feminism is the radical notion that all women are people."

Don't be afraid of the label. If you can't help yourself, okay. Don't call yourself a feminist. But, for God's sake, BE ONE! One of the women I interviewed for this book told me, "I'm no feminist," and I had to laugh to myself. Her whole life is being a feminist. She's worked hard, cut new trails, fought for her place and demanded equal treatment.

Sure sounds like a feminist to me.

That is exactly what happens to women who stand out front breaking trail. Even if you are competent, driven and in the right, the machine of the status quo can treat you like *you* are the one with the problem. You aren't. Unfortunately, changing the world takes time because there are so many people out there who are comfortable with things as they are.

Looking the Other Way

There's enough inequity out there. You don't have to notice everything, said Dr. Nancy Dickey, the first woman to lead the American Medical Association.
She's got a point.

One hundred and fifty years after Elizabeth Blackwell became the first woman physician, the American Medical Association appointed Dickey its first woman president in 1998.

Dickey came up in the old school when doctors ran an old boys' club. She learned to play by the old boys' rules. She remembers a moment in her residency when she was studying orthopedics. A patient came in for surgery who had driven a large carpenter nail through his kneecap. The professor was a real chauvinist, she said, and knowing the physical limitations that she might have, he told her, "OK, you get the nail out." "His intention was that I wouldn't be able to get the nail out and then he could lecture me on how women had to choose women's professions. But I would have physically ruptured myself rather than not get that nail out. So, I finally got it out and said, 'OK, here you go.'"

It's a story she laughs about, but one that might well have infuriated others in the same place. The key to getting through the inequity, she said, is by not focusing on the inequity. Now, 41 percent of the students in medical school are female and about 15 percent of the practicing physicians are women. By 2010, we can expect that to be 20 percent and a decade after that, 30 percent. "But, I was one of seven women in my medical school class," she said. "Some saw that as a real problem because we stood out and every professor knew every one of our names. I saw that as a real opportunity. If you are one of one hundred, you have to really shine to stand out. If you are one of less than a dozen, you already stand out."

Dickey said the struggle for equality is harder if you focus on the negative. "I honestly felt well-accepted and that I was given good opportunities," she said. "But, I also recognized from talking to some of my colleagues that part of it was in the mind-set. I don't go looking for slights and insults. There is only so much energy that you've got. If you go out thinking someone is out to get you, there isn't enough time to do what you have to do. I have colleagues who were side-by-side with me who certainly perceived more discrimination than I did. I've been told I was just blind to it. I ignored it. If you are feeling the hostility in this all-consuming profession, it makes it very difficult."

> "I myself have never been able to find out precisely what feminism is. I only know that people call me a feminist whenever I express sentiments that differentiate me from a doormat or a prostitute."
>
> —Rebecca West "Mr. Chesterton in Hysterics,"The Clarion, November 14, 1913

It is so much easier to give up and blend back in with the majority that doesn't have the desire or courage or foresight to push the limits. Not everybody is cut out to take the naysaying, the criticism, the harassment and the potential career fallout that comes from confronting the way things are. I wish all women were born with a healthy dose of guts and outrage, but we aren't all the same. To those who have the stamina, be strong. To those who don't, show your support. And, if you can't do that, at least stay out of the way. We've got work to do.

Ground-Breaking 101

- **Be true to yourself.** Don't settle for what others think you should do or be.

- **Pick your battles.** You can't fight back every time something goes wrong or what you say will be disregarded. Don't be negative or a chronic complainer. If you are going to fight, make it count. Make it a battle worth winning.

- **Have a strong support network.** These friends act as your cheering section no matter how tough things get.

- **Persevere.** You know the saying: "Never, never, never, never, never give up."

- **If you get the "troublemaker" label, make allies.** Do a great job. Learn to live with the tension that exists while bringing together a powerful support group. If it stays tough, think about looking elsewhere for work.

- **Give others the kind of support you want.**

- **Do your homework!** Always be prepared, know your facts and back them up with data, charts and reports.

- **Don't waste energy** trying to figure out why you haven't gotten respect from people you don't respect.

- **You can't possibly keep everyone happy.** Don't kill yourself trying.

- **Accept that it's not always going to go your way.** Try to keep your emotions in check.

- **Laugh a little.** At the absurdity of the situation—and at yourself. It's only a job!

A MOMENT WITH . . .
BETTY WILLIAMS
Nobel Laureate and Founder of the Peace Movement in Northern
Ireland

"I tried to do what every mother was doing. I tried to protect my kids. I have to be honest. You become very self-centered when you are being protective of those you love. You get the '*my* syndrome.' As long as it's not *my* kids, *my* car, *my* husband, it's not *my* house. You really have to try to alienate yourself from the violence, try to live as best you can among it. That's what I was doing.

"I had two beautiful kids and quite a normal life in very abnormal circumstances.

"Back in the early 1960s, Ian Paisley founded the Free Presbyterian Church. He never lifted a gun to kill anyone, but from the pulpit he preached fear and hatred. In 1963, violence erupted on the Falls Road of Belfast, which is a very Catholic area. They began burning Catholics out of their homes. One of my uncles, who had thirteen children, was burned out of his home. Then the fear grew within the Catholic community. Before that time, there was no Provisional IRA. It was born out of that situation.

"We tried to get back to some sort of local stability but hatred was festering. The Catholics didn't have a voice. They couldn't hold a decent job and very few Catholics ever got to the university level. That kind of injustice just festers. It sits in the living room, and people talk in the living room, they sit around and resentments build and divisions become wider and wider and the fear grows. Fear cripples communities, and that's what happened.

"Then in 1969 a series of events led to the explosion of what became the Northern Irish War. They call it the 'troubles.' I don't call it the troubles. It was a war. I saw far too much. People blown up in bomb blasts, soldiers shot from the halls of churches.

"I would see my own people begin to commit terrible acts of violence. Their motto was 'Peace with Justice,' but they weren't handing any out.

"The suffering of the women struck me because they were losing their husbands, their sons, their daughters. Women are the losers in war. We are. It's so difficult to give life. Every time a child is born I say a woman commits a miracle. There's nobody who can understand the kind of love it brings. So when a woman loses a child, recovery never takes place, it just doesn't happen. There is no way to come back. There are many women I've seen with dead eyes.

"For some—like Anne Maguire who lost three children in one day—there was no recovery possible. I was there when it happened to her children on the tenth of August, 1976. That was the day when I knew I could not bear it anymore.

"We started door-knocking campaigns, talking to women. Catholics, Protestants—everyone. The majority felt like I did. The insanity's got to stop. We called a rally and wondered if anyone would show up. There were ten thousand people there! At the second, there were twenty thousand. The third, thirty thousand. Then a quarter million in Trafalgar Square at our last rally. We had twelve rallies in all.

"Tears without action are wasted sentiment. While the rallies were very important, they weren't going to solve the problem. You have to solve it on a daily basis.

"Women would come up and say 'What can you do to make peace in our area?' I would say, 'That's your job to tell me, not my job to tell you. You need to ask people what it's going to take to make your area a better place to live.'

"To empower people to come up with their own solutions is not difficult at all."

AFTERWORD

Y OU KNOW WHY I WROTE this book? Politics were killing me at work. When I went looking for a book that would tell me how to deal with the emotional battlefields in the workplace, all I could find were books telling me how to dress and talk. I needed a book that would tell me how to survive.

I am not the same woman I was when I started asking these bold women for their mentoring advice. They have taken me to the place where I understand the challenges strong women face while trying to gain equality in a world that is not yet equal. They've shown me that there are times to fight about it, cry about it and even laugh about it. And while we enjoy our share of tough times and triumphs, we need to better connect with each other so we aren't fighting or reveling alone.

I'm sitting here, finishing up my book. This dream of mine has only about eight hundred more words left in it, then I have to figure out what's next. If this experience has taught me anything, it's that your work becomes a joy—not a job—when you are doing what is in your heart. Every moment of this experience has been a growth milestone. I'm happy, just sitting here at my keyboard writing for you.

And, that's the point. I know how hokey some of those self-help books can sound as they promise you fortune and success if you just follow those seven or eight or ten magical rules.

But, there is really only one rule: Be true to you. Stop worrying about meeting the expectations you think others have for you. What matters is that you honor your own self, set your own expectations and dare to bet on you. You can achieve your vision. It won't be easy.

When things get tough—and you know they'll get tough because they always do—lift yourself out of the turmoil by knowing who you are and what you want. You have so many options in this life. Stay, go, rest, grow—it's all your choice. When others pressure you into thinking you have no choice but to do it their way, always, *always* remember that you hold the power. You may have to play by their rules in the short-term, but you can always move on to your next dream.

All you need is faith in yourself, a clear vision of what you want and the guts to try. I've talked with so many women who tell me they wish they could do this or that with their lives, but something holds them back. Often, it's a lack of confidence, or a sense that their time has passed. Get it together! You *can* live your dream, and your time is *now*. Every person goes through spells of uncertainty, but, when you are in the middle of these spells, recognize them for what they are: Just nagging doubts that should be put in their place. Even when I'm not feeling sure of myself, I have enough faith to try to live what's in my heart. Do that. Don't talk yourself out of success and don't forget to enjoy it as it comes to you. In those moments when you lack confidence or you see your self-esteem starting to lag, try to laugh about it. Only us women could be this hard on ourselves. It's time we get on with it and live. Enjoy the moment and forgive our imperfections.

You don't have to do what Carly Fiorina or Jane Goodall or Jody Williams did in order to succeed. You don't need an Academy Award, a Nobel Peace Prize or your face on the cover of a magazine to say you count. You count, as much as any other person on this earth. Do what you want to do, and do it the best you can.

The next time you have a bad day at work or face troubles at home, come back to your mentors here and remember how big this world is, and see how much possibility exists for you. You don't have to live your life feeling insecure or out of control.

You have so much power. It's up to you whether or not you use it.

INDEX

MORE WISDOM

Once Oprah told the world how inspiring Fawn was, she became one of the nation's most sought-after keynote speakers.

IF YOU THINK HARD WORK plus excellent performance puts you on the fast track, you're wrong. It puts you on no track at all.

Two-time best-selling author Fawn Germer has now gone to the nation's most powerful corporate leaders to ask what it takes to take charge. She was told this: Performance is mandatory. But, it is only one piece of what Fawn has identified as a three-pronged strategy that has been used to achieve stratospheric success. The interviews are featured in her latest book, *The NEW Woman Rules.*

Fawn's seven new keynote presentations are feature breakthrough insights gleaned from her personal interviews with the CEOs of Fortune 500 companies — as well as the senior leaders who are positioned to take charge next .

From those interviews, the four-time Pulitzer-nominated journalist distilled success and leadership strategies that no other speaker can offer. Only Fawn Germer has gone to the CEOs, company presidents, CFOs, COOs, EVPs, and SVPs who have broken the barriers that hold us back. They told her exactly how they did it: what worked, and what didn't.

Oprah told the world that Fawn's writing is "very inspiring," and it is. Fawn is also one of the most entertaining speakers on the circuit today. After a recent keynote, Coca-Cola President Sandy Douglas asked her, "Have you thought of doing standup?"

She brings together her inspiration and humor in new presentations that show:

- Networking *is* working. Relationships drive careers.

- Success often comes when you dare to do something you know nothing about.

- The path to the senior office is usually not a straight line up. It may involve lateral or even downward moves to expand expertise.

- You create your next job promotion by volunteering for additional duties, then overdelivering results.

- There is a specific "language" of leadership unique to women.

- This generation of leaders can't waste time on perfection in a marketplace that moves faster than you can line up your ducks.

Fawn's interviews resulted in the 200 core rules for leadership and career success. Those rules are the cornerstones of her new series of keynote presentations.

www.fawngermer.com   info@fawngermer.com
(727) 467-0202

ABOUT FAWN GERMER

FAWN GERMER ONCE HAD A BOSS SIT HER DOWN and tell her that she'd never be more than she was at the time: a newspaper reporter. In the decade since, Fawn has written two best-selling books and has become one of the nation's most sought-after women's leadership speakers, key-noting for the nation's largest corporations.

This marks the release of her greatest effort yet, *The NEW Woman Rules*, which was published by the Network of Executive Women and includes interviews with more than fifty of America's most powerful women in the retail industry   .

When Fawn left daily journalism to write her first book, it was rejected fifteen times—by every major publisher in the country. She persevered, and then had her choice of publishers. She received her first copy of *Hard Won Wisdom* one day before the Sept. 11 tragedies, and had to promote her book—and herself—at the most difficult moment in our history.

She worked tirelessly to market the book, even sending Oprah's producers twenty-nine letters. Once Oprah told the world, "If you want to read a very inspiring book, read *Hard Won Wisdom*," Fawn's speaking career took off.

Her second book, *Mustang Sallies*, hit best-seller lists within two weeks of its release. The book looks at how strong women can find success by being themselves in a world in which there is so much pressure to be like everybody else. If features personal interviews with everyone from Hillary Clinton to Martina Navratilova to Erin Brockovich   .

This acclaimed investigative reporter has worked as a Florida correspondent for both *The Washington Post* and *U.S. News and World Report*. Her distinguished reporting career earned her numerous state and national awards, including four Pulitzer Prize nominations. She has worked as a staff writer for *The Miami Herald* and *Denver's Rocky Mountain News* and was an editor for *The Tampa Tribune*.

Fawn looks back on that old bully boss who tried to hold her back and says, "Some people have mentors. I had a tormentor." If not for him, she'd never have looked for anything different from her career. And the one thing she has learned again and again is, it's all about the obstacles.

For speaking information or to contact the author:

Telephone: (727) 467-0202
E-mail: info@fawngermer.com
Web site: www.fawngermer.com